SLAVERY, SMALLHOLDING AND TOURISM

SLAVERY, SMALLHOLDING AND TOURISM

Social Transformations in the British Virgin Islands

BY

MICHAEL E. O'NEAL

Classic Dissertation Series

Quid Pro Books

New Orleans, Louisiana

SLAVERY, SMALLHOLDING AND TOURISM

Published by Quid Pro Books.

QUID PRO, LLC
5860 Citrus Blvd., Suite D-101
New Orleans, Louisiana 70123
U.S.A.
www.quidprobooks.com

ISBN 978-1-61027-118-9 (pbk)
ISBN 978-1-61027-120-2 (hc)

Back cover photograph of author copyright © by Curtis De Ravariere, Paul's Photo Studio, BVI, used with permission. Background cover images copyright © by Rory Childress. The map of the modern Caribbean and British Virgin Islands is copyright © 2011 by Town and Country Planning Department, Premier's Office, Government of the BVI (through the generous efforts of Ron Beard, Deputy Chief Planner), and is used here with their permission and, as with all the images noted above, with the sincere gratitude of the author and publisher.

This book is also available in all leading eBook formats.

Publisher's Cataloging-in-Publication

O'Neal, Michael E.
    Slavery, smallholding and tourism: social transformations in the British Virgin Islands / Michael E. O'Neal.
        p. cm. — (Classic dissertation series)
        Includes bibliographical references, tables and index.
        ISBN 978-1-61027-118-9 (pbk)
1. Slavery—British Virgin Islands—history. 2. Tourism—British Virgin Islands. 3. British Virgin Islands—History. 4. Slavery—Law and legislation—Caribbean Islands—history. 5. British Virgin Islands—Politics and government. I. Title. II. Series.
F2129.O63 2012   972.66'72'88—dc21
                                                         201249792

FOR MY FAMILY

TABLE OF CONTENTS

Foreword i

Preface v

Introduction 1

Part I. The Historical Context 9
1 · The Era of the Plantation 11
2 · Manumission and Rebellion 27
3 · Between Plantation and Tourism: The Post-Emancipation
    Interregnum 51

Part II. The Contemporary Situation 73
4 · The Era of Tourism 75
5 · Perceptions of Tourism and Development 97

Part III. Reprise 125
6 · The Present as History 127

Afterword 133

Notes 139

Bibliography 147

Appendices
    A. Glossary 171
    B. Symposium Programme 172
    C. Tables 174

Index 183

About the Author 187

LIST OF FIGURES

Figure 1. Map of the British Virgin Islands 7

Figure 2. Map of Plantations on Tortola, 1798. 37

Foreword

Colleen Ballerino Cohen

IN THE LATE 1970s, when Michael O'Neal began research for this book, tourism studies were in their infancy. *The Annals of Tourism Research* had been publishing less than a decade, and the first edition of Valene Smith's *Hosts and Guests* (1977), and Dean MacCannell's *The Tourist, A New Theory of the Leisure Class* (1976)—both recognized today as classics—had just come out. Tourism was hardly on the radar of scholars in anthropology and sociology, and cultural studies—under which rubric I am inclined to place O'Neal's work—wasn't even a nascent discipline. Finally, as Dr. O'Neal points out in his Introduction, at the time that he undertook his research, scholarship on the Caribbean was far less highly regarded than it is today. Indeed, where today one would be hard-put to find an ethnographic study that does *not* address local-global intersections and histories, when O'Neal wrote this work in 1983, the Caribbean posed a real analytical problem for traditional anthropology, precisely because of its long-standing and complex connection with global economies and flows. What I find so remarkable about this work is that it *insists* on understanding the British Virgin Islands present as part of a long-standing involvement in global flows. We never get a sense of a static before and after sequence of events; rather, O'Neal shows us that the turn to tourism in the British Virgin Islands is the most recent phase in a historical reliance on a "monocrop" economy.

Read in the historical context of tourism and Caribbean research, Michael O'Neal's work stands out as an early and significant contribution. But even apart from its pioneering status, this is an important book. A quarter of a century after the original research, the work is fresh, innovative, and ethnographically rich. One of the things that makes this book so important—to Caribbean, ethnographic, and tourism studies alike—is that it documents a moment when a society is being transformed socially, culturally, and economically by tourism. There are several studies that look historically at the development of a tourist economy in a particular country (Ghodsee 2005) or even in the Caribbean region (Pattullo 1996, Sheller 2003). But with the possible exception of Bruner's collected essays on Balinese tourism (2005), none give us what this study does: an in-depth account of the transformations activated by tourism, as they are happening.

To emphasize the enormity of the transformation of the British Virgin Islands through tourism, O'Neal provides a solid historical background.

His treatment of the British Virgin Islands plantation and post-emancipation periods in the first three chapters makes extensive use of planter's reports, travelers' reports and government and court records, such that the reader achieves a rich sense of the time and place. The material on the 1776 manumission of the enslaved population of the Long Look plantation in Tortola's East End and the material on the Josiah's Bay Estate rebellion are particularly effective in conveying a sense of the active political and economic life of the Virgin Islands during the plantation period. Importantly, and with particular regard to the Josiah's Bay rebellion, O'Neal highlights the "relative impunity with which Virgin Islands slaves were able to defy the established authority of the planter-class" and documents "the slaves' recognition of the degree of bargaining power which their labour represented within the context of the social relations of production of a declining plantation economy" (p.48). Indeed, in light of the paucity of historical materials on the Caribbean's small islands during the plantation and post-emancipation periods, the first three chapters of the book alone must be considered an important historical intervention.

These initial chapters also set the stage for understanding the enormity of the move to tourism for this small British Dependent Territory. From before emancipation in 1834 to the middle of the twentieth century, the British Virgin Islands remained politically and economically marginal, a smallholding economy that, as O'Neal aptly points out, failed to generate "any sustained exploitative interest from the imperial center" (p.2). Throughout this period, the predominately Afro-Caribbean population of the British Virgin Islands was linked indirectly to a global economy, through exchange with neighboring St. Thomas, and through labor migration to the cane fields of Cuba, Puerto Rico, and Santo Domingo. But it was not until the mid twentieth century, when legislative groundwork was laid to encourage tourism development, that the British Virgin Islands began to become directly integrated again into the global economy.

Most of the records relevant to this important moment of transformation were destroyed in a 1950 fire in Antigua, where they were archived. So the information that O'Neal includes here—acquired through diligent historical research, interviews, and a 1982 symposium on tourism and social change—constitutes rare historical material related to this period. While all of this material is fresh and detailed, some of the most original pertains to the Wickham's Cay and Anegada Development Agreements of 1967, in which large amounts of British Virgin Islands land were leased for a period of 199 years to outside developers. This action promoted large-scale local protest; the same spirit of defiance that O'Neal documents during the plantation period was evidenced again in this early period of tourism development, when public outcry against the lease resulted in the abrogation of the original agreement.

To read O'Neal's account of the beginnings of tourism in the British Virgin Islands is to step back in time in a more immediate sense, for in this account the players are living and giving testimony about their experiences. One of the most compelling chapters of this book is Chapter 5, "Perceptions of Tourism and Development," in which we hear the voices of British Virgin Islanders as they consider the impact and future of tourism in their country. In the first part of this chapter, participants in a symposium organized and convened by O'Neal in May 1982 reflect upon the impacts of an ascendant tourist economy upon the lives of British Virgin Islanders: "From McWelling Todman's extraordinary oral-historical *tour de force*, to Elihu Rhymer's wry observations, the dialogue . . . affords perspicuous insight into British Virgin Islanders' perceptions about their existential circumstances" (p.97). These reflections are followed by excerpts from interviews that O'Neal conducted with individuals from all walks of British Virgin Islands life—a teacher, an expatriate charter-boat company manager, a development planning consultant, a civil servant, a student, to name a few. Weaving all of these voices together with a review of scholarship on tourism's impact, O'Neal provides a rich and nuanced view of a country on the cusp of extraordinary social and economic transformation. Twenty-five years later, our perspective on this transformation is brought into sharp focus by this exceptional account.

In his Introduction, O'Neal locates his work "in the expanding tradition of indigenous ethnography"—of studies done by "native" subjects of their own cultures and societies (p.2). It is this aspect of the work, as much as any other, that is worthy of note. Even today, a quarter century after the research for this work was begun, there are regrettably fewer works of scholarship being produced by cultural "insiders" world-wide than O'Neal's optimistic note of an "expanding tradition" suggested. Fortunately, the British Virgin Islands is an exception to this trend. The past several decades in the British Virgin Islands has seen the publication of several local memoirs, many works of original poetry and stories and several notable works of scholarship (Harrigan and Varlack 1970, 1975, 1988; O'Neal 2001). This book represents a significant contribution to this corpus: It opens a window on a critical period of British Virgin Islands contemporary history, and provides a backdrop for understanding the contemporary BVI, in which tourism revenues, combined with revenues from a robust financial services sector, are estimated to generate a GDP in excess of one billion dollars in 2007.

As important as this work is to Caribbean scholarship, tourism studies, ethnography, and scholarship on the British Virgin Islands, it bears noting that O'Neal has contributed to his country and the region in equally important ways, instituting a jazz and classical music series, spearheading distance education, and playing a leadership role in the movement to develop tertiary education in the British Virgin Islands. I have been privileged to have Michael O'Neal as a friend and colleague for close to twenty-five years. During that time, in addition to sharing our passion for scholarship on the Virgin Islands, we worked together at the H. Lavity Stoutt Community College, I as a member of the Board of Governors, and he as an officer of the College, initially Vice President and subsequently President of the institution. Thus, I am especially pleased to see this work finally reach publication. For in addition to its scholarly importance, it is a testimony to a life of dedication to indigenous scholarship and universally accessible higher education. Most importantly, it is a fitting legacy to the people on whose behalf this "son of the soil" has labored so selflessly.

COLLEEN BALLERINO COHEN, Ph. D.
Professor of Anthropology & Women's Studies
Vassar College
Poughkeepsie, New York

References

Bruner, Edward
  2005   *Culture on Tour: Ethnographies of Travel.* Chicago: University of Chicago Press.
Ghodsee, Kristen
  2005   *The Red Riviera: Gender, Tourism, and Postsocialism on the Black Sea.* Durham and London: Duke University Press.
Harrigan, Norwell and Pearl Varlack
  1988   *Ye Islands of Enchantment: A Profile of the British Virgins.* St. Thomas, USVI: Research and Consulting Services, Ltd.
O'Neal, Eugenia
  2001   *From the Field to the Legislature: A History of Women in the Virgin Islands.* Westport, CT: Greenwood Press.
Pattullo, Polly
  1996   *Last Resorts: The Cost of Tourism in the Caribbean.* London: Cassell.
Sheller, Mimi
  2003   *Consuming the Caribbean: From Arawaks to Zombies.* London and New York: Routledge.

Preface

The British Virgin Islands (BVI) have undergone tremendous change during the past half-century, as the society has been transformed from an essentially rural existence to one whose economy is now primarily based on tourism and financial services. This study places these transformations—up to the point of the ascendancy of tourism—in broad theoretico-historical perspective, while at the same time grounding that totalizing perspective in the existential realities of British Virgin Islanders.

The study is divided into three parts. Part I consists of three chapters, two on the plantation era and one on the post-emancipation period. This constitutes a prolegomenon to Part II, which treats the current era of tourism economy. Part III consists of a closing chapter, "The Present as History," titular inspiration of which is derived from Paul Sweezy's book of the same title. The final chapter is essentially a reprise and a plea for a sense of historical perspective.

This document saw its first incarnation as a doctoral dissertation, originally entitled "British Virgin Islands Transformations: Anthropological Perspectives" (Union, 1983). And while it was present within the so-called "grey literature" of academe, it was not really accessible. Its publication by Quid Pro Books in the Classic Dissertation Series now makes the study more readily available. I am especially grateful to publisher Dr Alan Childress, the Conrad Meyer III Professor of Law at Tulane University, and to my editor, Lee D. Scheingold, for patiently and graciously shepherding the manuscript through the process of publication.

I should like to acknowledge with gratitude the early and valued mentorship of two scholars—Dr William Brisk, political scientist and lawyer, and Dr Edward Towle, late founder and Chairman of Island Resources Foundation—both of whom sparked my interest in pursuing postgraduate studies in anthropology. I remain grateful also to Prof. Stanley Diamond, late Chairman of Anthropology at the Graduate Faculty, New School for Social Research, for having encouraged me to persevere in my postgraduate studies in anthropology, notwithstanding the then-competing exigencies of a family business.

I similarly acknowledge with profound gratitude my indebtedness to all the members of my doctoral committee of many years ago—Drs. Rayna Rapp, Michael Bone, Melvin Silverman, Judith Bernardi, Sylvia Hill, and, in memoriam, Halloway C. Sells. Their combination of constructive criticism, timely confrontation and empathetic support were crucial to my completion of this undertaking.

I am greatly indebted to Rita Georges, then-Director of the BVI Government's Mental Health Programme, as well as to the British Virgin Islands Mental Health Association, for providing the locus for an internship undertaken as part of my doctoral program. Segments of the unpublished transcript of the proceedings of an Association-sponsored symposium on social change in the British Virgin Islands are presented in this monograph. I am privileged that this document thus serves as the medium by which at least a portion of this important narrative material is preserved and disseminated. I am grateful to Judith Grigg-Charles for her meticulous transcription of the tape-recorded proceedings of the symposium.

To all those consultant-informants whose personal observations constitute a central part of this study, I also extend my sincere gratitude; I am truly grateful to them for having graciously countenanced many impositions upon their time and expertise. In the presentation of the contemporary ethnographic material, pseudonyms have been given to all subjects, with the exception of those whose statements were delivered in open forum.

Throughout the course of conducting this research, I benefited from frequent consultations with Dr. Norwell Harrigan (late Director, Caribbean Research Institute, University of the Virgin Islands), and Dr. Pearl Varlack (Professor Emeritus of Education, University of the Virgin Islands), whose pioneering historical work is much utilized in this study. Sociologist (now lawyer) Mitchell Codrington, geographer Christopher Howell, and anthropologists Karen Olwig, Frank McGlynn and James Lett—contemporaries who had each conducted postgraduate fieldwork in the Virgin Islands—were valued sources of scholarly support and engagement during the course of my own research.

Material derived from Chapter 2, "Manumission and Rebellion," has recently been published in the book *Negotiating Enslavement*, edited by Professor Arnold Highfield and George Tyson (Antilles Press 2009), and grateful acknowledgement is hereby recorded.

A number of friends and colleagues did me the favor of perusing the manuscript in its final, pre-publication stages and I have, thereby, been the beneficiary of their encouragement and feedback. They are, in alphabetical order: Deputy Governor, Inez Archibald; Dr. Paul Feldman; former Deputy Governor, Elton Georges; Attorney Terrance Neale; my brother, Attorney Colin O'Neal; businessman and former Chairman, H L Stoutt Community College, Elihu Rhymer; Attorney Helene Simonette-Lewis; and Vice President, Island Resources Foundation, Judith Towle.

I am honored to have had two anthropologist colleagues, Professor Colleen Ballerino Cohen of Vassar College, and Professor Bill Maurer of the University of California at Irvine, write a Foreword and an Afterword, respectively, for this volume. Both scholars have done extensive research in the British Virgin Islands and their valued contributions place the present study in the context of more recent Caribbean anthropology and the ethnography of the financial services industry, which became ascendant in the British Virgin Islands after this study was completed.

And finally, to my wife Verney Seymour O'Neal, I express heartfelt gratitude for her crucial role in the preparation of the manuscript for submission to the publisher and, more especially, for her steadfast support and encouragement.

M. E. O.

SLAVERY,

SMALLHOLDING

AND

TOURISM

Introduction

This monograph constitutes a study of the socioeconomic transformation of the British Virgin Islands over time—from plantation economy, through the development of a society of free Black "smallholders," to the recent development of a predominantly tourism-based economy.

The disciplinary field within which the study falls is Development Anthropology, and the methodological orientation derives from the critical anthropological perspective.

> [The anthropological] perspective has two primary moments. First, it is *totalizing*. The entire sweep of human history, from its most arcane origins to its most sophisticated current status, is within the purview of anthropology. Moreover, the anthropological perspective is totalizing in its attempt to grasp all the structures of human cultural life, from the economic "base" to the religious and artistic "super-structure." In other words, the totalizing character of anthropology is both a diachronic and synchronic one.
>
> Secondly, the anthropological perspective is *concrete*. Fieldwork as the first step in ethnological research has necessitated the de-distancing of the observer. The ethnographer must experience the society he studies from within, if he is to understand it at all. This means that all ethnologic conclusions, being based on data derived through participant observation, must share this concrete character. Thus anthropology is radical not only in its search for the roots of human reality and culture but also in its rootedness in concrete human experience. Critical anthropology attempts to view the world from the perspective of this concrete universality of research. (Editorial statement, *Critical Anthropology*, vol. 2, No. 1, 1971)

The field of study is dubbed "Development Anthropology" and the object of its study—British Virgin Islands society—is conceptualized as "an historically conditioned, dialectically developing entity" (Wilbur 1973).

This study is not a conventional work of Caribbean ethnography, with its characteristic emphasis on domestic organization, but rather, is conceived in the spirit of what has been referred to—perhaps with some optimism—as the current "rapprochement between history and anthro-

1

pology" (Mintz 1975:479). It is also a work in the expanding tradition of indigenous ethnography (Hsu 1973, Maruyama 1974, Hurston 1935, Drake 1945, Gwaltney 1980):

> The general stance of the anthropological establishment not very many years ago was that one could not do research on one's own people because as an insider one could neither be objective nor even actually see the sociocultural system because of one's intimate participation in it. Hence, only trained outsiders were considered qualified to be able to view a society both holistically and objectively. Another issue, so implicit as not to need to be voiced, was inherent in the nature of the science. Anthropologists from "civilized," highly developed (at least technologically) Western societies studied the "primitives," the "natives," the "stone age people" (Walker 1980:3).[1]

The emic perspectives embodied in the personal statements of "native" subjects—whose observations constitute the core of Chapter 5, "Perceptions of Tourism and Development"—can stand on their own, without recourse to etic constraints.

THE STUDY AREA

The British Virgin Islands, located some sixty miles east of Puerto Rico, were happened upon by Christopher Columbus during his second voyage to the West Indies in 1493. The group has a total land area of approximately sixty-nine square miles and numbers some sixty or so islands, cays and rocks, many of which are uninhabited.[2] They are all of volcanic origin with rugged, precipitous topography, with the notable exception of Anegada, which is flat and of limestone formation. Tortola is the largest of the group and is the site of the capital, Road Town (cf. West Indies and Caribbean Map, p.7).

Agriculturally marginal historically, the British Virgin Islands were brought into production as a sugarcane-producing plantation economy later than most British Caribbean plantation colonies. Thus, although claimed by British nationals around the mid-1500s, the era of prosperity experienced by British Virgin Islands plantation society was relatively short-lived. By the time slavery was abolished in 1834, British Virgin Islands plantation economy was in a moribund state. With the virtual obliteration of the British Virgin Islands plantation system by the end of the nineteenth century, the erstwhile slaves were left to eke out an existence for themselves within the framework of a petty commodity mode of production, a situation which would obtain until the fairly recent past. The British Virgin Islands economy had simply become too marginal to generate any sustained exploitative interest from the imperial center. Almost a century would pass and a new "monocrop"—tourism—would gain predominance before such interest would be revived.

RATIONALE

Historical and/or social scientific investigation regarding the British Virgin Islands is, by and large, a fairly recent phenomenon[3] and has been more or less concurrent with the dramatic socioeconomic transformations which have occurred in the BVI as the economic mode shifted from an essentially smallholding economy to one based almost exclusively on tourism, beginning in the early 1960s. As a result, there still exists only a fairly scant body of what might be termed sociocultural self-knowledge, upon which British Virgin Islanders can draw in an attempt to chart a course for the future.

This study, therefore, constitutes a contribution to the continuing effort to fill this lacuna. The study approaches the problematic of the idiographic characteristics of each British Virgin Islands socio-historical development phase—i.e., plantation economy, smallholding economy, and tourism economy—from the perspective of a nomothetic or generalizing conceptualization of the phase in question.

RESEARCH DESIGN

The plantation and smallholding phases of social formation in the British Virgin Islands are observed through library and archival research while, in the case of the current tourism phase, this approach is supplemented by fieldwork.

Library and Archival Research

In treating the slave-plantation system in the British Virgin Islands, local peculiarities are placed within a larger Caribbean context (Gurney 1840, Letter . . . 1843, Goveia 1965, Patterson 1967, Craton 1974). Excerpts from contemporary documents pertaining to British Virgin Islands plantation society are quoted *in extenso* for the color and detail that they impart to the picture of the British Virgin Islands plantation society and especially for the insight that is thus afforded into the dialectics of slave-master relations in the declining years of British Virgin Islands plantation economy (Parliamentary Papers 1824, 1825). This approach is partly informed by Stanley Diamond's (1974:347) admonition not to ". . . overlook the individual event and actor in the attempt to delineate overall patterns and structures . . . , [but rather] to confront the living flux of people making events," as well as by Edward Brathwaite's (1977:611) observation that too often research disregards "the face within the archive."

As with the treatment of slavery and the plantation era, the peculiarities of the British Virgin Islands smallholding/petty commodity mode of production are analyzed from the perspective of a broad conceptualization of that mode of production (Wolf 1966, Mintz 1973, Dalton 1972, Foster 1965, Shanin 1971, Meillassoux 1973). This, in turn, is situated within the larger British Caribbean context (Mintz 1974, Hall 1971, Marshall 1978, Beckford 1978). The relevancy of the concept of "peasantry" with respect to the post-emancipation social formation in the British Virgin Islands is questioned (cf. Mills 1976, Ennew et al.) and an alternative conceptualization is advanced.

The current phase—tourism economy—is, similarly, approached from the perspective of a generalizing conceptualization of the phenomenon of tourism (Smith 1977, MacCannell 1975, Turner and Ash 1975). The notion of tourism as development strategy is critically appraised (Young 1973, Bryden 1973) and examined through an analytical overview of the evolution of British Virgin Islands government policy directed towards the promotion of tourism economy (O'Loughlin 1962, Phillips 1966, BVI Economic Development Programme, 1979).

Field Research

The formal fieldwork phase of this study encompassed the period of April 1981 through December 1982. Initial emphasis was placed on informant (or, as John Gwaltney [1980] put it, "key consultant informant") interviewing and participant observation—essentially, a sort of "hanging-out" immersion in the sub-culture of BVI tourism.

Shortly, however, a required doctoral internship—in which I served as anthropologist-consultant/resource-person bilaterally to the Government's (Medical and Health Department) Mental Health Programme and to the British Virgin Islands Mental Health Association[4]—began to provide specific focus to the direction of my field research.

In this capacity, in October 1981, I assisted in conducting a "needs assessment" exercise for the Mental Health Programme. Input was obtained from various sectors of the community—including representatives from the clergy, education, the Immigration Department, the Police Department, the Ministry of Social Services—and areas of concern were identified. This exercise seemed to indicate, among other things, a fairly pervasive concern over the social dislocations—attrition of family ties and influences, alienation among youth, increasing incidence of drug abuse, etc.—concomitant with the rapid socioeconomic change experienced by the British Virgin Islands over the recent past. This perceived concern led to a decision to provide a forum in the form of a conference or symposium at which these issues could be further addressed. I was given the responsibility for conceptualizing and designing this forum (see Appendix).

The symposium, entitled "Social Change: Implications for the British Virgin Islands", was held in Tortola on 21, 22 May 1982. The proceedings were tape-recorded and subsequently transcribed. From this body of unpublished material, extensive portions are incorporated herein as Chapter 5, "Perceptions of Tourism and Development." This material is presented without any interposition on my part since—as John Gwaltney says of the key consultant informants in his book, *Drylongso*—"The people whose voices are heard in these pages are eminently capable of self expression, and I have relied on them to speak for themselves" (Gwaltney 1980: xxii).

The content of the transcribed material was analyzed, the themes thus identified leading to further exploration thereof by means of an adaptation of the so-called Delbecq Technique. This involved the selection of a "panel" of individuals who were asked to respond in writing to a series of statements or propositions regarding tourism, development, and the socioeconomic state of the Territory (cf. Delbecq and Van de Ven 1971).[5] The intention here was, as Van Maanen (1979:520) puts it, to "come to terms with the meaning, not the frequency," of certain aspects of BVI tourism economy. As with the Symposium material, the individual perceptions elicited by this method of data collection are presented at length in Chapter 5.

Taken as a whole, then, this approach provides a perspective on the socioeconomic transformation of the British Virgin Islands that is both diachronic (via library/archival research) and synchronic (via contemporary fieldwork).

LIMITATIONS

Societies such as the British Virgin Islands which were historically marginal to the interests of the imperial center are characterized by a corresponding paucity of historical records. This is especially so with regard to the smallholding period (post-emancipation to, say, 1950), which might be characterized as a period of imperial disinterest. Moreover, some of the more potentially useful records pertaining to the British Virgin Islands were transferred to Antigua for centralized storage and were subsequently destroyed by fire (1950). In some cases, therefore, while bibliographic references exist, the material no longer does. Thus, while the sweep of this study is broad, its scale is inherently narrowed by the paucity of available primary material for certain periods. Evidence for the contemporary tourism era is less problematic and was generated largely by my fieldwork.

In this latter regard, perusal of the narrative material thus derived (see Chapter 5) renders it readily apparent that the informants' perception concerning tourism and development presented in this study reflect an obvious class-bias. This is a function of the cohort of respondents selected—senior civil servants, university students, development consultants, hotel managers, and so on. The narrative material reflects a remarkable candor and provides useful insight into the contradictions which have been engendered by the rather abrupt transition from a smallholding economy to a tourism-based economy. It must be acknowledged, however, that the social perspective represented in the present study is, necessarily, only partial.

SIGNIFICANCE OF THE RESEARCH

It is my hope that this study will constitute a worthwhile contribution to the literature on the Caribbean in general and, more specifically, to an increased understanding of what has been called "the other Caribbean" (Hannerz 1974): those small, historically marginal economies (the British Virgin Islands, the Cayman Islands, Anguilla, and so on) which, after the demise of plantation economy in the 1800's, have only recently—with the recognition of their tourism potential—evoked a rekindling of interest from the imperial center. But perhaps more importantly, the availability of a study such as this should constitute a useful addition to the resources which British Virgin Islanders might utilize in the necessary attempt to place current circumstances in socio-historical perspective.

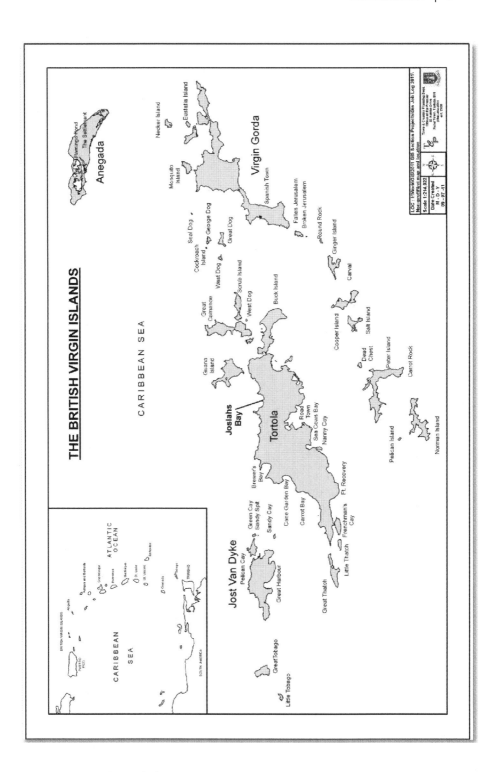

PART I

THE HISTORICAL CONTEXT

1

The Era of the Plantation

I am an advocate for humanity, and in consequence of this principle not an advocate for the liberation of the slave. I am an advocate for all that can make him comfortable and happy, for his
removal from his natal soil, that he may taste the comforts of
protection, the fruits of humanity, and the blessings of religion.

— William Beckford, Jr., *The Gentleman's Magazine*, 1788

AN HISTORICAL OVERVIEW

Euuropean settlement in the British Virgin Islands in the early years
following the Columbus encounter appears to have been sporadic
and insignificant, although the Islands' peculiar geographic characteristics, with their many bays and coves, rendered them the ideal haunt of
pirates and buccaneers of various nationalities. In 1565 a band of English
"adventurers" captured Tortola from a small group of Dutch nationals who
had settled there. It was not until 1680, however, that sustained English
settlement was begun, a few English planters having transferred from
Anguilla. Shortly thereafter, the European presence was further increased
by settlers "such as had fled from Barbados and the greater islands for
debt or to avoid punishment for their crimes and have since been increased by pirates who have come in upon acts of grace and are married
and settled there, whose posterity not knowing the world remain there and
cultivate the ground for a wretched subsistence" (Calendar of State Papers:
Colonial Series, America and the West Indies, No. 260; cited in Harrigan
and Varlack 1975:8).

Their "wretched subsistence" notwithstanding, the early white settlers
of the Virgin Islands colony deemed it necessary and found it possible to
avail themselves of black slave labour. Indeed, some of the settlers who
had transferred to the Virgin Islands had brought slaves with them. Subsequently, slave inventories were supplemented through purchase from
Danish St. Thomas, and after the 1730s, when cotton and subsistence
farming began to be supplanted by relatively large scale sugar production
for export, by direct importation of slaves from Africa (Dookhan 1975:71).

11

Until 1759, however, the economy of the British Virgin Islands colony continued to be centered primarily on the production of cotton.[1] In that year, the export value of sugar for the first time exceeded that of cotton (Harrigan and Varlack 1975:58).

The gradual shift from cotton and subsistence farming to sugar production—the production of the latter being considerably more labour-intensive than the former—was dramatically reflected in the demographic statistics. The first Virgin Islands census, taken in 1717, reveals a population of 547 blacks and 795 whites; in 1720 the population stood at 1,509 blacks and 1,222 whites, the latter figures remaining fairly stable throughout the heyday of Virgin Islands plantation society. The next census, in 1756, at the dawn of the transformation of the Virgin Islands' economy from one based on cotton farming to one based on sugar production, reveals a black population which had increased to 6,121.

The final quarter of the eighteenth century saw what might be termed the golden era of Virgin Islands plantation society, which produced a prosperity based in no small part on the energetic activities of Virgin Islands privateers during the War of American Independence. The Virgin Islands census of 1774, accordingly, reveals a black population which had risen to 9,000.

The early 1780s in particular was a pivotal period in the history of Virgin Islands plantation society. During this period, a transition took place from a society of small yeoman farmers and their slaves engaged in the cultivation of tobacco, cotton, and provisions, to one based on the production of sugar (and, incidentally, of rum) by relatively large estates. The outcome of this process was the decline and virtual disappearance of the small cotton planter as a result of real estate consolidation precipitated by the expansionist pressures of the larger sugar planters. As Herman Merivale (1841:75-76) noted in respect of the British Caribbean as a whole,

> the early settlers who occupied in such numbers the soil of the Antilles, seem to have been chiefly small proprietors, who lived on the produce of their estates. When the cultivation of sugar was introduced about 1670, the free white population rapidly diminished, and continued to do so for a century afterwards. . . . Sugar requires . . . the simultaneous application of much labour at particular seasons. Thus this species of agriculture resembles in some respects a manufacture; and, as in manufactures, the large capitalists have great advantages. . . . Hence all accounts of our West Indian colonies, in the first half of the last century, teem with complaints of the decay of small proprietors, and the consolidation of all classes of society into two, the wealthy planters and the slaves.

Thus in 1784, John Fahie, President of the Virgin Islands Council, reported in this regard that "it is here, as it is elsewhere, the large fish swallow up the small. The estates of the poor cotton planter which were contiguous to sugar estates have been swallowed up by them" (C.O. 152/53, cited in Goveia 1965:103). This expansionist period also saw considerable "expropriation" of slaves' allotted provision grounds.

The Virgin Islands census of 1805 reveals a population peaking at 10,520 persons, of whom 9,220 were blacks and 1,300 were whites.[2] In fact, however, the Virgin Islands plantation economy was by this time already well on its way along the path of economic decline. The economy had prospered and grown during a period encompassing two major wars—the Seven Years War (1756-63) and the American War of Independence (1776-83)—during which time what amounted to a sellers' market existed. But the termination of the War in 1783, together with incipient realignments of the world economic system, combined to bring about the demise of the Virgin Islands plantation economy. The Virgin Islands plantocracy had gotten caught up in the euphoria of a "bullish" market and had over-expanded. Thus, as early as 1790, Thomas Woolrich, a former resident of the Virgin Islands colony, could testify to the Select Committee of the House of Commons that "divers of their estates mortgaged in England to the merchants there have been sold at public vendue upon low terms by reason that there were very few able to buy and pay for them" (cited in Harrigan and Varlack 1975:60).

Clearly, then, the population peak revealed in the 1805 census was no longer indicative of a coincidence of prosperity. Indeed, "the problem," as Elsa Goveia has written of the British Leeward Islands generally, "was the very numerous slave population which had to be supported out of the proceeds of an economy which was no longer expanding" (Goveia 1965: 126).

By the early nineteenth century a number of critical factors were combining to bring about the decline of British Caribbean plantation economy and ultimately, of British Caribbean slavery itself. Among these interrelated factors were: (1) the ending of the War of American Independence in 1783; (2) the shift in Britain from the protectionism of a mercantilist capitalism to the laissez faire thrust of a growing industrial capitalist economy; (3) the increasing importance of British East India as an alternative source of sugar; and, as a consequence of all of these factors, (4) the increasing effectiveness of an humanitarian abolitionist-emancipation argument (see Craton 1974:239; cf. Williams 1970, Goveia 1965).

In the case of the British Virgin Islands plantation colony, the contrast between its era of prosperity and its subsequent decline may be demonstrated by consideration of accounts left to posterity by persons who visited the colony at different stages of its economic well-being.

Thus, a participant in a North American naval expedition against Tortola during the closing years of the War of American Independence—in an unsuccessful attempt at retribution for Virgin Islands colonists' privateering against American shipping—has left the following report:

> That part of Tortola which presented to our view appeared greatly cultivated & in a very flourishing state. The plantations exten-

sive and slaves numerous. The Town is compact but small; its situation low, & the air consequently confined by mountains adjacent which were exceeding high. The harbour is not large, but from its situation may reasonable be judged a place of security, from the severity of bad weather. At each fortified part of the Island were a cluster of Houses, pleasantly situated, which I supposed to be the residence of principle planters. (1781-2 "The Log of the [S/S] Pilgrim"; cited in Tyson 1977:92).[3]

Some forty years later, the economic picture had changed completely for the worse. A devastating hurricane in 1819 completed the process of degeneration which had begun with the ending of the War of American Independence and the subsequent decreasing economic significance to Britain of her Caribbean Colonies.[4] British Mercantilism was on its death-bed and so, consequently, were the British Caribbean plantation colonies. In Tortola, "many large proprietors who before [the hurricane of] 1819 had been considered persons of opulence found great difficulty in obtaining sufficient credit to enable them to carry on the cultivation of their estates, little prospect being attached to their ability to repay" (Dookhan 1975:65).

Trelawney Wentworth's account of his visit to Tortola shortly after the hurricane of 1819 informs us that

> extensive tracts of land which bore the marks of tillage, but which were no longer in cultivation, lay before us in every side; and the soil had been so much washed by the heavy rains, and impoverished by long culture, as to afford only a scanty herbage to a considerable number of sheep (Wentworth 1834:175).

Under such circumstances of progressive degeneration, the "compensation" which the British Virgin Islands planter class received from the British Treasury on emancipation of its slaves in 1834 was undoubtedly, from its perspective, a most timely windfall. In the perverted logic of slavery, the metropolitan Government indemnified not the victims, but rather the beneficiaries of slavery. "It was," as Eric Williams (1970:331-2) puts it, "compensation not for the deprivation of liberty but for the expropriation of property." Pursuant to the provisions of the British Emancipation Act of 1833, 382 claims for compensation were submitted by British Virgin Islands slave-owners (Williams, Eric 1970:283). Against this "property", British Virgin Islands planters were compensated in the amount of some £70,177 (Williams, Eric 1970:332).

By 1841 only four European plantation proprietors remained in the colony, and by 1845 "landed property which was principally in the hands of representatives of absentees and persons having no fixed interest in the colony was much deteriorated in value" (cited in Harrigan and Varlack 1975:64). In a very real sense, plantation society no longer existed in the British Virgin Islands after the 1840s. The sale of several major encumbered estates by the Virgin Islands legislature in 1864 to various erstwhile slaves effectively ended the era of Virgin Islands plantation society.

THE PLANTATION SYSTEM:
CARIBBEAN PERSPECTIVES AND BRITISH
VIRGIN ISLANDS PECULIARITIES

The term "plantation" is defined in the *International Encyclopedia of the Social Sciences* as

> an economic unit producing agricultural commodities (field crops or horticultural products, but not livestock) for sale and employing a relatively large number of unskilled laborers whose activities are closely supervised. Plantations usually employ a year-round labor crew of some size, and they usually specialize in the production of only one or two marketable products. They differ from other kinds of farms in the way in which the factors of production, primarily management and labor, are combined (Jones 1968:154).

As regards the Caribbean, it would seem fairly clear that there was an historically inextricable relationship between the development of the plantation system and European colonization.[5] For present purposes, European colonies in the New World can be classified according to a three-fold typology as posited by George Beckford. Some of these colonies were "settlement" colonies, being based on fairly large-scale European immigration (as, for example, in North America, Australia, and New Zealand). Others were "conquest" colonies, being established primarily to effect the physical transfer of wealth—especially precious metals—from the colony to the mother-country. The third type was the colony of "exploitation," established for the purpose of commodity production for trade (Beckford 1972:8). While there was obviously some overlapping between colonial types, "the plantation," as Beckford points out, "was the institution best suited to metropolitan needs in colonies of exploitation" (ibid.; cf. Thompson 1960).

In the Caribbean, moreover, "plantation development", as Sidney Mintz has observed, "was always linked to sub-tropical commodities (particularly sugar), into the production of which climate and topography entered importantly" (Mintz 1977a:257). The further observation should be made that in the Caribbean, the sugar plantation constituted the quintessential form of that institution. Significantly also, the development of the Caribbean plantation prototype was historically linked with and, in fact, based upon a system of coerced labour, more specifically, of enslaved African labour.

> When one analyzed . . . the phenomenon of the sugar plantation, with the perspective of an entrepreneur intending to establish an

enterprise in the best possible place, one understands that plantations and slavery (together) are a very Antillean phenomenon,
although both earlier and later they are found in other zones.
(Fraginals, in Mintz 1966a:258)

At this point, it might be appropriate to offer another definition of the
plantation, one which more specifically encompasses the characteristics of
the Caribbean slave/sugar plantation. The plantation is here conceived as
"a capitalistic type of agricultural organization in which a considerable
number of unfree labourers were employed under unified direction and
control in the production of a staple crop" (Gray 1941:444). Drawing on
Gray's work, Sidney Mintz has distilled the following factors as being
characteristic of the plantation system:

> (1) the roles of the laboring and employing classes were set
> sharply apart; (2) the aim of the system was continuous com-
> mercial (that is, market-oriented) agriculture; (3) the trend was
> to specialization in monocrop production; and (4) the enterprise
> was capitalistic in character in that the value of slaves, land, and
> equipment required the investment of money capital, frequently
> in large sums and frequently borrowed, while the planter tended
> to assume the role of businessman, testing success by the yield of
> income relative to the capital invested. (Mintz 1974:96)

Having thus defined the nature of the Caribbean plantation, we will
now consider some of the more salient characteristics of the plantation,
both as a system of production and as a social institution, as regards the
British Caribbean in general and the British colony of the Virgin Islands in
particular.

The Physical Setting

The most visually imposing object on the typical British Caribbean plantation was invariably the planter's residence or the Great House, as it was
generally called. Orlando Patterson, in his seminal work *The Sociology of
Slavery*, rather uncharacteristically devotes very little descriptive attention to the Great House, noting simply that "they were constructed of
roughly cut stones and wood; the rooms were extremely large, centered on
an enormous hall and the furniture 'generally plain but genteel.'" Patterson further dismisses these edifices as evincing little architectural merit
(Patterson 1967:53-4).

In the case of the British Virgin Islands, however, we are provided with
a detailed description of a planter's residence:

> The dwelling . . . consisted merely of one floor, composed of a
> frame-work in the form of a parallelogram, clap-boarded at the
> sides and extremities, and with the ordinary span roof planked

and covered with small pieces of wood called shingles. The interior was divided, as high as the cross-beams, into three compartments, one occupying nearly half the area, which was designated "the hall" and appropriated to the ordinary daily purposes of drawing and dining-room; the other two served as sleeping rooms, each having communication with the other, as well as access and egress by a door opening on a stone pavement on which the whole fabric stood, and which also supported an open gallery or corridor projecting about four feet from the roof. . . . The floor was planked, but without carpeting, and the articles of furniture were such as necessity and convenience required, rather than such as elegance or caprice might have suggested. A common hall lamp was suspended from one of the center beams; on one side of the room stood a small mahogany sideboard, bearing such articles of plate and glassware as were in use, the two ends of a dining-table forming a circle, stood in the center, and the other portion of it occupied a position on one side, to await occasions which might require accommodation for a larger party; a few cherry-tree chairs completed the arrangement. (Wentworth 1934:152-3)

The slaves' housing was, as one might expect, considerably less substantial. As Michael Craton points out, "no expenditure on slave housing was allowed for in the capitalization of estates" (Craton 1974:189). Typically, therefore,

slaves were expected to build their own houses and consequently constructed them as they would in Africa, of wattle and daub, with the thatch of guinea grass, cane tops or palmetto, the "poor man's shingle". Absolutely vulnerable to fire, flood, and hurricane, unlike the stone-built sugar factories and the more substantial Great Houses, they have left no traces behind. Old prints and maps, however, show that they were generally situated close to the estate factory (with its sickening stench of the final sugar waste product called "dunder") and within sight of the overseer's house, and were either clustered together like a collection of beehives or laid out in rows. . . .

Barely larger than twelve feet square, they were generally divided into two rooms, without floors or windows, "sometimes suffocating with heat and smoke; at others, when the fire subsides, especially at night, admitting the cold damp air through innumerable crevices and holes". (ibid.)

The appurtenances of the slave hut were correspondingly meager:

Furnishings were very poor: "a few wooden bowls and calabashes, a water-jug, a wooden mortar for pounding their Indian corn, and an iron pot for boiling the farrago of vegetable ingredients which comprised their daily meal, composed almost all their furniture".

Sometimes a crude bed was constructed out of a raised platform on which a mat made of . . . [trash] was placed; but most slaves slept on the ground. (Patterson 1967:55)

Even in this context, it is interesting to note, a sort of social stratification manifested itself in the "zoning" patterns within the slave compound, for

sometimes the huts of the headmen, denoting their occupiers' status, were somewhat larger and stood slightly apart, significantly closer to the plank-built houses of the managerial whites. (Craton 1974:189)

Each plantation had a building designated as a "hospital" or "hothouse" for the slaves.

In addition to the room for sick Negroes, it also contained a room for mothers during their period of confinement, room for the doctor and one or more storerooms where some goods belonging to the plantation were kept. (Patterson 1967:56)

The architectural survey of the Caribbean plantation is completed with the inclusion of the sugarcane-grinding mill—in a very real sense the heart of the physical setting of the plantation—and the ancillary boiling, curing, and distilling buildings.

The Productive Milieu

The slaves' workday was long and arduous, beginning, as the saying goes, at "can see" and ending at "can't see." Work began at dawn with the sounding of the slave driver's conch shell, and continued without break until around nine o'clock when a period of forty-five minutes or so was allowed for breakfast (see Goveia 1965; Patterson 1967). Work was then continued until around midday when a break varying in length of time from ninety minutes to three hours was allowed. "However, few slaves ate a midday meal at this time, especially if they were required to bring in a bundle of grass when they reassembled at one or two o'clock in the afternoon" (Goveia, Elsa 1965:130).

The Caribbean slaves' diet was invariably inadequate:

Slaves on sugar estates were regularly issued sugar, cane juice, or molasses, and rum whenever the weather was foul or the work particularly hard. At best—where masters were comparatively generous with issues and slaves were given sufficient time and ground to grow their own provisions—the slave diet was barely adequate; monotonous, starch-heavy, and deficient in protein and vitamins. At its worst—on constricted or severely managed estates when foreign supplies were cut off—the slave diet was totally inadequate. In times of war, hurricane, or exceptional drought, actual starvation was not unknown. (Craton 1974:192)

In any case, after the midday interlude,

[the slaves] were again mustered and set to work in an afternoon spell which lasted until about half an hour before sunset. Then they were turned out once more to pick grass before the light faded. The slaves, therefore, worked at least ten hours in the field each day and to this must be added the extra time spent on the task of grass picking. In crop-time even longer hours were sometimes worked, since the mill which was grinding all night, had to be kept supplied with canes and also with fuel for the boilers. (Goveia 1965:130)

The majority of the slaves on the sugar plantation were involved in field labour:

The field that was to be holed was first divided up, laying down reasonably accessible roads or intervals within the boundaries. Then it was cut into smaller squares, and the slaves were put to work in a long line using their hoes to dig up holes in each square. As each line of squares was holed, the gang moved on to the next line, and the process was repeated. When the land had been manured and was ready for planting, cane cuttings were laid longitudinally in these holes and covered with mould. . . . On steep lands the siting of the squares was a matter of great importance as the banks had to be used to prevent . . . ruinous washes of soil. . . . It was reckoned a tolerable day's work for forty slaves to hole one acre of land. (Goveia 1965:120)

The reaping of the crops was a similarly strenuous, highly regimented operation (see Patterson 1967). Once the sugarcane was cut, it had to be transported fairly quickly from the fields to the site of the grinding-boiling-distilling process. Animals or animal-driven carts were generally used for this purpose, although, as Elsa Goveia has observed, "the planters were often more careful of their [animals] than of their slaves, preferring to transfer heavy loads from the animals to the Negroes 'as soon as the steep became severe'" (Goveia 1965:118; citing Caines 1801).

In the British Virgin Islands, however, because of topographical constraints, the planters resorted to an apparently unique sled-like means of
transferring the harvested cane from the hillside fields to the mill. According to an English traveller who visited the Virgin Islands sometime during
the first quarter of the nineteenth century,

> the steepness and irregularity of the upland sides, rendering
> carts impracticable, caused the use of wooden spouts or troughs
> to convey the canes to the mill. These troughs being ranged on
> the inclined plane, in a line as direct as possible to the works, or
> to the nearest vicinity, whence the canes are conveyed by carts,
> necessarily intersect at different intervals, the zigzag paths which
> lead to the mountain summits. (Wentworth 1834:153)

This trough mechanism, while perhaps an efficient means of convey-
ance of the harvested sugarcane, was not without inherent danger, as our
English raconteur was to discover. Indeed, he recounts almost having been
killed by a "sweetened arrow" when,

> in stepping across the range at a moment of imagined security, a
> single cane was thrown down the trough, and came with the ve-
> locity of an arrow impelled from a bow, and having received a
> check in the channel of the trough, it ascended in a curved direc-
> tion to the height of our head, and passed within an inch of our
> existence. Many instances of injury to the negroes have occurred
> from this cause, and two who had lost their leg or arm, were af-
> terwards pointed out to us. (ibid.)

Once the sugarcane was received at the processing site, it was put
through the grinding mill and the juice extracted. The extracted cane juice
was then subjected to the dual process of boiling and clarification, the end
product of which was a soft, heavy form of sugar.

During the boiling and clarification process, the resultant "scum was
ladled off as the juice boiled" (Goveia 1965:132).

> The . . . last boiler, called the teache, required very careful tim-
> ing, since it was necessary to watch for the moment when the fire
> should be extinguished and the liquor ladled into a cooler to al-
> low crystals to form. The process was known as "striking" and
> was regarded as one of the most difficult in the craft of sugar
> manufacture and was of great importance in determining the
> quantity and quality of sugar which eventually reached the mar-
> ket. When the sugar had finally crystallized in coolers, it was
> usually potted in hogsheads which were then hung over a large
> cistern to be drained of their surplus molasses. After this last
> process of curing, the sugar was ready to be shipped. (ibid.; cf.
> Edwards 1793, vol. II:259-75)

At virtually every stage of the plantation productive process, the health of the slaves was in jeopardy:

> Setting off for work in the chilling predawn mists, the field slaves were alternately broiled and soaked with tropical sun and rain, with no protection save their hats of felt or straw or the flimsy shelters erected at the edge of the fields. Factory slaves were shielded from the rain, but the hellish heat and stink of the boiling, curing and distilling houses were scarcely more healthy than the fields. In all phases of work, pulmonary infections and fevers had ideal conditions in which to flourish and spread. (Craton 1974:192)

Given such conditions, it should hardly be surprising that by the time they had attained the age of forty-five, most slaves, especially those involved in the productive process, were considered to have passed their prime (Patterson 1967:175).

The Socioeconomic Setting

SLAVES AND MASTERS

Slaves were perceived and utilized as factors of production and as such, a monetary value was ascribed to each slave according to skills possessed. In the British Caribbean, newly imported African slaves were sold on average for around £70 for males and £63 to £68 for females; seasoned Creole praedial slaves went for £80 to £125 for males and £70 to £110 for females; artisans averaged £130 to £300, according to trade and skills. The higher prices for "seasoned" Creole slaves reflected "the costs of breeding and subsisting slaves till they could be used or sold as labourers" (Goveia 1965:122-3).

Obviously, the skills which were most highly valued by the master-class were those which were considered most critical to the proper functioning of the plantation system. It follows, therefore, that "social stratification and the division of labour among the slaves were functions of their socioeconomic relation to the white group" (Patterson 1967:57). Thus, for example,

> the boilerman was in many respects the most valued slave on the estate. On his skill depended the quality of the sugar produced and one false move on his part could ruin an entire field of cane. Naturally, he had considerable independence and few overseers dared to antagonize him as he had it so much in his power to exact vengeance. (ibid.:62)

At the other extreme were those slaves who had the misfortune of working the so-called jobbing gang:

These gangs were usually owned by small-scale proprietors or sometimes adventurers seeking a quick fortune. Often they were communally owned, the owner of the largest batch usually being the supervisor of the gang for which task he was paid a commission by the other owners. Jobbing gangs were not only hired to dig holes, but also to make and repair roads, clear forests and in general, to do the most arduous work on the estates and elsewhere. They had no permanent homes and slept wherever night overcame them, in sugar mills, on the roadside, or in the huts of friendly estate slaves. It is easy to understand why the life expectancy of such a gang was estimated at seven years. (ibid.:66)

In contrast to the black slave majority, whose presence in the British Caribbean was involuntary, members of the white master-class—planters, overseers, bookkeepers and the like—were under no such constraints. Generally, however,

the first generation of West Indian planters did not enjoy sufficient wealth to visit their homeland, but sent their sons for an education that would equip them for their plantocratic duties. The third generation stayed in England. . . . Thereafter, the plantations were in the hands of overseers and attorneys. (Craton 1974:201)

Given the overarching need in British Caribbean plantation society for the white master class to maintain the subjugation of the black slave majority, it is not surprising that a somewhat contrived social solidarity evolved among the colonists. This point was noted by the plantocrat, Bryan Edwards, when he observed, with some misgivings, that

the poorest white person seems to consider himself nearly on a level with the richest, and emboldened by this idea approaches his employer with extended hand and a freedom, which in the countries in Europe, is seldom displayed by men in the lower orders of life towards their superiors. It is not difficult to trace the origin of this principle. It arises without doubt, from the preeminence and distinction which are necessarily attached even to the complexion of a White Man, in a country when the complexion, generally speaking, distinguishes freedom from slavery. (Edwards 1783:11:7-8)

By the late eighteenth century most of the British Caribbean plantations were absentee-owned, their management being entrusted to attorneys and overseers, a group which Michael Craton has characterized as "the most mediocre members of the imperial middle class" (Craton, 1974:202). "Many plantation whites", Craton further asserts, "sank into a hopeless moral torpor, eating, drinking and fornicating themselves into an early grave" (ibid.:205-6). Indeed, Edward Long, the renowned Jamaican plantocrat, felt obliged to concede that these creole whites were so degenerate that even the "better sort" of slaves despised them (Long 1774:289).

THE LAW IN PLANTATION SOCIETY

Societies in which slavery played a significant role have historically generated extensive corpora of judicial fabrications, the primary purpose of which has been the absolute regulation of the slaves.

In the particular case of the plantation society of the British Virgin Islands colony, the slave laws were undoubtedly epitomized by the Slave Act of 1783, entitled, "An Act for the good Government of Negro and other Slaves. . . ." As was the case in many instances throughout the British Caribbean, slave laws in the Virgin Islands colony were invariably concerned with effecting the socioeconomic subjugation of the slaves on the one hand, and what might be termed the police regulation of the slave majority on the other. These two concerns were, of course, not mutually exclusive.

The Virgin Islands Slave Act of 1783 arose in part because of certain contradictions which had developed within the society as regards the slaves' status. Thus the Virgin Islands legislature found it necessary in the Act to censor

> the unwary Indulgences of Proprietors of Slaves [which] have crept imperceptibly into great Excess within these islands, by granting them a Licence of owning and purchasing Slaves or Cattle, by which they become aggrandized, insolent, and contumacious, disregarding the necessary Decorum which ought to be supported in a prudent and well regulated Police, and most probably will be fraught with most fatal, ruinous, and destructive Events, unless timely checked and prevented. (Slave Act of 1783; in Goveia 1965:180)

A different aspect of the Act's economic regulatory preoccupations is evident in its position on compensation to planters for runaway slaves. Under the terms of the Act it was provided that

> runaway slaves were not valued by appraisement [since] the owner received compensation at the fixed rate of £50 per man and £45 per woman slave condemned to death for this crime. When the slaves ran away in gangs of ten or more, and only the leader suffered capital punishment, the full appraised value of this slave was paid to his owner. (Goveia 1965:177)

It is significant in this regard that the economic value of the slave as a factor of production was reflected in the Virgin Islands justices' discretionary powers regarding capital punishment in the case of runaways.

Thus, "even the ringleader of a runaway gang could be punished in some other way than by death" (Goveia 1965:178). In the same vein, Orlando Patterson asserts that

> quite often a master would resist all attempts by the constable to arrest a valuable slave. . . . Crimes committed by these slaves would often go undetected and it was not uncommon for slaves whose services could be more easily dispensed with to be substituted for the more valuable ones who had committed the crime. Even more pernicious was the practice, though not common, of masters falsely accusing weak or old slaves of capital crimes so as to be awarded the legal compensation for them. (Patterson 1967:88)

The police regulatory functions of British Virgin Islands slave law attempted to effect the complete subjugation of the slave in virtually every facet of his existence.

> To prevent dangerous assemblies of slaves, it was laid down that owners should not permit their slaves to get together and beat drums, or blow horns, or make great feasts, or meet with strange slaves on their plantations. The penalty for neglect was £20 for every offence. A fine of £50 was inflicted upon every owner who failed to have his Negro houses searched, once every three months, to discover hidden guns, weapons, and stolen goods. A slave informing on other slaves planning revolt or escape was to receive £3 reward if his information was certified to be good, but could be whipped if it proved frivolous. Slaves found to be planning to procure offensive weapons, to mutiny, or to desert the island, were declared felons, and were to suffer death or other punishment, at discretion. Any slave who struck or opposed a white, on proof before a justice, was sentenced to whipping. If he had been guilty of serious resistance, his punishment was mutilation, dismemberment, or death, except only in cases where slaves were acting on orders from the master. Any Negro who attempted to poison or otherwise murder any person was to die, with all his accomplices, upon conviction. (Goveia 1965:184; citing the Virgin Islands Slave Act of 1783)

The physical punishment meted out to slaves was harsh indeed. Patterson posits that "until about the middle of the second quarter of the eighteenth century brutality to the slaves was the norm" (Patterson 1967:82). On the evidence of Sir Hans Sloane, a contemporary pro-slavery writer, we learn that for participation in rebellion, slaves could be punished by

> burning them by nailing them down on the ground with crooked sticks on every limb and then applying the Fire by degrees from

the feet and hands, burning them gradually up to the head, whereby their pains were extravagant. . . .

For crimes of lesser nature, Gelding, or chopping off half of the foot with an Ax. . . . For running away they put Iron Rings of great weight on their Ankles, or Pottocks about their Necks, which are iron rings with two long necks riveted to them, or a Spur in the Mouth. . . . For Negligence, they were usually whipped by the overseer with Lance-wood Switches, till they be bloody, and several of the Switches broken, being first tied up by the hands in the Mill-Houses. . . . After they were whip'd till they are Raw, Some put on their Skins Pepper and Salt to make them smart; at other times their Masters will drop melted Wax on their skins and use several exquisite tortures. (Cited in Patterson 1967:82-3)

The inextricable connection between the unflinching ability of the white master-class to inflict such brutal punishments on their black slaves and the prevailing racist ideology is made starkly evident and is typified by one of the inane pronouncements of that "lady of quality," Janet Schaw, who tendered the observation that

when one comes to be better acquainted with the nature of Negroes, the horror of it must wear off. It is the suffering of the human mind that constitutes the greatest misery of punishment, but with them it is merely corporeal. As to the brutes, it inflicts no wound on their minds, whose Natures seem made to bear it, and whose sufferings are not attended with shame or pain beyond the present moment. (Schaw 1939; cited in Goveia 1965: 134)

Given such a perspective, it was easy for the master class to adopt an attitude that was at once both casual and unpremeditated in the administration of punishment to their bondsmen (cf. Gratus 1973:155).

SLAVERY AND SUBSISTENCE CULTIVATION

Throughout most of the Caribbean, the custom evolved whereby slaves were allowed, indeed encouraged, to cultivate provisions on plantation lands deemed unsuitable for cultivation of primary export crops. Writing in 1790, William Beckford provides a useful description of the phenomenon:

The slaves . . . prepare their land, and put in their crops on the Saturdays that are given to them, and they bring home their provisions at night and if their grounds be at a considerable distance from the plantation, as they often are, the journey backwards and forwards makes this rather a day of labour and fatigue, than of enjoyment and rest; but if, on the contrary, they be within any tolerable reach, it may be said to partake of both. . . .

Upon these occasions they move, with all their family, into the place of cultivation; the children of different ages are loaded with baskets, which are burdened in proportion to their strength and age; and it is pleasing to observe under what considerable weights they will bear themselves up, without either murmur or fatigue. The infants are flung at the backs of the mothers, and very little incommode them in their walks or labour. (Beckford 1790, II:151-87, passim; cited in Mintz 1974:186)

Another contemporary observer (Stewart 1823:267; ibid.:187) furnishes a descriptive distinction between the kitchen-garden or house-lot and the provision ground:

Adjoining to the house is usually a small spot of ground, laid out into a sort of garden, and shaded by various fruit trees. Here the family deposit their dead, to whose memory they invariably, if they can afford it, erect a rude tomb. Each slave has, besides this spot, a piece of ground (about half an acre) allotted to him as a provision ground. This is the principal means of his support; and so productive is the soil, where it is good and the seasons regular, that this spot will not only furnish him with sufficient food for his own consumption, but an over-plus to carry to market. By means of this ground, and of the hogs and poultry which he may raise (most of which he sells), an industrious Negro may not only support himself comfortably, but save something. If he has a family, an additional proportion of ground is allowed him, and all his children from five years upward assist him in his labours in some way or other.

Over time, as Sidney Mintz suggests, "a wholly distinctive crop repertory . . . was created by combining familiar African crops, such as 'guinea yams' and okra, with native . . . crops, including corn [and] sweet potatoes; European vegetables, such as cabbage and carrots; and Southeast Asian cultigens, including the breadfruit" (1974:236). But most importantly, the slaves' evolving extra-plantation horticultural repertoire would later constitute, in large measure, the basis of their ability to survive the demise of the plantation system.

Having thus considered certain salient characteristics of British Caribbean plantation society—indicating wherever possible within that framework, some of the peculiarities of the British Virgin Islands case—attention will be directed in the next chapter to the consideration of aspects of the social relations of production in British Virgin Islands plantation society.

2

Manumission and Rebellion

This chapter considers the social relations of production in British Virgin Islands plantation society via examination of instances of slave manumission and rebellion in the colony. The approach adopted in examining slave-master relations in the Virgin Islands colony involves the presentation and analysis of selected documentary material, with the intention of attempting to flesh out the picture of the Virgin Islands plantation society.

The first set of documents under consideration relates mainly to the controversy which resulted in England as a consequence of the freeing in 1775 of the slaves on the Long Look estate of the Quaker planter Samuel Nottingham. This occurred considerably before Britain had decreed either the cessation of the slave trade or the emancipation of slaves in her colonies.

THE NOTTINGHAM FREE PEOPLE

In June 1776,[1] Samuel and Mary Nottingham, who were at the time residing in Long Island, New York, effected a deed of manumission as regards slaves on their Tortola plantation called Longlook (review of the Quarterly Review. . . . 1824:91), also deeding to them in perpetuity their fifty-acre estate (Harrigan and Varlack 1975:24).

The documentary material under consideration here is derived from the journalistic debate which occurred in England in 1824 on the question of the viability—indeed, of the desirability or lack thereof—of free black communities in the New World colonies. The case of the Nottingham Free People, as they came to be called, was cited by both sides of the debate in support of their respective arguments.

James McQueen, the pro-slavery writer in the debate, paints an exceedingly pejorative picture of the Nottingham Free People by means of extensive quotation of various Tortolian planter correspondents:

> Instead of living together upon the plantation . . . the males ramble here and there, every where forming TRANSITORY CONNEXIONS among and with the female Slaves, upon the

27

neighbouring estates. Upon these females, with other precarious means, they are altogether dependent for sustenance. Most of the males have female Slaves for their wives, and consequently their children, when they have any, are born Slaves. They do not cultivate their own land or any other in exportable Colonial produce. They possess little stock of any sort. They may, indeed, be pretty clear of debt, as I am sure no one would be silly enough to credit them to the smallest amount. In short they are an intolerable nuisance to people of all ranks, wherever they take up their abode, which seldom is in one place. . . . The principal increase amongst these people proceeds from a connexion with Slaves and free people unconnected with the Nottingham family. GRACE, the wife of Jeffrey is an enfranchised female, formerly belonging to MRS. FRETT. Such is their low and mean condition that there are only two decent houses on the establishment of LONGLOOK, the one built by JASPER RAPSOT, a freeman and a shipwright, who lives with EVE NOTTINGHAM: and the other built by JEFFREY, a Slave belonging to Mr. PICKERING, a neighbouring proprietor, and which Slave Jeffrey lived with DIANA NOTTINGHAM. The ground belonging to this woman was partly cultivated by Mr. Pickering's Slaves, hired by their fellow Slave Jeffrey to do so during their time when not engaged in labour for their masters. The greatest part of the females liberated by Mr. Nottingham died without issue. Most of the males connected themselves with female Slaves, and were consequently relieved from the trouble of providing for, and supporting their children.

Besides their liberty and the land, Mr. Nottingham's negroes were left a legacy of £316.15s sterling by his sister, and which was paid to them by DR. DAWSON of Tortola. Not a fourth part of the property left to them, and some negroes also manumitted by Mr. Perceval, and Mrs. Vanterpool, and Mrs. Frett, remains in their hands. They do not raise one single article of exportable produce for the European market. They rear nothing that produces either taxes to the Colony or revenue to the Mother Country. By the labour of Slaves belonging to the neighbouring plantations they collect some means of barter, such as a little firewood, and perhaps some country provisions, which they carry to the Danish island of St. Thomas, to market, and bring back from there in exchange the coarsest American productions and imports, such as a few boards and shingles, salt-fish and similar articles not one of which is the production of the soil, skill, or manufacture of Great Britain. (Cited in McQueen 1824:171-2)

The implication of Mr. McQueen's carefully marshaled evidence on the Nottingham ex-slaves is clear: even given a head start with free land and monetary windfalls, free black communities in the colonies would inevitably be economically and perhaps even genetically nonviable.

By way of buttressing his argument and underscoring the presumed validity of his evidence on the degeneration of the Nottingham Free People, McQueen also cites the case of the Virgin Islands plantation proprietor, Mrs. Elizabeth Frett, who

> before her death emancipated seven Slaves, viz. William, George, Peter, Eve, Grace, Bice and Mary-Ann. William was the oldest, and at the time of his emancipation was 40 years of age: three months after the death of his mistress, William owned and possessed a house, 2 sailing boats, both decked and sloop rigged; the largest was worth 700, the smaller worth 160 dollars. He was also the master and owner of four Slaves, four horses worth about 70 dollars each, and several head of horned cattle, and one acre of land. He died in July 1821, in great want, brought on entirely by indolence. He had got rid of all the preceding property except the house, a cow, and the land. George died about four years ago and, while he lived, depended for support upon his friends and would never labour nor cultivate any land. Mary-Ann lives in Broadtown [sic], a common prostitute: and Bice exists by huxtering canes, and other estates' produce; she has a house and cow left by her father, and a piece of land which she never cultivates. (ibid.: 321-2)

Ultimately, however, the racist assumptions which underlay McQueen's argument become glaringly obvious, for he concludes that "such is the fate and fortune of [free blacks]. Amongst the natives of the temperate zones industry is general and indolence rare: but amongst the natives of the torrid zone the case is the reverse, indolence and sloth are general—industry rare" (ibid.).

Apart from the racist implications of McQueen's deductions from the evidence which he presents on free blacks within the larger context of the slave/plantation society of the Virgin Islands colony, the assertion that the freed slaves—through "indolence and sloth"—dissipated their inheritance, should be viewed with some skepticism.

In the first place, the Virgin Islands, at the time McQueen was writing (1824), had only recently suffered a series of natural disasters. In 1815, it has been observed, "scarcely one-fifth of Tortola was under cultivation due to severe drought" (Harrigan and Varlack:21). This was followed in 1819 by a devastating hurricane. The combination of these factors alone meant that the Virgin Islands plantation economy as a whole, let alone a relatively small class of free blacks within a slave-labour economy, could hardly have been prospering. And in any case, it is extremely doubtful whether a putatively prospering free black planter class developing within Virgin Islands plantation society would have been tolerated by the white master class.

Finally, it would seem fairly clear that the kinship networks that were established between the Nottingham Free People and slaves on surrounding estates were of much greater significance than simply being "transitory connections," as McQueen disparagingly dubbed them.

Totally apart from the social and affective implications of these relationships, there are also two economic implications: First, the incidence of slaves working the grounds of their kin and/or acquaintances among the Nottingham Free People was beneficial to both parties, with arrangements undoubtedly being developed among themselves for the sharing of the proceeds.

Second, the fact that the Nottingham ex-slaves were free to travel to, and trade in, the neighbouring Danish West Indies enabled them to serve as a sort of conduit for the sale of their own and their slave relatives' and associates' surplus produce.

Shortly after the publication of McQueen's pejorative analysis of the predicament of free blacks in Virgin Islands plantation society, an article in rebuttal appeared in the emancipationist journal, *The Edinburgh Review.* "Mr. McQueen has endeavoured," the author of the essay in question asserted,

> . . . by producing a long detail by a Mr. D. Frazer of Tortola, to show that the Nottinghams are an idle, profligate, pilfering set. All this proves nothing . . . [although] it would be easy to show several palpable contradictions, even in this latest detail of Mr. Frazer. But, admitting the whole to be as true, as it evidently is untrue and exaggerated, it only makes the case of the Nottinghams a more remarkable proof of the beneficial effects of freedom, as compared with slavery. If they, though idle and profligate, immoral and vicious, have contrived to maintain themselves for nearly fifty years, without any burden on the community, without contracting debts, without being convicted, or even judicially accused, of any crime, and have in that time increased from 26 to 44, while the slave community around them has been rapidly decreasing; is it possible to mark more strongly than by these facts the comparatively destructive nature of slavery? But the case, when all the circumstances of it are known, establishes this position still more strongly. Although Mr. Nottingham emancipated his slaves in 1776, he being then a resident in America, yet owing to the war which intervened, it was at least eight years later before they were put in possession of their freedom. In 1790 their number had diminished from 26 to 20. From that time, however, they increased; and their number has since has been more than doubled, notwithstanding all the harsh epithets bestowed on them by Mr. McQueen's friend. How much more rapidly must they have multiplied, had they been sober, industrious, and moral! As for the charges of profligacy and vice, they are charges which affect not the Nottinghams only, but the

Methodist Society, of which so many of them are members; and it behooves the Methodist Ministers at Tortola to explain how it is that such worthless characters continue to be connected with them. (Review of the Quarterly Review . . . 1824:42)

The author then proceeded to support his argument by means of a comparative demographic analysis of what might be termed the genetic or reproductive viability of Virgin Islands blacks in slavery and in freedom. As regards the Nottingham blacks, it should be parenthetically noted here (see also note no. 1) that although the English Nottinghams had initially decreed the emancipation of their slaves in 1776, their full freedom was not attained until 1790. Thus the observation was made that

in the interval . . . between 1776 and 1790, during at least eight or nine years of which the Nottinghams continued in a state of slavery in the hands of agents, their number appears to have been reduced from twenty-six to twenty, being above the average rate of decrease among the slaves of Tortola at that period. But from whatever cause this decrease may have proceeded, it would seem, from the deed of Hannah Abbott, that in 1790 the Nottinghams were only twenty in number—viz. eight males, and twelve females. In 1823, however, the number which had sprung from these twelve females, including such of the original stock as were yet alive, amounted to forty-four. The increase, therefore, had been at the rate of 120 percent: in thirty-three years. (ibid.: 92)

By way of contrast, demographic evidence was marshaled to demonstrate that those blacks who remained enslaved fared considerably worse than the Nottingham Free People:

In 1788 the slave population of [Tortola] amounted, according to the Privy-Council Report, to 9000. From the returns made to the House of Commons, in subsequent years, it appears, that from 1790 to 1806, 1009 slaves had been imported into that island from Africa, and retained in it. The imports from 1790 to 1796 are wanting. Taking, however, the number imported to be no more than the returns actually made specify, namely, 1009, the whole number to be accounted for will be 10,009. But in 1822, when the last census was taken, the slave population amounted only to 6,178, being a decrease, in 34 years, of 3431, from which the manumissions which have taken place in that time, amounting to 304, are to be deducted. And let it not be imagined that this ratio of decrease is a diminishing ratio. On the contrary, the decrease in the four years from 1818 to 1822, has been in full as high a proportion; as will appear on a reference to the returns of the registry of slaves in that island, made by Mr. Richard King, the Registrar. According to these returns the slave population in 1818 amounted to 6,815. But the slaves belonging to two estates—namely, those of the deceased Arthur Hodge, amounting in 1822 to thirty-nine, and those of Mrs. Simpson, amounting to forty-seven, having been omitted, the number ought to have been 6,901.

In 1822 the total number in the island proved to be only 6,178, leaving a deficiency in four years of 432. The number of manumissions, however, in these four years having amounted to 101, the real deficiency is so much less—namely, 322 making a decrease of upwards of four and a half per cent in that time. (ibid.:93)

It was further pointed out that "this, however, is only the average decrease. If the returns of particular estates are examined, the mortality will be found to be much greater" (ibid.). The article then proceeds to cite specific instances:

1. On the estates of the late Mrs. Ruth Lettsom, on which, in 1796, there is said to have been 1120 slaves, the number is stated in the Registry of 1818 to be 708, but in that of 1822 only 641. Here we have a decrease in four years (one slave having been manumitted) of sixty-six; being nearly nine and a half per cent. in that time, or two three-eighths per cent. per annum.

2. In 1818 Richard Hetherington possessed 458 slaves. This number in 1822 had been reduced to 404, being a decrease in four years (one having been manumitted) of fifty-three slaves, or upwards of eleven and a half per cent. in that time, or nearly three per cent. per annum.

3. In 1818 Thomasson and Thornton possessed 145 slaves. These in 1822 were reduced to 125; a decrease of twenty, or nearly fourteen per cent. in four years, or three and a half per cent. per annum.

4. On the estate of Archdeacon Wynne in 1818 there were 121 slaves, the remains, it is said, of a gang much more numerous: but in 1822 they had decreased to eighty-nine; a decrease of thirty-two, or of nearly twenty-seven per cent. in that time, being at the rate of six and three-quarters per cent. per annum (ibid.:93-94).

"And," it was wryly observed,

if such are the effects of the slave system, even in Tortola, where according to certain statistical returns, the slaves actually wallow in the abundance of all that can contribute to render them both the happiest and the richest peasantry in the world, what must the case be in other less favoured colonies?

Clearly, then, the case of the Virgin Islands plantation colony constituted, it was felt, an irrefutable argument for general emancipation.

Finally, lest the incontrovertibility of his argument be doubted, the author documents the prosperity of the free black and colored sectors of Virgin Islands plantation society: "The following facts, deduced from the Registry of Tortola," he avers,

> will afford some proof of the growing prosperity of the free Black and Coloured population of that island, notwithstanding the unjust and degrading disabilities to which they are yet subject, and all the abuse poured out upon them.
>
> In 1818 the number of free Black and Coloured persons possessing slaves had increased to 120; while the slaves belonging to them, in consequence of some large bequests of this species of property, had more than trebled their number. In that year (1822) they amounted to 1766, being more than a fourth; indeed now—since the deportation to Trinidad of a large body of Creole slaves long rooted in the island, which has recently taken place—to nearly a third of the whole slave population. (ibid.:95)

The intended implication here was presumably that—contrary to allegations of inherent "indolence and sloth"—free blacks were, in fact, as industrious and enterprising as their white counterparts, indeed, to the point of owning their own slaves. Such were the dialectics of plantation economy.

The second set of contemporary materials under consideration relates to the considerable documentary evidence which was generated as a result of a rebellion in 1823 by slaves on the Josiah's Bay Estate of the absentee planter, Isaac Pickering. This particular material is especially significant for the insight that is afforded into the existential relationships of Virgin Islands slaves and an increasingly constrained master class during the declining years of Virgin Islands plantation economy.

THE SLAVES OF ISAAC PICKERING:
ALLEGATIONS OF INSUBORDINATION
AND REBELLION

In 1823, a rebellion of sorts occurred at the Josiah's Bay estate of the absentee planter, Isaac Pickering, as a result of which five of the slaves implicated were brought to trial. The transcript of the trial proceedings (Parliamentary Papers, 1825) reads, in part, as follows:

Monday 17th November 1823

Before a Board of Magistrates

Present,—The Honourable John Stobo esquire Sitting Magistrate
----------------George R. Porter
----------------Wiliam R. Isaacs
----------------Wilson Lawson

The King
versus

Bristol. Sciah, and Lankey
(Felony)

Slaves the property of the Honourable Isaac Pickering, esq.

also

Chance and Ruthy's George

Witnesses

Johnny, a Slave the property of said estate.
Harry   .   ..   do
Michel   .   ..   do

APPEARED personally Mr. Charles Cother, a manager of Josiah's Bay, the property of the said Isaac Pickering, and charged the first three Slaves, Bristol, Sciah, and Lankey, for that they on the twenty-second day of October were prominent characters in quitting their work, and surrounding the said manager with their bill in a threatening manner; which conduct was followed by the . . . gang consisting of two-and-twenty, then at work, excepting two. The said manager also charges Bristol and Lankey with threatening the life of Johnny the head watchman on the estate; and the said manager further charges the said five Slaves, Bristol, Sciah, Lankey, Chance and Ruthy's George, with being in a state of actual rebellion at the time above-mentioned; and that they committed violent and rebellious acts for some days, and that twenty of the men gang, among whom were the aforesaid five men, run away from said estate, and were absent for some days, until they were driven in by hunters; and that during the time of their absence, the boat belonging to said estate was stolen by the said slaves.

The prisoners severally arraigned, and pleaded Not Guilty. John I. F. Pickering, esq. attorney to the Honourable Isaac Pickering, esq., present, and consented to the trial.

The Magistrate after hearing the evidence produced against the said Slaves, and also what they had to say in justification of themselves, retired; and on their return, Ordered, That the said prisoners be remanded to the jail, and to be brought up tomorrow at the hour of twelve of the clock in the afternoon, then to hear their sentence.

The following day, the magistrates handed down their verdict. The transcript continues:

Tuesday, 18th November 1823

The board of Magistrates met pursuant to adjournment.

The Magistrates unanimously find the prisoners guilty. They were then brought up and the following sentence passed upon them: viz. That Bristol, Lankey and Sciah receive each tomorrow forenoon, between the hours of ten and twelve of the clock, sixty-three lashes on their bare backs with a cat-o-nine tails, twenty-one of which number to be inflicted on each by the corner of Blyden's Cane-piece, the same number opposite the Court House, and the same number at the foot of Clifton Hill.

That Ruthy's George and Chance do likewise receive each thirty-nine lashes in like manner with a cat-o-nine tails opposite the jail, and that after the infliction of the said punishment, they be remanded to gaol, there to be kept in close confinement in irons, until they can be transported from this colony. . . .

The various testimonies submitted during the course of the trial afford a relatively rare glimpse at both slaves and masters as real, interacting people. A copy of the evidence (Parliamentary Papers, 1825) taken at the trial further reveals the following:

Johnny (a slave of Mr. Pickering) sworn, (cautioned to state nothing but the truth; an intelligent youth).

Andre, the overseer, met witness, and told him, the manager ordered him to bring Santlo the watchman to him; witness went down to the field on the south side and told the driver, that the manager sent him for Santlo, that the driver told Santlo the manager called him; Santlo asked what for: . . . Bristol said to Santlo, if you go they will make mutton out of your bottom; Lankey and Sciah said, if their own father came to the field for them, he must put up with what he got, . . . Lankey, Bristol and Sciah particularly came up close to witness; Sciah said, wherever he and witness met, there should be grave for one and gallows for t'other; Michelle and Phoenix tried all they could to keep them off witness (Johnny); Lankey particularly struck at witness; witness then went away and came to his master in town, as he was afraid to stay on the estate. . . .

. . . Michelle, driver, belonging to Mr. Pickering, sworn,—says, . . . in the afternoon the manager came into the field and told witness he must order Santlo over, and ordered George and Phoenix, being nearest to Santlo, to lay hold of him; they both refused to do so, saying Santlo had a bill on his hand; manager then told witness he must drive George and Phoenix out to the field, after they won't obey orders: they refused to go, after that they all began to quarrel with the manager; witness ordered them twice to mind their work, they would not; the manager then put his hand in his pocket and showed a pistol; someone said, if you shoot one you can't shoot two, and they all left their work. . . .

Mr. Pickering came up on Friday, when the gang saw him coming, all except three (Cornelius . . . Mosey and John) went away; sent three messages to call the negroes back, but they refused to come; sent one message by John, who himself stopped and did not come back; Sciah asked witness if he neglected his work, says, no, except when he take a day for himself, which he very often did; none of the other prisoners asked witness any question.

The trial, it might be recalled, concerned acts of rebellion and insubordination which occurred on the 22nd October 1823 and for which five of Mr. Isaac Pickering's Josiah's Bay Estate slaves were convicted and punished. But the trouble had not ended there, as the evidence (Parliamentary Papers, 1825) indicates:

Virgin Islands, Tortola

AT a Meeting of Privy Council, on Saturday the 25th October 1823

Present,—The Honourable GEO. RICHARDSON PORTER, Esquire,
President

-------------- MARK D. FRENCH   )
-------------- WILLIAM R. ISAACS)   Esquire

John F. Pickering, Esquire, attended and laid before the Board a letter he received this morning from Mr. C. Cother, his manager on Josiah's Bay Estate, which was read, and is as follows:

[*trial account continues page 38*]

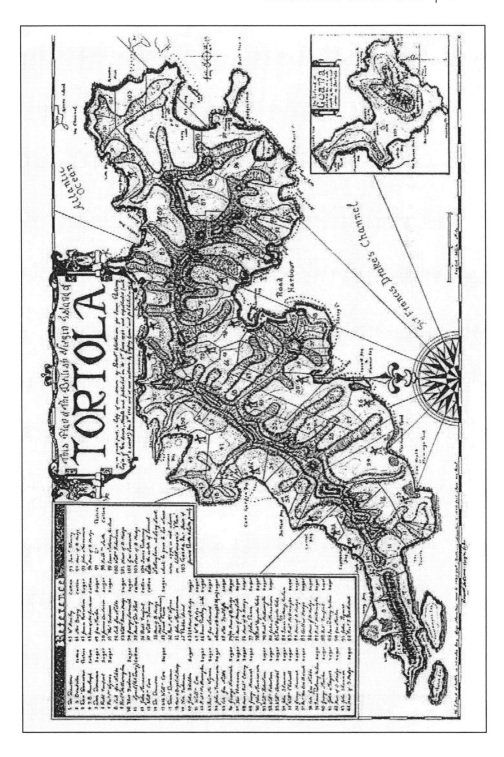

To J. F. Pickering, Esquire

DEAR SIR,

THIS morning, about four o'clock, the negro men passed through yard, armed with cutlasses, and some with bayonets and sticks. Phoenix accosted Harry, who was watching the yard, and asked him if he would not join. Harry observed, Join in what: Phoenix reply was, Join to go into the bush to fight. Harry told him No: that he would not have anything to do with him. Sciah immediately knocked Harry down with a stick, and gave him a broken head, and a severe blow on the neck. After this they went off to the south side, with destroying a few more of Andrew's stock. From their manner this morning it shows what their intentions are. I have not waited to learn of any of them, if any of them intends coming to their work this morning, as I think it best to give you the earliest information of their behaviour. Could you get the loan of a pair of pistols for me until this business is over? It will be no harm for me to be prepared in case they should make an attack.

> I remain respectfully yours,
> C. Cother.

The Josiah's Bay Estate manager, Mr. Cother, was not alone in his concern. The Virgin Islands plantocracy found itself in an increasingly embattled situation, as the minutes of the Privy Council further reveal:

AFTER some discussion on the matter contained in [Cother's] letter. It was resolved, That His Honour the President should issue circulars to the respective managers in the Island, requesting they would send out as many hunters[2] as they could spare on Monday morning before break of day, and if possible to accompany them, to meet at the late Mr. Hetherington's Retreat estate, and from thence to proceed in such manner as they should judge proper, to apprehend and secure the runaway negroes from Josiah's Bay estate, who have behaved in a very riotous manner, and thereby involving the general vital interest and safety of all the Slaveholders of the island.

A true copy of the Minutes of the Privy Council held October 25, 1823.

> (signed) Daniel Fraser,
> Clerk of Council.

As in the case of the Nottingham Free People, the 1823 rebellion of the Pickering slaves attracted the attention of protagonists in the British Parliamentary debate on slavery and on the material condition of slaves in the colonies.

On the basis of the Parliamentary evidence, a recent historical work on the British Virgin Islands declares that

> none of the disturbances of the nineteenth century was due directly to discontent over bad living and working condition. Neither can dissatisfaction with the system of slavery in general adequately explain the sporadic outbursts. In 1823 the negroes on Pickering's Josiah Bay Estate were reported to be in a state of rebellion. Investigation showed that the insubordination of the slaves was due to their refusal to be removed to Trinidad on the insistence of their master. The slaves on the Pickering estates, imbued with a greater sense of freedom and independence fostered by absenteeism, had a reputation for disorderly conduct. (Dookhan 1975:85, citing Parliamentary Papers 1825)

This is precisely the impression that the colonial officers concerned had contrived to convey to Parliament (although, as shall be shortly demonstrated, the argument is contradicted by the evidence). Thus, Governor Charles W. Maxwell—Captain General and Governor-in-Chief, headquartered at St. Kitts—on the basis of a lengthy report on the rebellion from the President of the Virgin Islands colony, George R. Porter, officially assured the Right Honourable the Earl Bathurst that

> . . . Mr. Pickering, the proprietor of Josiah's Bay estate, having arranged to remove the whole of his negroes to Trinidad, the latter had, in the first instance, expressed their readiness to undergo the change, but afterwards objected to it; some disturbance took place in consequence, and twenty of the most refractory escaped in a boat from the Island. They have since been brought back, and by the sentence of a bench of magistrates banished the Island; and, on the 22nd November, were embarked for Trinidad. (Parliamentary Papers 1825: Maxwell to Bathurst, 16th February 1824)

In a subsequent dispatch, Governor Maxwell further assured the Earl Bathurst that

> . . . the insubordinate conduct of Mr. Pickering's negroes did not arise from or was [it] in any [way] connected with the recent discussions in Parliament, on the amelioration of the negro condition . . . . (op cit.: Maxwell to Bathurst, 6th July 1824, with two enclosures)

The Pickering slaves, it was asserted, had always been "turbulent and hard to be ruled". Thus, according to the personal testimony of President Porter, "early in the year 1789," for example,

> the whole gang attacked the late Colonel Thomasons (Mr. Pickering's then attorney), Mr. Edward Coke, a very respectable gentleman of the Island, who accompanied the Colonel to the estate . . . and other overseers who were present; they stoned them, and compelled them to take refuge in the house, which they repeatedly endeavoured to force; they continued stoning the house for hours, until assistance was procured from other estates, who liberated these gentlemen from their perilous situation and guarded them in safety through the estate. On this occasion, several were tried; two were condemned to death and executed, and three . . . banished. (ibid.)

President Porter further posited that on another occasion,

> the whole gang except four, left their work, and most of them the estate, and did not return until the fourth of October, nor would they consent to return there, until they compelled the attorney to discharge the overseer, with whose conduct he was so well satisfied, that although he did not want an overseer, he gave him employment on his own estate. (ibid.)

By way of further buttressing their contention that the Pickering slaves had persistently been insubordinate and riotous prior to their acts of rebellion in 1823, Governor Maxwell and President Porter proffered the following deposition:

> Copy of a Letter from Mr. Robert Lewis (who was the Manager on Mr. Pickering's Josiah's Bay Estate during the hurricane in 1820 and for some time after) to the Honourable G. R. Porter.
>
> DEAR SIR,
>
> I EXPECTED you out yesterday, for to see the wounded; but as you did not come, I concluded it was for want of a horse; I therefore send a horse for you. When you are coming out, you will oblige me by calling on the Reverend Mr. Whitworth, and ask him for to ride out to the estate with you. Josiah's Bay negroes are in a state of open rebellion and I make no doubt but a few words from their parson might have a good effect, and bring them to their duty. They will obey no orders; they only think of plunder and destroying the property. Last night about seventy of them passed through the yard, and went to the south side, where there was two puncheons of corn meal, which they took by force

from the watchman, and plundered every grain; the night before they took six sheep out of the pen. This ought to be represented and taken notice of by the government, and an immediate stop put to it, before it goes too far and spreads.

> I remain, etc. etc. etc.
> (signed) Josiah's Bay
> Robert Lewis

(Parliamentary Papers 1825).

Similarly, a deposition from Isaac Pearson—a former manager (ca. 1821) of Josiah's Bay Estate—regarding antecedent rebellious behaviour on the part of the Pickering slaves, was also enclosed in the Porter-Maxwell dispatch to the Earl Bathurst:

Virgin Islands, Tortola

Before His Honour the PRESIDENT, and the Honourable Members hereinafter named, in Privy Council; viz

> The Honourable M. D. FRENCH
> ------------------- WILLIAM GEORGE CRABB
> ------------------- WILLIAM GORDON, Esquire

APPEARED personally, Isaac Pearson of Tortola, planter, who being duly sworn, made oath and said, That he took charge of Mr. Pickering's East End estate in April last; that until six weeks ago, the Slaves belonging to that estate behaved very well, from which time they have occasionally absented themselves, to the numbers of ten, twenty, and even thirty, two or three times in a week; that on his ordering some of them to be flogged for such gross misconduct, they defied him, and told the driver it was at his peril to touch him, he would be the worse for it; in consequence of which, the driver gave up the attempt he made to take hold of one of them.

Deponent further saith, that Harry is, in his opinion, one of the principal ringleaders; that he has been absent a week together frequently; Mary Ann's John, Phoenix and Marian's Stephen, three brothers, are also ringleaders, and have committed the same offence, that Stephen was watchman in the yard one night in the last week, when deponent called him, and ordered him to go on his watch; he said that it was customary for the manager to give the watch supper and grog, which deponent refused; whereupon the said Stephen quitted the door, and when he was at a short distance from the door, he said "I'll be damned, if I should meet Mr. Lettsom, or Mr. Pearson (the deponent) in the night, I should not mind much breaking their heads with a stone." That on the same night, a calf, a sheep, and a hog, were taken out of the yard, and have not been heard of since; that he has reason to believe Stephen was concerned in the robbery, as in the middle of the night deponent called out, and could not discover any watchman in the yard. That Thomas, in the hearing of deponent made use of the following expression, "That if Mr. Lettsom [Mr. Pickering's attorney/agent] did not put provisions on the estate, he must not show his face on the estate again." That at this time the allowance to each negro was two quarts of corn meal, and two mackerel, and also had Saturdays to themselves; that soon after, when provisions were scarce on the property, deponent was obliged to reduce the allowance to three pints per week, and two mackerel, which the whole gang refused on that occasion, and thirty-five of them took the afternoon to themselves.

That since deponent has been on the estate, the dungeon has been twice broken open, and the prisoners liberated, but by whom deponent cannot say.

Deponent further saith, That Bristol, Abrahan, Scipio and Jeffry, Sciah and Lankey his brother, as also Sessman, are among the most insubordinate of the gang; that upon Maryann's Stephen being absent for two or three days, on his return, deponent ordered him to be taken out of the field to be flogged, but upon Andrew, who was then the driver, attempting to bring him forward, he dared the said driver to lay hold of him, that he threw down his hoe; and said he could go to where he had been the day before, and went away; that on Friday night last, three hogs, two turkies and eight fowls were stolen from deponent, and on his accusing Lankey, who watched that night, of the theft, he said he took them, and would continue to take his hogs and fowls when he pleased.

(signed) Isaac Pearson

But the inclusion of the testimonies of Lewis and Pearson by Governor Maxwell and President Porter in their dispatch to Parliament was ill-conceived, for these testimonies inadvertently revealed considerably more than Maxwell and Porter had apparently intended or realized. In fact, both of these testimonies contained substantial evidence which strongly contradicted the Porter-Maxwell attempt to assure Parliament that the "insubordinate, riotous, if not actually rebellious conduct" of the Pickering slaves was in no way related to the material conditions of their existence. (Maxwell to Bathurst, 6th July 1824; op. cit.)

It perhaps bears reiteration that in the early 1820s, when most of the riotous activity occurred, the Virgin Islands plantation system had recently suffered the effects of a devastating combination of severe drought (1815) and hurricane (1819). There can hardly be any question, therefore, but that the material conditions of the slaves' existence must have been adversely affected. It is in this light that the estate manager, Robert Lewis' charge that "seventy of [the slaves] . . . went to the south side, where there was two puncheons of corn meal . . . and plundered every grain" must be understood. Similarly, Mr. Pearson's allegation regarding the slave Thomas's threat that ". . . if Mr. Lettsome [the estate owner's attorney] did not put provisions on the estate, he must not show his face on the estate again," must also be viewed in this context.

Given the facts of an economy in sharp decline and with a large resultant surplus of slave labour, many Virgin Islands planters sought to remove their slaves to other colonies—particularly to the newer Crown colonies of Trinidad and Guyana, where the demand for slave labour was then on the rise (cf. Craton 1974:258-71).

> Between 1808 and 1822 a total of 95 slaves were exported from the Virgin Islands to several Caribbean territories including St. John, St. Christopher, Nevis, Anguilla, Trinidad and Demarara. . . . In 1825, 1055 slaves consisting of 492 males and 563 females were removed. (Dookhan 1975:93, footnote)

Moreover, despite British Parliamentary regulations which attempted to curtail this inter-colonial slave trade, planters often "removed their slaves illicitly by taking advantage of the lax enforcement of the regulations and by having the slaves sentenced to transportation in the law courts" (ibid.).

The determination of the absentee Virgin Islands planter, Isaac Pickering, to remove his Josiah's Bay Estate slaves to Trinidad was, therefore, not without precedent. Indeed, one wonders whether the judicial machinations which followed the 1823 rebellion might not have been contrived in large measure to enable a member of the Virgin Islands plantocracy to effect the removal of his surplus slave labour to a colony where the returns on that species of property would be more lucrative.

None of this escaped the notice of the emancipationists in England. Earlier, in 1790, Thomas Woolrich, a former British resident of Tortola, had testified to a Select Committee of the House of Commons that he "never saw a gang of negroes that appeared anything like sufficiently fed; their appearance to the eye fully proves their want and hardships" (cited in Dookhan, 1975:80). In the intervening war years, however, the interest of the British public in the condition of slaves in the colonies had waned considerably. Thus,

> as early as 1809 Wilberforce was expressing disappointment with the effects of abolition on slave conditions, and in 1811 the publicizing by Brougham and others of the Huggins and Hodge

cruelty cases in Nevis and Tortola indicated serious attempts to arouse the public. (Craton 1974:270)

Indeed, the trial of the Tortolian planter Arthur Hodge for the murder of his slave Prosper was a precedent-setting case. In the words of a contemporary observer:

> Great things were at stake as to the issue. If the killing were proved and the murderer were to escape because of his complexion, wealth and standing, alas for the poor slaves in that and other islands! If on the other hand he should be found guilty and be executed for the murder of a slave, the fact would be established far and wide that the blacks, though in bondage, were regarded as human beings; and if killing a human being maliciously was murder, then killing a slave was murder also. (Kidder 1852:92; cited in Harrigan and Varlack 1975:33)

Governor Ellis—an avowed abolitionist who invoked martial law and saw that the sentence to capital punishment was carried out—wryly observed that Hodge's "enormities were not likely to have ever been subjected to public investigation, had it not been for the accidental and personal quarrels of this guilty being with some of his former associates and friends" (Goveia 1965:201; citing C.O. 152/97, Elliot to Liverpool, no. 44, 18 May 1811). In this context, therefore, the case of the Pickering slaves provided welcome ammunition to the emancipationists—as did that of the Nottingham Free People, considered earlier in this chapter.

In this regard, an emancipationist writer—commenting on the Porter-Maxwell contention that the Pickering slaves had always been "turbulent characters"—made the following observation:

> Supposing this were true, what had it to do with this particular transaction [the removal of the slaves to Trinidad] except to relieve the actors in it from some of the odium it must have tended to excite? But that there had been occasionally sufficient ground for their insubordination in the excitement of that most painful of sensations, especially to men called to work under the lash, we mean hunger, comes out incidentally on the deposition of a man that had been their manager; for in testifying to one instance of great insubordination, which had happened while he was in charge of them, he proves that they must actually have been in a state of starvation. The weekly allowance to each Negro, he says, had been only two quarts of corn meal, and two mackerel; provisions becoming scarce, the deponent had reduced the allowance to three pints per week; the regular allowance, be it remembered, in the Bahamas, as well as the prison allowance of Jamaica, being twenty-one pints per week. (*The Slave Colonies of Great Britain . . .* 1825)

Moreover,

> They were almost all Creoles, natives of the island, who had near connections on all the neighbouring estates, and who had, according to Dr. Stobo, one of the Judges who afterwards tried them, amassed some property, but nearly the whole of which they would now be obliged to sacrifice. (ibid.)

In this light, it should be small wonder that the Pickering slaves reacted in a rebellious manner to their predicament of virtual starvation and impending separation from kin and property.[3]

On the Dialectics of Slave-Master Relations

While the harsh reality of starvation and the threat of separation from kin and property constituted the immediate causes of the 1823 rebellion of the Pickering slaves, the underlying causes must be sought in certain contradictions which had developed in the Virgin Islands plantation economy during its phase of decline.

In the first place, the very fact of ownership of property by chattel-slaves was a logical incongruity, and the evidence indicates that by 1823, the property owned by British Virgin Islands slaves was not inconsiderable. Slave property estimates at that time were as follows:

38 horse at £7.10s each	£285.	0s
938 horned cattle at £5. each	4690.	0s
2125 goats at 10/ - each	1062.	10
1208 pigs at 10/ - each	604.	0
33120 poultry at 1/6	2484.	0
23 boats at £5 each	115.	0
Fishpots and Fishing Tackle	123.	10
Property in building chiefly in town	700.	0
Furniture and utensils at 15/ - per head	4698.	8
	£14,762.	8s

> These estimates did not include the disposable portion of esculents and fruits, and cotton produced by the slaves on about 1,675 acres of land whose estimated yield annually totalled £5,862. (Dookhan 1975:84)

But such relatively extensive slave ownership of property was more than simply incongruous; in fact, it reflected the degenerate state of the Virgin Islands plantation economy itself.

As has been previously observed, by the 1820s the combination of adverse economic and environmental factors had drastically reduced the viability of the Virgin Islands plantation system. Thus, the contemporary writer Trelawney Wentworth observed (ca. 1820) that, on Tortola,

the extensive ranges of waste land and pasturage, afford the negroes an opportunity of cultivating provisions to an almost un-
limited extent, and they were not generally restricted, as in most
of the islands where cultivation is more extended, in the rearing
of any particular description of live stock. Some of them possess
several head of horned cattle, as well as goats and sheep, which
range over the mountain wastes, or herd with the stock belonging to the estates. (Wentworth 1834:178)

It might further be noted in this connection that where provision-
gardening by slaves was encouraged, or evolved out of necessity, there
often developed among the slaves notions of customary ownership of the
particular grounds worked by the slaves concerned, to the extent that
slaves would "bequeath their grounds or gardens to such of their fellow-
slaves as they think proper" (Edwards 1793, II:133). Writing from his
Jamaican experience, the plantocrat Edward Long observed that

... the black grandfather, or father (as they are called) directs in
what manner his money, his hogs, poultry, furniture, cloaths,
and other effects and acquisitions shall descend, or be disposed
of, after his decease. He nominates a sort of trustees, or execu-
tors, from the nearest of kin, who distribute them among the
legatees, according to the will of the testator, without any moles-
tation or interpretation, most often without the enquire of their
master. (Long 1774, Vol. II:410)

This phenomenon would appear to have been fairly generalized throughout British Caribbean plantation society (cf. Mintz and Price 1976).
   In agriculturally marginal economies such as that of the Virgin Islands
plantation system, the acquiescence of the planter class to the slaves'
customary land rights was, in any case, largely academic. And therein lay
another far-reaching contradiction within the social relations of production in Virgin Islands society, for, as Karen Olwig has observed in a similar
context,

though the planters had to grant the slaves the right to use the
land, they could not in effect deny the slaves this right, because
the planters were not able to provide for the slaves except by let-
ting them grow their own food. (Olwig 1977:103)

Mintz and Price, moreover, argue persuasively that a strong relationship between kinship and slaves' customary land rights very probably
emerged quite early in the process of creolization or cultural synthesis.

Let us begin, once again, with a hypothetical aggregate of recent-
ly-enslaved Africans on a new plantation in the Americas. What,
if anything, might have constituted a set of broadly shared ideas

brought from Africa in the realm of kinship? Tentatively and provisionally, we would suggest that there may have been widespread fundamental ideas and assumptions about kinship in West Africa. Among these, we might single out the sheer importance of kinship in structuring inter-personal relations and in defining an individual's place in his society; the emphasis on unilineal descent, and the importance to each individual of the resulting lines of kinsmen, living and dead, stretching backward and forward through time; or, on a more abstract level, the use of land as a means of defining both time and descent, with ancestors venerated *locally,* and with history and genealogy both being particularized in specific pieces of ground. The aggregate of newly-arrived slaves, though they had been torn from their local kinship networks, would have continued to view kinship as the normal idiom of social relations. (Mintz and Price 1976:34)

It would seem plausible to infer, therefore, that even prior to emancipation, and apart from land deeded to them by more or less benevolent masters, Virgin Islands slaves would have developed individual and/or corporate interests in specific plots of land (cf. Mintz and Price 1976:38). The evidence on both the Nottingham and Pickering slaves lends credence to this assertion.

In aggregate, these contradictions which had developed within Virgin Islands plantation society were ultimately incompatible with the perpetuation of "normal" slave-master relations. The blacks, while still in bondage, had begun to acquire many of the attributes normally associated with freedmen, particularly as regards land rights and property ownership. At the same time, in a moribund economy with a declining white presence, there was a correspondingly declining capacity on the part of the planter class to effectively constrict the increasingly independent existence of the slaves. Trelawney Wentworth's surprise at this phenomenon is understandable:

At an auction we witnessed in the Road Town the number of negroes perhaps exceeded that of the white and coloured portion of the assemblage, and we were naturally led to inquire into that apparent independence in the use of their time, which their attendance seemed to bespeak. (Wentworth 1834:219)

In fact, however, this was merely yet another manifestation of the shift in the social relations of production which necessarily accompanied the decline of the plantation mode of production in the British Virgin Islands. The older order was dying, and a new social order was struggling to be born. The planter class, however, was determined to maintain the *status quo ante,* and this inevitably exacerbated the inherent antagonism of the slave-master relationship. In the plantation system, as Leslie Manigat (1977:431) points out, two cultures were juxtaposed: a dominating one (the . . . whites) and a subordinate one (the . . . blacks). The racism of the former, with its differentiating privileges, helped the latter to become aware of the culturally explosive content of the opposition and to define itself by the conflicting character of the relationship.

In the case of the 1823 rebellion of the Pickering slaves, it would seem fairly clear that they were acutely cognizant of the existing differential access to the means of subsistence. In an economy which was then generally suffering the effects of drought and hurricane and in which consequently the slaves' provision grounds and cultigens must have accordingly suffered, this differential access became, as we have seen, a source of overt conflict.

Apart from the distributive appropriation of food from the plantation store and engagement in certain retributive "predatory acts against property," many of the Pickering slaves defiantly left the plantation, their act of flight or *marronage*[4] thus constituting "the extreme form of reacting negatively against the conditions of work . . . a stopping dead of work and running away," or as Leslie Manigat dubs it, "the marronage strike." (Manigat 1977:428-9)

The act of flight dramatically exemplified, moreover, "the rejection (momentary, lasting, or even final) of the institutional orthodoxy and of the cultural norms of the existing social order" (ibid.:422). Indeed, the slave's deliberate, and—from the standpoint of the planter class—illegal, removal of himself from the subjugation of the plantation system constituted an effective negation of the planter's claim to rights of ownership in the slave. It should hardly be surprising, therefore, that some of the harshest punishments prescribed by the 1783 Virgin Islands Slave Act ". . . for the good government of negro and other slaves . . ." were reserved for apprehended runaways.[5]

The case of the Pickering slaves also illustrates quite clearly the slaves' recognition of the degree of bargaining power which their labour represented within the context of the social relations of production of a declining plantation economy. Thus, as we have seen, by means of a work stoppage, the Pickering slaves were able to force the removal of a disliked overseer.[6]

In the final analysis, however, the relative impunity with which Virgin Islands slaves were able to defy the established authority of the planter class rested in the paucity of the latter and the considerable distance of the Virgin Islands colony from the nearest major British military bastion.[7]

CONCLUSION

The collapse of British Virgin Islands plantation economy was largely reflective of shifts which were occurring in what Immanuel Wallerstein (1974) has called the "European world-economy," and which produced an attenuation of British mercantilist interest in the Caribbean sugar islands in general, and especially in marginal producers such as the British Virgin Islands plantation system. Agriculturally marginal plantation systems such as that of the British colony in the Virgin Islands[8] were, in any case, economically viable only when profits had been high and costs low. Finally, a combination of adverse environmental conditions (drought and hurricane) dealt the mortal blow to the Virgin Islands plantation economy.

The Virgin Islands sugar-plantation economy was a highly specialized mono-crop system of production which was almost totally externally oriented. The *raison d'être* of the plantation system was the local production of sugar for export to the metropolitan markets. Similarly, the presence of the white planter class in the Virgin Islands colony was predicated upon the profit-potential/realization of the plantation economy. With the advent of economic decline, the planter class lost the basis of its social reproductive ability; its economic base had disintegrated and it was consequently no longer viable as a social class. Finally, with much of its property in receivership, the Virgin Islands planter class had little choice but to physically abandon the colony. Thus, by the time emancipation was declared in 1834, there were only 477 whites left in the colony, whereas there had been 1300 whites in 1805; by the final decade of the nineteenth century (1891) there were only 32 whites in the colony.

The Virgin Islands slaves, of course, did not have the option of abandoning the colony upon the demise of the plantation economy. More importantly, the institutional arrangements which the slaves had forged over time—their kinship systems (both genealogical and fictive),[9] their notions of customary land rights, their methods of provision gardening—constituted a system of social reproduction which, having evolved within the context of plantation economy, would enable the slaves to survive the demise of King Sugar.

It might be fitting to conclude, therefore, by noting Karl Marx's (1857) observation that

> there is something in human history like retribution and it is a rule of historical retribution that its instrument be forged not by the offended but by the offender himself,

and by concurring with Sidney Mintz's embellishment thereon:

> Nothing else during the history of slavery was so important as marketing and provision cultivation in making it possible for the free man . . . to adapt himself to freedom without the blessings of his former master. (Mintz 1978:95)

The process of transition from a European-dominated Virgin Islands plantation society to a society of free, black "smallholders" could hardly be more appropriately aphorized.

3

Between Plantation and Tourism:
The Post-Emancipation Interregnum

By the late 1850s the emergent social formation which was superseding the old order of the plantation society was contemplated with a certain degree of chagrin by the resident Crown representative: "All these material blessings," President A. W. Moir disingenuously lamented,

> are now almost exclusively in the hands of the coloured population who do not have much capital and who are averse to the judicious outlay of that which they possess. . . . I could not see but with sad disappointment sugar estate after sugar estate totally abandoned or parceled out in patches of cane yielding but poor returns to unscientific and prescribed cultivation bestowed on them.
>
> I have seldom seen a better opportunity than is presented in Tortola for a few men [read Europeans] of practical experience having a little capital to commence with to make a comfortable livelihood and in a few years to add considerably to their original capital in a healthy tropical climate. (Despatch to Leeward Islands Governor, 1869)

President Moir's hopes for a resuscitation of the British Virgin Islands' plantation economy were not to be realized. The British Virgin Islands economy, for the duration of the intervening period, had simply become too marginal to generate any sustained exploitative interest from the imperial center. Almost a century would pass before Moir's exhortation would bear fruit, when the exploitative potential of the colony would once more become evident with respect to a new "monocrop"—tourism.

SEQUEL TO SLAVERY

It was strongly felt by some proponents of the English emancipation movement that the slaves, once freed, would willingly continue to constitute the labor force on the plantations. As prognosticated by the Quaker abolitionist Joseph Sturge:

51

in a state of freedom it may be expected that the conditions and resources of . . . [the former slave], working for regulated wages, will be, as they are in England, superior to those of a paltry agriculturist, cultivating his little plot of land with his own hands; and it is evident therefore that the negroes will generally prefer working on the estates. Their strong attachment to the place of their birth, to their houses and gardens, to the graves of their parents and kindred, exceeding what has been recorded of any other people, is another circumstance which favours their continuance as labourers on the estates to which they are now respectively attached. (cited in Mintz 1974:158)

Indeed, emancipation was in large measure conceived as a potentially demonstrative triumph for the presumed efficacy of free (i.e., non-slave) labor. Thus, Joseph John Gurney (1840:178-9), on the basis of observations made during a visit to Tortola and several other West Indian islands, was led to the conclusion that "the whole quantity of work, obtained by the stimulus of wages, is considerably greater than the amount formerly procured by the terror of the whip":

When I speak of the stimulus of wages, I allude especially to its most effective form—payment by the piece, or job. The peasantry of the county of Norfolk, in England, afford a fair specimen of industrious labor on day's wages, in a cool climate. My own observation has led me to the conclusion that a free negro in the West Indies, paid by the day, will, in general, perform about three quarters of the quantity of work which would be called a fair day's labor in Norfolk. But employ and pay him by the job, or piece, and he will soon equal, and even exceed the day-labor standard of the Norfolk peasant.

With respect to the islands visited, Gurney (1840:224) asserted that "the peasantry are working well—I may almost say without any exception." This was not, however, a viewpoint which was shared by the plantation proprietors of the early post-emancipation era. In the words of one of their protagonists,

the great evil under which the planters now labour is, the enormous price of wages which the free negro exacts, by the abolition of the apprenticeship and the change in our laws, for the cultivation of the soil, and the very unsatisfactory, capricious, and unsteady supply of that labour, however enormously overpaid. The rate of wages in many of the colonies is double that of an English labourer, though a negro's wants are comparatively so small; but the mischief is considerably augmented by the uncertainty of his labour, inasmuch as he supplies it quite at his own caprice, and according to the fluctuation of his temper. Sometimes he will

work only two days in a week, and pass the rest in a kind of sen-
sual torpor; sometimes he will abstain from work altogether, to
the great cost of his employer, whose plantation thereby becomes overrun with weeds, which, growing with a tropical luxu-
riance unknown to other countries, will shortly gain such a firm
hold on the soil, that the season of cultivation and harvest will be
entirely lost to the owner. (cited in Letters . . . 1843:232)

For the planter, then, a major concern arising from the transformation
of the labor force from slave to free, was the difficulty in ensuring regular
and continuous labor on the plantation.

The problem, in fact, had been anticipated by Lord Howick, Secretary
of State, even before emancipation:

The great problem to be solved in drawing up any plan for the
emancipation of the slaves in our colonies, is to devise some
mode of inducing them when relieved from the fear of the driver
and his whip, to undergo the regular and continuous labour
which is indispensable in carrying on the production of sugar. . . .
Their [the planters'] inability . . . to pay liberal wages seems beyond all question; but even if this were otherwise, the experience
of other countries warrants the belief, that while land is so easily
obtainable as it is at this moment, even liberal wages would fail
to purchase the sort of labour which is required for the cultivation and manufacture of sugar. . . . The examples of the western
states of America, of Canada, of the Cape of Good Hope, and of
the Australian Colonies, may all be cited in order to show that
even amongst a population in a much higher state of civilization
than that to which the slaves in the West Indies have attained,
the facility of obtaining land effectually prevents the prosecution
by voluntary labour of any enterprise requiring the cooperation
of many hands. It is impossible therefore to suppose that the
slaves (who, though as I believe not more given to idleness than
other men are certainly not less so) would if freed from control
be induced even by high wages to continue to submit to a drudg-
ery which they detest, while without doing so they could obtain
land sufficient for their support. . . .
    I think that it would be greatly for the real happiness of the
Negroes themselves, if the facility of acquiring land could be so
far restrained as to prevent them, on the abolition of slavery,
from abandoning their habits of regular industry. . . . Accordingly it is to the imposition of a considerable tax upon land that I
chiefly look for the means of enabling the planter to continue his
business when emancipation shall have taken place. . . . (Lord
Howick, Memo, 1832; cited in Williams 1970:328-9)

"Thus," as Eric Williams (1970:329) wryly observed, "was the law of the superiority of free labour repealed in the interest of a single class, and metropolitan legislation reinforced the colonial tradition of debarring the Negro from land ownership."

Having defined the central problem as that of control of the freed labor force in a manner ensuring "regular and continuous labor," the planters proceeded to combine Lord Howick's recommended restrictive land policy with a congeries of oppressive rents and taxes applicable only to the freed blacks.[1] This inevitably led to conflict between the plantation proprietor and his erstwhile slave. In the British Virgin Islands,

> the major source of continuous irritation between planter and labourer was the question of rent and labour. It arose primarily from the undefined position of the labourer in possession of a house and provision grounds on the estate, as a tenant-at-will. Instead of a money payment labourers satisfied rental charges by working on the estates. But they also received a small remuneration from the planters for their labour. The dual employer-employee, landlord-tenant relationship between planters and labourers, was the fundamental cause of differences between them. In return for their inadequate wages, labourers did as little work as they could, and the planters were inclined when they observed a disposition by labourers to withhold their services from the plantations, even for the shortest time, to consider themselves in order defrauded. At first they were content to use threats of coercive action in order to remind labourers of their responsibility, but by 1842 several of them were beginning to assert a right summarily to eject from his cottage and provision grounds, any labourer who absented himself from the service of the plantation, or who refused to renew his weekly contract". (Dookhan 1975:130)

Overt conflict between planter and labourer occurred with considerable frequency in the British Virgin Islands during the period between emancipation in 1838 and the demise in the early 1860s of such vestiges of plantation economy as still prevailed. These conflictual relations are epitomized by a "peasant insurrection" (Harrigan and Varlack 1970:22) in 1853, incited by the imposition of an invidious and oppressive tax on the cattle of the blacks.

> On the day when the tax should have come into effect large numbers of the rural population converged on Road Town. Though the crowd was non-violent, the Riot Act was read and two arrests were made. Violence followed and some constables and magistrates were beaten. On the following day nearly 2,000 persons re-entered Road Town and marched on Government House appealing to President Chads to intervene on their behalf.

His answer was a promise to put their case before the legislature if, indeed, he were properly petitioned. In the ensuing confusion one of the demonstrators was shot. Certain that no redress would be forthcoming and full of bitterness and a feeling of revenge, the people went on the rampage for three days. The greater part of Road Town was burned down and a large number of country houses plundered, destruction being halted only when military assistance arrived from St. Thomas and Antigua. By this time all members of the legislature had fled to St. Thomas for refuge along with the majority of the white population. (Harrigan and Varlack 1975:95)

The observation was made by Governor Henry Barkly of British Guiana that "the disadvantages under which most of the British Colonies labour . . . do not arise . . . from the dearness of Free Labour. [They] are attributable almost entirely to the great difficulty of commanding continuous labour, which always constituted a crying evel [sic] in countries where there exists a great deal of waste land and a very small population" (C.O. 111/269. Barkly to Grey, 30 October 1849; cited in Adamson 1975:462). In the case of the British Virgin Islands, a greatly diminished *white* population, more specifically, relative to that of the blacks, played a determining role in the ultimate resolution of the planter-labor conflict. With an economy continuing in a decline begun even before the abolition of slavery (1834), the British Virgin Islands legislature was forced in 1864 to take steps to effect the sale of encumbered estates. In this manner,

eight estates totaling 780 acres were sold under decrees of the local Commissioner at a total cost of £979. Five of these estates (Cotton Bay, Spring Gut, Johnson's Gut, Appleby and Capoon's Bay) had been in Chancery for 35 years, while three others (Joe's Hill, Diamond, and Hawk's Nest) had been similarly encumbered for 44 years. (Dookhan 1975:135)

With the sale of these properties at an average price of £1.53 per acre falling well within the purchasing power of many of the former slaves (ibid.), this event constituted both the symbolic and effective demise of plantation economy in the British Virgin Islands. And thus was born a society of free black smallholders.

THE CONTEXT OF FREEDOM: ASPECTS
OF POLITICAL ECONOMY

Writing from the perspective of the first decade of the twentieth century, the resident Crown representative observed:

[T]he history of the British Virgin Islands since 1815 has been one almost uninterrupted record of retrogression and decay, broken only for an instance by the exceptional situation caused by the American Civil War, when cotton was for a few years shipped from here and sold at famine prices in England. The short revival of prosperity was followed by perhaps the most helpless decades in their history. The old Virgin Islands families abandoned their . . . estates to their former labourers, who raised degenerate stock and subsisted on fish and root crops, with the help of a certain amount of sugar and bad rum for local consumption. The Virgin Islands during these years were almost forgotten and no interest was taken in their inhabitants either in England or elsewhere. (BVI Government Report 1907; cited in Harrigan and Varlack 1975:74)

By "the old Virgin Islands families," the Commissioner meant, of course, the white planter class. Moreover, the British Virgin Islands were "forgotten" and "no interest" was taken in them precisely because, with the demise of plantation economy, the colony produced no surplus which could be extracted by the imperial center.

Economic and Constitutional Retrogression

Whereas the average value of imports and exports for the decade immediately following emancipation (1838-1847) stood at £103,000 and £144,000, respectively, the statistics reflect an overall pattern of economic decline, such that at the beginning of the twentieth century (1899-1903), these figures had declined to a low of £3,000 each[2] (cf. Table 3). Similarly, the demographic trajectory of the white planter class evinced dramatic correlation with that of the economy. Thus, whereas at the abolition of slavery in 1834, the white population stood at 477—down from a peak of 1,300 in 1805 during the heyday of the colony's prosperity—by 1891, the white presence had declined to 32 persons. The black population in 1891—while also evincing dramatic decline—stood at 4,607 (see Table 1).

The post-emancipation epoch is also characterized by a steady process of constitutional retrogression. In 1854 a representative government was abolished and a unicameral Legislature instituted in its stead. In 1859 membership of the Legislative Council was reduced from six to four. In 1867 elections were abolished: thus the Legislative Council was comprised solely of nominated members. Finally, in 1902 the Legislative Council itself was abolished. It was not until 1950 that, as a result of popular agitation, the Legislative Council was re-established and representative government reinstituted (cf. Harrigan and Varlack 1970).

It perhaps bears emphasizing that this process of constitutional retrogression was not unique to the British Virgin Islands. Throughout the British West Indies, the post-emancipation epoch witnessed a numerically inferior white population more or less voluntarily relinquishing local legislative control to progressively direct rule by the Colonial Office. This was an effort to subvert the possibility of politico-legislative dominance by

the numerically superior black population. The rationale was unquestionably racist. As one English colonist (ca. 1889) expressed it, "I know what
the black man is; he is incapable of the art of government, and . . . to trust
him in framing and working the laws for our islands is to condemn them
to inevitable ruin" (cited in Lowenthal 1972:64). It was further rationalized
that "those of European descent are most fitted to understand and enjoy
the blessings of the English Constitution," as Lieutenant-Governor Samuel
Blackhall of Dominica declared in an official dispatch (5 February 1854,
C.O. 71/117; in Lowenthal, ibid.). But the process of constitutional retrogression towards Crown Colony Government or direct imperial control
locally was also reflective of an imperial thrust towards rationalization and
centralization of its colonial fiscal and administrative structures in the
West Indies (cf. Codrington 1977:199) as that section of empire declined in
its contribution to imperial wealth.

This phenomenon of constitutional retrogression in effect debarred the
black majority from meaningful participation in the political process.
Fiscal mechanisms in the form of a series of Tax Acts were also utilized in
the British Virgin Islands as a means of politico-economic control. Thus, in
anticipation of emancipation, the Tax Act of 1837 imposed a tax of 20/- an
acre "on lands other than those devoted to the cultivation of sugar and
cotton" (Dookhan 1975:152). Since, as Dookhan points out, "the tax did
not extend to the owners of estates, the aim was obviously to extend the
system of taxation to include those Negroes who sought to establish themselves as independent proprietors. The fact that . . . lands belonging to
estates were exempt from the tax emphasized the intention of the planter-
legislators to prevent the drift away from the estates by the ex-slaves"
(1975:152-3). As time passed and the British Virgin Islands plantation
economy went into irrevocable decline, the emphasis of fiscal control
shifted accordingly. Thus, the mid-nineteenth century (1840s-50s) witnessed the promulgation of a plethora of taxes levied on the British Virgin
Islander's items of production (especially livestock), real property and
income, as well as upon the boats used in inter-island trade with the
neighbouring Danish colonies. The situation was, therefore, literally
taxation without representation. Given these circumstances, it is hardly
surprising that this period is characterized by frequent conflict between
government and governed. The so-called "peasant insurrection" of 1853
has already been noted as one instance of popular response to an oppressive taxation on cattle. Widespread smuggling became a generalized
response to taxation, and conflict between Crown and subject was often
related to maritime issues.

> On being informed on November 24, 1856 that a boat belonging
> to an inhabitant of Thatch Island was trading without a licence,
> the subtreasurer of Tortola proceeded to seize it. He soon had to
> abandon the seizure, however, when he was assaulted and the
> crew of his boat badly beaten. Two days later, a force consisting
> of four constables was dispatched by the stipendiary magistrate

to arrest the offenders. On landing they were obstructed by forty to fifty people, and when they persevered and made their arrest were also severely beaten. On the following day, a large force comprising thirty men, principally rural constables, twelve of whom were armed, was dispatched to quell the spirit of insubordination and to apprehend the offenders. Despite this show of force, it was only the assistance of the Wesleyan missionaries who were influential among the inhabitants, which enabled sixteen arrests to be made without active opposition. (Dookhan 1975:151)

Similarly,

riotous disturbances threatened again in 1890 when smugglers openly defied the customs officer over the seizure of a boat and a large crowd marched on Road Town from Long Look and demanded its release, firing shots for emphasis. The commissioner deserted his government and decamped to St. Thomas, ostensibly, at least, in search of help. (Harrigan and Varlack 1975:96)

Civic Retrenchment

Prior to Emancipation, the colonial legislatures in the West Indies had no need to concern themselves with matters of social welfare. The black majority as slaves was by definition property of the plantation proprietors. The care, maintenance, and control of this human property was effected within the context of the individual plantation.

The estate-owners were responsible for the maintenance of their aged and infirm slaves; so there was no general provision of poor relief for those unable to work. Each estate contained some 'hospital' or sick-bay, attended, as required, by a doctor employed by the estate-owner: so there was no need for large considerations of public health, except in times of danger of island-wide spread of infectious disease. Each island had its militia, but this was a force intended to meet foreign invaders or to stamp out slave rebellion, not to carry out the ordinary daily routines of keeping the peace; and the daily maintenance of discipline and good order were the business of the slave-owner of every estate: thus there was no general police force. Petty misdemeanours, and even more serious ones, committed by slaves were usually discovered and punished on the estates by the masters, who were themselves the local magistracy anyway: so there was no adequate provision of law courts to meet the demands of the whole population for access to justice. Religious teaching and other education for the masses were in the hands of the clergy of the Church of England and, more actively, of the dissenting churches; and in any case the opportunities allowed to slaves to improve themselves by these means were small, and not all slave-owners were convinced that benefits would follow: consequently there was no general provision for schools and teachers. (Hall 1971:14)

After Emancipation, with the British Virgin Islands economy in serious decline, the resources upon which the State was able to draw in fulfilling its precipitously expanded civic responsibilities were correspondingly constrained. Thus,

> the greater part of outdoor relief granted after 1864 was given in small allowances of 9d, 1/- or 1/6 a week. Around ten percent of the gross revenue was expended, but ten percent of a small amount of total revenue was inadequate. For the purposes of economy, tight control was exercised over the selection of candidates. No assistance was granted unless the applicant was quite incapacitated for work, and without relatives who could give assistance. In 1871 there were 56 outdoor paupers; by 1881 these had been reduced to 28 . . . .
>
> The support of paupers in the infirmary was equally deficient; allowances averaged only 21/2d. a day, food was scant, and equipment and utensils inadequate. Apart from the matron who was too old and inefficient, there was no other nurse or attendant attached to the institution, and the inmates were obliged to look after each other's everyday wants. Most of the people suffered from extreme old age, and from such incurable diseases as chronic rheumatism, chronic ulcers, asthma and syphilis. (Dookhan 1975:174)

If the sorry state of the social services was reflective of economic decline, so was the machinery of government in general. The response to fiscal constraints was increasingly the "amalgamation or abolition" (Dookhan 1975:160) of posts within Government. Thus, by way of further illustration,

> following the death of the Chief Justice in April, 1866, approval was given to the proposal to combine the offices of Judge and Magistrate. In 1868 and 1869 the offices of stipendiary magistrate and of Queen's Council respectively were abolished. More important than these was the abolition of the office of Colonial Secretary in 1869, and the transfer of his duties to the Provost Marshal, in whom was vested the duties of Registrar, clerk to the magistrate and clerk to the President. Further changes were affected during the same year following the dismissal of the Treasurer-Postmaster who was implicated in the illegal sale of a foreign vessel, the *Telegrapho*. The Inspectorship of Police was

abolished and in the holder of that office was vested the duties in the Treasury, and Landing Waiter of Customs. Because of the vacancy in the Postmastership, advantage was taken of these changes to transfer the business of the Post Office to the Treasury. Towards the end of 1870 the offices of jailer and clerk to the Provost Marshal were united to allow the saving of £25 a year to be appropriated to the superannuation of the Colonial Surgeon. Yet further changes were made in 1872: the duties of the Treasury devolved upon a sub-Treasurer under the superintendence of the President; the offices of coroner and crown prosecutor were united, later to be fused with that of surgeon; the salary of the rector was abolished and this was followed by the disendowment of the Established Church; and finally the office of the jailer was abolished and the salary of the turnkey reduced. (Dookhan 1975:160-1)

This process of progressive governmental retrenchment served as a further source of popular alienation. It is not altogether surprising, therefore, that as the twentieth century dawned, the resident Crown representative, E. J. Cameron, felt impelled to make the observation that

the Government is not popular and does not possess the confidence of the people, partly owing to the small amount of attention bestowed on them, the high duties payable on certain articles especially breadstuff and the fact that they do not realize what becomes of the money they pay. . . . (BVI Government Report 1887; cited in Harrigan and Varlack 1975:152)

Dependent Relations with the Danish West Indies

One of the most far-reaching consequences of the decline of the British Virgin Islands economy and its concomitant removal from economic intercourse with the European "World Economy" (cf. Wallerstein 1974) was the development of an increasingly dependent relationship with the neighbouring Danish West Indies, particularly St. Thomas. From the 1850s onwards, St. Thomas became not only the primary external market for the British Virgin Islands' items of production—agricultural produce, livestock, fish, charcoal—and labor power, but also came to constitute the colony's medium of contact with the outside world.

The historical reasons for the ascendancy of St. Thomas as a commercial entrepot are usefully summarized by Professor Richard Sheridan in his "Introduction" to Dookhan's *History of the Virgin Islands of the United States* (1974):

Not only was [St. Thomas] a distributing point for its sister islands, but it carried on an extensive trade with neighbouring foreign islands and the Spanish Main. European manufactures, North American foodstuffs and building materials, and African slaves crowded the wharves and warehouses of the port city of Charlotte Amalie. The kingdom of Denmark-Norway remained neutral during the numerous wars of the later part of the seventeenth and eighteenth centuries. This meant that St. Thomas was able to conduct a lucrative neutral trade with the colonies of belligerent nations. Here was found a money market for sale of captured ships and cargoes and courts to dispose of prizes brought in by the privateers of different nations. In time, St. Thomas became a free port which attracted foreign traders in times of peace.

Indeed, while local and international economic circumstances were resulting in imperial disinterest in the British Virgin Islands, there was a simultaneous increase in British commercial interest in St. Thomas. Thus, when in 1819, the facilities of the Royal Mail Steam Packet Company in Tortola were destroyed by hurricane, they were removed to St. Thomas. By 1839, British investment in the Danish colony had grown to a point where, of 41 major import establishments, 13 were British (cf. Dookhan 1974: 100-2; Krigger 1980: B-49). The demise of the Tortola-based financial-trading firm of Reid, Irving and Company in 1847 resulted in St. Thomas also becoming the British Virgin Islands' sole nexus with international finance.

These developments were the cause of some official alarm, as evidenced by a British Virgin Islands Government Report of 1854 in which the President observed:

> [T]he immediate vicinity of St. Thomas is, I am inclined to think, in many respects injurious to these islands. The intercourse carried on by means of small boats is so frequent that the inhabitants of this colony have learnt to regard St. Thomas as the market town for the sale of their produce and for the purchase of all the supplies they require. So little support or encouragement is afforded the few individuals who have opened small shops in Tortola, that their establishments never can rise above the level of the most petty shops in an English village. (cited in Harrigan and Varlack 1975:68)

To be sure, the prosperity of the Danish islands was not consistent. The plantation economy of St. Croix—which never evolved into a major trade emporium, as did St. Thomas—was, by the end of the first quarter of the nineteenth century, suffering a serious economic decline.

> After 1850, St. Thomas joined St. Croix on the path of economic decline. The competition of other Caribbean ports which eased their restrictions on foreign commerce, the replacement of sail-

ing ships by steamships which found it easier to call at more ports, a terrible cholera epidemic in St. Thomas in 1853-54 which killed more than 1,500 people and gave St. Thomas a reputation as unhealthy, all contributed to a decrease in the trade and shipping activities of St. Thomas, which proved to be permanent despite spirited efforts to reverse it. From the middle of the 19th Century, therefore, until the 1930s—a span of about nine decades, the population of the [Danish West Indies/U.S. Virgin Islands] continually decreased as people kept leaving for the United States, Cuba, Santo Domingo, Panama or . . . [wherever] there was more lucrative work to be found. . . . (Krigger 1980:B-49)

The economic fate of the British Virgin Islands had become inextricably intertwined with the fortunes of the neighbouring Danish colonies. "Reliance on the St. Thomas market meant," as Dookhan points out, "that any disruptions there, as had been the experience with Britain, would seriously affect the trade of the (British) Virgin Islands" (1975:142), a situation which was to persist well into the third quarter of the twentieth century.

THE LATER YEARS: TOWARDS TOURISM

On a visit to the British Virgin Islands in 1913, Charles F. Jenkins, a Quaker of Philadelphia, Pennsylvania, made the observation that "Tortola's commerce today is practically nil, the islanders growing enough for their own use and not much more" (Jenkins 1923:58).

Everywhere were ruined stone houses, unroofed by some former hurricane, broken arches of one-time big estates tumbled by earthquakes, and evidences on all sides, of a departed prosperity. The inhabitants were living in small frame or thatch cottages, many with the corrugated iron roof so common in the tropics. (ibid.)

A decade later, in a letter to Jenkins, Commissioner H. W. Peebles reported that

considerable improvement is to be noted in Tortola, dilapidated ruins are renovated and many new dwelling houses are erected. A market place has been laid out in Road Town. Much improved roads throughout Tortola. Street lamps have been erected in the main road in Road Town. A cricket ground and a race course have been laid out on a five-acre recreation ground, affording much recreation for the young folk. A bandstand is also erected at the grounds. A bonded warehouse has been erected and the matter of enlargening this building compatible with increased trade, is now under consideration. A library consisting of some

200 or more up-to-date novels has been established. A Peasants' Agricultural Bank has also been established. This has proved itself a great blessing to the peasant inhabitants. Money is loaned at reasonable rates on good securities. A motor boat service has been established. A 13-ton launch, capable of carrying thirty or more passengers with five tons of cargo, carries the mails to and from St. Thomas. The journey to and from St. Thomas by sailing sloop is thus made less tedious. (cited in Jenkins 1923:93)

In further noting that "two new estates [had been] opened up by English settlers," Commissioner Peebles optimistically averred that "there is still opportunity in these wonderfully productive islands for fresh settlers" (ibid.). The ethnic affiliation of those who would bring economic salvation to the colony was hardly left in doubt.

Emigration of labor constituted one of the more salient socioeconomic characteristics of the British Virgin Islands during the early years of the twentieth century, continuing a trend begun immediately after emancipation. Initially, as already noted, the neighbouring Danish colonies constituted the primary market for this labor power, with Puerto Rico, Haiti and especially the Dominican Republic subsequently playing central roles in this regard. "The majority, I may almost say *all* the able bodied men, emigrate during the months of October and November to Santo Domingo," the resident Crown representative observed, "where they find ready and lucrative employment at from 3/- to 6/- per day at the sugar factories, returning in July. . . [to] spend the interval in recuperative ease" (in Harrigan and Varlack 1975:119). In fact, this historical phenomenon of labor migration was not altogether seasonal and bi-directional; many of the emigrants never returned. Thus the period between the 1850s and the turn of the century witnessed a dramatic decline in the population of the British Virgin Islands, from 5,892 in 1859 to 4,607 in 1899 (cf. Dookhan 1975:141).

As the twentieth century marched into its second quarter, the economic activity of the colony continued to be comprised of small-scale agriculture, fishing, charcoal production, and livestock rearing, with continuing dependence on the United States Virgin Islands (the former Danish West Indies) and the sale of emigrant labor power.

With respect to agriculture, an advisory report of the early 1960s proffers the observation that

> all the farms are peasant owned and are operated on a family basis with practically no wage labour but with a certain amount of free reciprocal farm help. Cultivation is almost entirely by hand, the system being one of shifting or rotational cultivation in which food crops are alternated with pastures and ultimately scrub bush. The cycle begins after the land has rested for a period of two or three years. (Faulkner 1962:8)

The report further noted:

> [A]griculture is left largely to the older people although, even in
> their case, it is often subsidiary to wage earning occupation and
> to trades. . . . The conditions of life in the hilly areas of the is-
> lands under which agriculture has to be conducted is such that it
> is unlikely to encourage the young people either to stay there or
> to return in order to make it their place of residence or liveli-
> hood. (ibid.)

In St. Thomas, where fish, agricultural produce and charcoal from the
British Virgin Islands found a relatively lucrative market, "a 'strap of fish'
[sold] for 10 cents [ca. 1930s], charcoal fuel, sold in heaps or butter pans,"
commanded two to five cents per units and "a heap of vegetables or fruit"
brought the vendor five cents (Irish 1980:B-9). British Virgin Islanders
who found work re-fuelling ships on the St. Thomas docks earned "two
cents a basket for carrying 98 pounds of coal on their heads from the dock,
up to the gang-way, dropping it into the ship's hold." Others found employment as "'trimmers' in the ship's hold, spreading the coal for 40 cents
a day" (ibid.).

There were relatively brief spurts of economic prosperity occasioned by
the extension of the United States [liquor] Prohibition laws to the US
Virgin Islands. These laws gave profitable encouragement to British Virgin
Islanders' historic propensity for smuggling. There were also employment
opportunities consequent to the construction of American military facilities in St. Thomas in the 1940s. Apart from these, little change occurred in
the political economy of the British Virgin Islands during the first half of
the twentieth century. "Up to the outbreak of the Second World War," as
was later noted in a Government report,

> the traditional agricultural economy—small holdings with the
> raising of livestock and production of fruit, vegetables, and
> ground provisions for subsistence and a small cash income—
> went on relatively unaffected by the outside world, but the de-
> mand for labour in the United States Virgin Islands for military
> construction and later in the tourist industry seriously depleted
> the local labour force and has led to an increasing decline in ag-
> ricultural and livestock production. (in Harrigan and Varlack
> 1975:130)

During the 1950s and particularly with the closing of Cuba to tourists
from the United States after the Revolution in 1959, the United States
Virgin Islands experienced a dramatic increase in tourism, the number of
tourists increasing from 16,000 in 1949 to 164,000 in 1959, to 1,122,317 in
1969 (Dookhan 1974:286). This windfall phenomenon prompted the
British Virgin Islands Government to express the hope that "some of this
influx may eventually spill over" into the British Virgin Islands, while at

the same time recognizing that "conditions are different and the initial obstacles to tourist development are greater" (in Harrigan and Varlack 1975:130).

As one means of surmounting these obstacles, the British Virgin Islands Government in 1953 passed incentive legislation in the form of a Hotel Aid Ordinance. The 1950s consequently witnessed the opening of a small American-owned private club/resort on Guana Island as well as a small hotel in Road Town. The British Virgin Islands Government Report for 1961-62 observed:

> [A]lthough the basic economic structure has undergone no fundamental change (the livestock industry, despite a tendency to decline, still being the backbone of the economy), there is a growing consciousness of the substantial tourist potential which the Colony possesses and every effort is being made to exploit it. (in Harrigan and Varlack 1975:131)

In 1962, "A Survey of Economic Potential, Fiscal Structure and Capital Requirements of the British Virgin Islands" was undertaken on behalf of the Government by Dr. Carleen O'Loughlin of the University of the West Indies. The study recommended pursuit of tourism as the primary vehicle of economic development, with fishing and agriculture becoming ancillary activities, since tourism was more "likely to bring higher living standards to all economic classes in the population than . . . a primary industry" (O'Loughlin 1962:passim).

The acceptance of the basic premise of the 1962 O'Loughlin Report marked a watershed in the development planning approach of the British Virgin Islands Government. Henceforth, the promotion of tourism as development strategy was to be pursued as a "firm policy" of Government (cf. Dookhan 1975: 231). The construction of Laurance Rockefeller's Little Dix Bay Hotel in Virgin Gorda—completed in 1964—constituted the "economic takeoff" in that regard. The so-called peasant economy was dead. The era of tourism had arrived.

CODA

We have thus delineated a general profile of the British Virgin Islands' social formation for the period between emancipation and the advent of tourism. This epoch, as we have seen, is ubiquitously characterized in the literature by some implicit notion of "peasantry" or "peasant society". It might be useful at this point, before closing this chapter, to digress at some length upon the question of the peasantry.

The notion of the peasantry is invariably invoked at some point by most observers, both contemporary and modern, who comment on the post-emancipation epoch in the British Virgin Islands. Gurney (1840:244) assured his audience that in Tortola, as in other Caribbean islands visited, "the peasantry are working well—I may say almost without any exception."

More recently, the essence of the transformation which occurred in the post-emancipation British Virgin Islands was described in this way: "The former African slave very quickly was converted from a *res* incapable of possessing legal rights, to a landed or, at least, a peasant proprietor" (Todman 1969:550). A recent anthropological study points out that as the post-emancipation British Virgin Islands were "characterized by both cheap land and cheap labor . . . , no amount of punitive law would abort the process of social formation giving birth to a freehold peasantry underway in Tortola" (McGlynn 1980:80). Still more recently, another scholar (Harrigan 1982:8), in addressing the topic of social change, questioned, in passing, the relevance of "the concept 'peasant'" with respect to the British Virgin Islands. Nowhere in any of these works is the operative concept of "peasantry" defined or explicitly conceptualized.

On the Problematic of
"the Peasantry"

The historian E. J. Hobsbaum, in an essay on "Peasants and Politics," offers a rather interesting allegorical commentary on the concept of the peasantry and its concomitant definitional constraints. "It may well be," he suggests, "a very complex matter for a zoologist to define a horse, but this does not normally mean that there is any real difficulty in recognizing one. I shall therefore assume that most of us most of the time know what the words 'peasants' and 'politics' refer to" (1973:3). The anthropologist, Sidney Mintz, on the other hand, contends that the difficulty with such a common-sense approach "inheres in the expectation that everyday terms [such as "peasant", for example] . . . are self-explanatory, simply because they are made prosaic by use, and because each of us thinks himself, by virtue of being human, to be an unwitting expert on what they supposedly mean" (1975:492). The appeal of Professor Hobsbaum's invocation of common sense notwithstanding, it would seem, appropriate to the task at hand to offer some definition of the concept, although no attempt will be made to be original.

One lexical source renders the term "peasantry" simply as "a chiefly European class of persons tilling the soil as small landowners or labourers" (Webster's Dictionary), a definition which quite appropriately implicates the European feudal derivation of the concept. Drawing on Wolf (1966) and Firth (1951), Mintz (1974:141) defines the term "peasantry" as "those small-scale cultivators who own or have access to land, who produce some commodities for sale, and who produce much of their own subsistence." Teodor Shanin defines the peasantry as consisting of "small agricultural producers who, with the help of simple equipment and the labour of their families, produce mainly for their own consumption and for the fulfillment of obligations to the holders of political and economic power" (1966:240). The intent here is to present at an early stage a few definitional instances on the assumption that these might serve as conceptual referents.

Current interest in peasant studies within Western social science was, to a large extent, precipitated by the work of the anthropologist A. L. Kroeber (1948), although as Teodor Shanin has suggested, the fact that Western anthropologists had begun "running short of small tribes and closed 'folk' communities" might well have contributed to the development of this interest. In Kroeber's conceptualization, the peasantry is defined as "constituting part societies with part cultures, definitely rural, yet [living] in a relation to a market town. . . . [They] lack the isolation, political autonomy and self-sufficiency of a tribal population, yet their local units maintain much of their old identity, integration and attachment to the soil" (1948:284). Kroeber's conceptualization of "a timeless, placeless, and institutionless peasantry" (Dalton 1972:399) continues to exert a powerful influence within Western social science. The problem with accepting Kroeber's definition as the basis for a nomothetic conceptualization of "the peasantry" lies in the Eurocentrism of his definition. Geertz comments:

> It was mainly the European peasantry of the nineteenth century and the early twentieth that was in Kroeber's mind as he wrote; but his stress on the fractional, incomplete quality of peasant society and culture has reappeared in virtually every anthropological study of peasant life from Mexico to India as well as in every theoretical treatise on the subject, that has since appeared. (Geertz 1962:1-2)

To be sure, conceptual contention regarding the peasantry is not an exclusive characteristic of "Western" social science. Among Russian Marxists, the peasantry has been variously referred to as "a class" by Stalin, a "petit bourgeois mass" by Kritsman, and "not a class but a notion . . . , non-existent, historically speaking" by Plakhanove (cited in Shanin 1971:239) and passim). Marx and Engels refer to the peasantry as a "class that represents the barbarism within civilization," an "undecipherable hieroglyphic to the understanding of the civilized" (cited in Shanin 1981:239). Marx himself, in a famous passage from *The Eighteenth Brumaire,* dismissed the French peasantry as an essentially undifferentiated "sackful of potatoes":

> The small peasants form a vast mass, the members of which live in similar conditions, but without entering into manifold relations with one another. Their mode of production isolates them from one another, instead of bringing them into mutual intercourse. . . . Their field of production, the small holding, admits of no division of labour in its cultivation, no application of science and, therefore, no multiplicity of development, no diversity of talents, no wealth of social relationships.
>
> Each individual peasant family is almost self-sufficient; it itself directly produces the major part of its consumption and thus acquires its means of life more through exchange with nature

than in intercourse with society. The small holding, the peasant and his family; alongside them another small holding, another peasant and another family. A few score of these make up a village, and a few score of villages make up a Department. In this way, the great mass of the French nation is formed by simple addition of homologous magnitudes, much as potatoes in a sack form a sackful of potatoes. In so far as millions of families live under economic conditions of existence that divide their mode of life, their interests and their culture from those of the other classes, and put them in hostile contrast to the latter, they form a class.

In so far as there is merely a local interconnection among these small peasants, and the identity of their interests begets no unity, no national union and no political organization, they do not form a class. (Marx [1852, orig.] 1972:515-6)

This characteristic "low classness" (Shanin 1971:passim) of the peasantry, as discerned by Marx, continues to bedevil subsequent attempts at approaching the peasant problem via class analysis. The problem, as Stephen Dunn points out, is that "unlike other classes, peasants do not show, wherever and whenever they are found, a distinctive and uniform relationship to the means of production, inasmuch as they include (or have included) medieval serfs, tenants holding land on various kinds of terms, and independent proprietors, as well as people occupying various positions intermediate between these" (1976:639). On the other hand, "it becomes apparent that the problem inheres less in any presumed deficiency in the methodology of class analysis than in definition / conceptualization of the peasantry, which remains amorphous enough to include "medieval serfs . . . , tenants . . . , and independent proprietors.""

The definitional dilemma has given rise to many typologies of the peasantry, predicated upon such criteria as "level of technology, cultural features, the existence of specific forms of exchange, agricultural practices" and so on. Unfortunately, such typologies merely "develop descriptive categories which are analytically useless," and simply "reproduce the given category 'peasant'" (Ennew et al. 1977:311).

In the received wisdom of anthropology, 'peasant' appears as an

> unproblematic descriptive category which only poses difficulties of definition and differentiation because of the varied forms of its concrete appearance. Thus statements about the difficulty of defining 'peasants', 'peasantry' or 'peasant economies' proliferate as the range of suggested typologies correspondingly increases. Meanwhile, no one doubts the existence of peasants. (ibid.:310)

With respect to the Caribbean, this definition/conceptual "confusion," as Sidney Mintz contends, "is confounded," and "sloppiness of usage" abounds (1974a:40). "Meanwhile," to reiterate the terse observation of Judith Ennew and associates, "no one doubts the existence of peasants."

Writing in 1936, Sir W. Arthur Lewis noted that "modern West Indian history begins without a peasantry . . . " and that this fact "is of particular interest because in tracing it, we trace the birth and development of an entirely new class which has profoundly affected the foundations of West Indian Society" (Lewis 1936:1). Given the "relatively shallow social history" (Mintz 1974a:140) of this new class—the putative Caribbean peasantry—it is clearly inappropriate to attempt to analyze its manifestations in terms of a Eurocentric notion of peasantry-in-general. It certainly does not constitute the "rural dimension of old civilizations," as Robert Redfield characterized the peasantry and about which, he maintained, there is "something generic" (1956:25-29).

Mintz locates the origins of Caribbean peasantries within the contradictions of the slave/plantation system, eventuating in the formation of what he terms a "proto-peasantry," wherein "the subsequent adaption to a peasant style of life was worked out [by the slaves] . . . while . . . still enslaved" (1974a:151). (This process was noted in the preceding chapter, although without adopting Professor Mintz' nomenclature.) The Caribbean peasantries which evolved after emancipation are, therefore, dubbed, "reconstituted peasantries" in Mintz' schema (1974a 146-156). Within this conceptual framework, Mintz—unquestionably one of the most percipient and prolific students of the Caribbean—has contributed much to the elucidation of the nature of post-emancipation social formations.

But George Dalton may have a point with his objection that "to use such terms as 'protopeasant' . . . is simply to signal distress with the concept of peasant" (1972:399n). Further, given the ambiguity and contention which pervades attempts at constructing a nomothetic conceptualization of "peasantry," it seems reasonable to question the analytical appropriateness of utilization of the term with respect to the Caribbean. Professor Frank Mills of the University of the Virgin Islands makes this point quite emphatically:

> Gross generalization and vagueness often accompany the use of the terms "peasant", "subsistence", and "traditional" in classifying non-plantation agriculture in the Caribbean. The term "peasant" does not mean the same to the anthropologist as the economist, for the former uses a way-of-life definition, the latter a way-of earning-a-living one. It is used repeatedly in the literature on tropical agriculture, but few writers are careful enough to define their use of the term. It usually implies a backwardness in agricultural methods that is taken for granted, the use of archaic tools, illiteracy, a strongly conservative attitude, great inefficiency in production, excessive poverty indexed by low per-capita income, implied low cultural values, etc. "Subsistence" or "traditional" embodies some of these characteristics to some degree. Even if the definition of "peasant" were limited to a tiller of the

soil as a small proprietor or labourer with no socioeconomic implications, it would be too vague to be analytically useful in any meaningful classification of farming type. This would not adequately describe the non-plantation agricultural producers in the Caribbean. Varying combinations of the level of consumption, the proportion of the crop marketed, the motivations prompting this marketing and the rate of change in time of production methods are all used in the literature to define "subsistence" farmers. Under the definition of complete self-sufficiency by the individual or household, Caribbean small-scale cultivators as a whole cannot be regarded as "subsistence" farmers, for here it is conceptually difficult and empirically impossible to distinguish between those who sell and barter and those who do not; and because there are no common indices for identifying degrees of "subsistence", all small-scale farmers with any unsold produce tend to be labeled "subsistence" farmers. An agricultural system in which output is based wholly on long-established methods of production is called "traditional", which is essentially a cultural characterization of the way particular people live. It is suggested that the concepts "peasant", "subsistence:, and "traditional" are not meaningful enough to be analytically useful as usually applied to Caribbean non-plantation agriculture, and should therefore be abandoned. (Mills 1976:165n)

For the purposes of this study, therefore, the term "smallholding" is used in respect of the social formation which immediately followed the demise of plantation economy in the British Virgin Islands. Although recognizing that the term "smallholding" is itself not without conceptual shortcomings,[3] it is here defined as a small plot of land utilized in the production of a mixture of cash crops and subsistence farming. With particular reference to the British Virgin Islands instance, "smallholding" incorporates fishing, charcoal production and livestock rearing, including the marketing and/or export of surplus after consumption needs have been met.

Toward an Alternative Perspective on British Virgin Islands "Peasant Society"

The position adopted herein is essentially derived from that of Judith Ennew and her colleagues, who argue that "a rigorous concept, of 'peasant mode of production' cannot be constructed because it is impossible to specify distinctly 'peasant' relations of production" (1977:319).

In the case of the British Virgin Islands, the social formation during the period between the abolition of slavery in 1834 and the increasingly dependent relations with the neighbouring Danish islands, circa 1850-1860, exhibits in many respects the characteristics of a petty commodity mode of production:

A petty commodity mode of production is characterized by a class of free, independent small producers. . . . They organize and control their own production process and sell their products on a market, thereby obtaining funds to purchase other commodities for their needs. . . . The petty commodity mode is an example of an incomplete or transitional mode. It often exists in a relation to another predominant mode or tends to become fairly quickly transformed into another mode. . . . (Edwards et al. 1978:40-1)

Further, in terms of class analysis, the petty commodity mode of production is conceived as being "based on the individual ownership of the means of production."

The individual petty producer performs necessary and surplus labor. This is seldom seen as a dominant class process and is generally found in conjunction with a number of other class processes. Petty production seems to be a transitional form resulting from the breakup of a clearly defined class process. The frequency of its historical appearance is greater in social formations in a transitional conjuncture. (Bluestein 1982:16)

Indeed, with the obliteration of the "clearly defined class process" of the plantation system on emancipation in 1838 and the virtual disappearance of the expropriating planter class not long after, a fair approximation of a petty commodity mode of production was evinced in the British Virgin Islands during the first few decades following emancipation. Moreover, as we have seen, attempts by the planter class after abolition to coerce the conversion of the former slaves into a class of free, wage-bound labourers were, ultimately, completely futile. Such a class process is, in any case, "particularly unlikely to 'appear' in situations" (such as the British Virgin Islands) "where land is available for squatter cultivation, police power to shut such cultivation off is lacking, and population density is low" (Mintz 1977:262).

While the concept of a petty commodity mode of production serves as a useful heuristic approach to the early years of the post-emancipation epoch, it affords little explanatory insight into developments after the 1850s/1860s. At this time, as noted, the British Virgin Islands descended into increasingly dependent relations with the nearby Danish colonies. At that point it becomes more appropriate to conceive of the British Virgin Islands' social formation as constituting a conglomeration of non-capitalist *forms* (rather than modes) of production—fishing, small scale livestock and agriculture, charcoal—all consonant with commercial capitalism (cf. Deere 1979), as mediated by trade relations with the Danish islands.

If the level of analysis is shifted to the family unit of production, a number of contradictions become evident. On the one hand, it is accurate to refer to the forms of productive activities engaged in by British Virgin Islanders during this period as non-capitalist. This is because, although individual members of the family unit of production ". . . may participate temporarily in capitalist relations of production" via the St. Thomas/Santo Domingo nexus, "access to the means of production of subsistence assures that the . . . [unit of production] is not dependent on the wage for the full production and reproduction of familial labor power" (Deere 1979:145n). On the other hand, as Werlhof and Neuhoff (1982:89) observe in another context (that of Yaracuy, Venezuela), the deceptively "capitalist character of the observed production relations is expressed in specific combinations of subsistence and commodity production which link even the most non-capitalist production to the market and therefore to capitalist exploitation." Thus, via the varied links with the Danish islands and the exportation of labor power to the sugar factories of Haiti and Santo Domingo, the apparently non-capitalist relations of production in the British Virgin Islands became subsumed under capital.

A further contradiction resided in the fact that St. Thomas—the primary medium through which the British Virgin Islands were linked "to the market and therefore to capitalist exploitation"—was itself a dependent entity, a Danish colonial possession. This peculiar development has been termed "subcolonization" (Codrington 1977), salient characteristics of which are as follows:

> critical exclusion from direct trading within the mainstream of the capitalist market system, based upon the territory's incapacity to produce sufficient surplus to deal adequately in such a matrix; creation of alternate links with nearby colony of some metropolitan power in a satellite relationship; own account small-scale agricultural production becomes the dominant form, together with petty merchant/commercial trading operations; migrant labor becomes the main form of wage labor, following capitalist projects to neighbouring countries; repatriated earnings [become] a central source of cash for domestic/familial maintenance; constitutional down-grading within the imperial/colonial hierarchy. (Codrington 1977:201)

This situation of subcolonization persisted at least until the mid-twentieth century, at which point "actualities and possibilities of surplus extraction" inherent in the British Virgin Islands' tourism potential became apparent to the British Colonial office. This recognition prompted the infrastructural spending consonant with an overall development strategy which looked to tourism as the vehicle of economic transformation. At that conjuncture (ca. mid-1960s), the British Virgin Islands social formation was directly reintegrated into the World economy. It is to the development of this tourism-based economy that attention is now directed in Chapter 4.

PART II

THE CONTEMPORARY SITUATION

4

The Era of Tourism

The promulgation of the 1953 Hotel Aid Ordinance constitutes an early stage of what would eventually become a "firm policy" on the part of the Government of the British Virgin Islands to pursue the promotion of tourism as development strategy. Such a strategy, however, was not initially unqualifiedly recommended by those involved in advising the Government on such matters. In fact, an advisory report of 1958 strongly recommended that an appropriate development strategy for the BVI would look to the revitalization of the agricultural sector, rather than to tourism. "It would clearly be unwise," the Report suggested, "to rely on [tourism] as a means of developing the Virgin Islands. On the other hand, there are good prospects for development in the fields of agriculture and fisheries" (Frampton and Briggs 1958:1).

The recommendation was no doubt regarded as being hopelessly retrograde. Moreover, given the historical marginality of the Colony as an agricultural producer, such a recommended development strategy would inevitably—and with some justification—be met with skepticism. In any event, circumstances external to the BVI would ultimately lead to tourism becoming the development strategy of "choice."

To begin with, the decolonization process of the immediate post-War period lent impetus to the devising of economic bases alternative to, or in addition to, the traditional neo-mercantilist monocrop economies. In many instances tourism was promoted as that alternative. Inevitably, over time, the requisite ideological rationale emerged. By the 1950s, tourism was almost universally being touted by the international development agencies as, in the words of the Paris-based Organisation for Economic Co-operation and Development, "a promising new resource for economic development" (cited in Hiller 1976:95). In a similar vein, a later (1969) study by the U.S. State Department suggested that whereas public sector development aid might not be justifiable on the basis of investment productivity, when coupled with "dollar-earning tourism, [such infrastructural development aid] would be more readily justifiable" (U.S. State Department 1969, ibid.).

The closing off of Cuba as a tourist mecca for North Americans after the revolution of 1959 and the advent of jet travel rendered other destinations within the Caribbean region increasingly attractive, accessible and exploitable. It should be noted in this regard that the early 1960s constituted a period of declining rates of profit for the North American hotel industry: the average return on investment declined to the region of 2%, "as jets shortened the hotel stays of businessmen in downtown areas, while motels sprang up along highways and near airports" (Geshekter 1978:59). Thus, as Mary Vaughan (1974:272) points out, "one means of escaping the depression and saturation at home was to move into the international market, which became more attractive as jets shortened the distance between parts of the globe."

It is within this broad context, then, that the pivotal O'Loughlin "Survey of Economic Potential, Fiscal Structure and Capital Requirements of the British Virgin Islands" (1962) should be considered. As noted in the preceding chapter, that study recommended the promotion of tourism as the primary medium of economic development. Agriculture and fishing—in contradistinction to the 1958 Frampton and Briggs Report—were relegated to ancillary activities. Tourism, to reiterate, was held to be more "likely to bring higher living standards to all economic classes in the population than . . . a primary industry" (O'Loughlin 1962).

With the acceptance by the BVI government of this basic premise, the O'Loughlin Study was followed over the years by a succession of Development Plans, all essentially sharing that premise, though each one rendering various idiosyncratic embellishments. Some of these plans will be considered later in this chapter.

In 1962 when the O'Loughlin Study was submitted, there were 28 hotel rooms in the BVI. Two years later, the total had jumped to 105 rooms. This increase reflected the completion in 1964 of Laurance Rockefeller's 66-room Little Dix Bay Resort on Virgin Gorda, at an unprecedented cost of some $7.5 million. By 1970, hotel rooms totaled 253 and by 1981, 674 rooms with the completion of the 131- room Prospect Reef Hotel in Road Town. Also during this period, tourist arrivals rose from 17,500 in 1967 to 154,500 in 1981 (Source: BVI Statistical Abstracts).

But the virtual unconditional positive regard with which the international development agencies and their clients apparently beheld tourism was increasingly challenged. In the case of the Commonwealth Caribbean, for example, it was suggested that the imputed magic of the so-called multiplier effect of tourist spending was "mystification multiplied," an ideological product of "a powerful metropolitan tourist lobby . . . [whose] purpose appears to be dissemination of misleading information concerning the economic benefits of tourism to poorer regions and countries" (Lewitt and Gulati 1970:326).

In the British Virgin Islands, considerable popular concern had evolved by the late 1960s (1968-9) regarding both the pace and scale of tourism-related development. The precipitating issue centered upon a popular perception that Government had "sold out" to a private British developer in extending 199-year leases on sizeable portions of local real estate. A period of reassessment, eventuating in the appointment of a Commission of Inquiry to investigate these leases and their projected socioeconomic effects, resulted in the termination of the leases. The onset of the 1970s witnessed a retrenchment of tourism development in the Territory, with a sustained upswing beginning around mid-decade.

This, then, is a thumbnail sketch of the evolution of tourism economy in the BVI. It soon becomes apparent, however, when one studies the phenomenon—and in particular, the various development plans which purport to plot the course of its trajectory—that tourism tends to be accorded a sort of *sui generis* mystique which has implications for its adoption as development strategy. For this reason, therefore, before proceeding to analyze the growth and consolidation of tourism in the BVI, we shall first turn our attention to the consideration of tourism *qua* phenomenon.

THE PHENOMENON OF TOURISM

Tourism may be defined as "voluntary, self-interested travel" (Graburn 1977:24). On a world scale, tourism constitutes an economic phenomenon of enormous proportions, as the 1983 edition of the Travel Industry World Yearbook indicates:

> Total world spending for . . . tourism is now more than $700 billion. Spending is expected to grow at about 5 percent a year in real non-inflationary terms during the coming decade. This world total is about 6 percent of the world's gross production of goods and services. It is larger than the GNP of all but four countries in the world. . . .
> . . . In the world trade, international tourism is the second largest single item, second only to oil. In many countries it is the largest foreign exchange earner and the leading growth sector in the economy. (Waters 1983)

It would appear, moreover, that the growth of this so-called "smokeless industry" will continue into the foreseeable future. As Herman Kahn (1980:16), Director of the Hudson Institute, prognosticates, "we do not expect tourism to top out at any point in the next fifty years for almost any country. Most other things, we do expect to top out. That is one of the reasons why we think of tourism as being the largest industry in the world by the end of the century."

Travel as Leisure

Tourism is generally associated with leisure or "non-work." Thus, while travel is an ancient and culturally ubiquitous human activity, tourism is a relatively recent phenomenon, especially in terms of the enormity of its present proportions.

Travel *at* leisure has traditionally been, as one might expect, the domain of the wealthy. For example, that elitist eighteenth century precursor of modern tourism—the European Grand Tour—served as an important medium of enculturation for the aristocracy (cf. Graburn 1977). Travel *as* leisure is a decidedly modern phenomenon:

> What we are in fact seeing is the transformation of "Play" into one of the stronger roles in our culture. This has not always been the case. In the past leisure has been seen primarily as "time remaining at one's disposal after work". Even into the 1950s, the majority of people still saw leisure as "time", rather than as an "activity". The general feeling thus still reflected the Protestant Ethic, which placed non-work activities in a limbo by conferring all its legitimacy on work.
>
> Gradually, rising affluence and greater time away from work have changed this situation and led to an increase in active leisure time pursuits. (Turner and Ash 1975:13)

From this perspective, then, tourism constitutes an "escape valve" from the alienation of which the work-play dichotomy is reflective.

Heliophilia: The Cult of the Suntan

Louis Turner and John Ash provide an intriguing explanation of the genesis of what might be termed the cult of the suntan and its relation to leisure travel. Since suntan tourism is a central aspect of the specific subject being treated here, it might be interesting to place the BVI situation in larger perspective.

The suntan, according to Turner and Ash (1975:79), was always regarded as a desideratum by the leisured classes of the North Atlantic countries. Historically, it is suggested,

> the ruling classes of white imperialist states avoided darkened skin tone when this was possible. Any deliberate cultivation of a tan would have savoured too much of identification with lower (largely rural) classes and coloured subject peoples. . . . For the females of the landed aristocracy in Europe, a pale complexion was the symbol of their superior delicacy, their idleness and seclusion.

Turner and Ash aver that "the deliberate cultivation of a darkened skin by a leisured class is not to be found before the 1920s" (1975:78), at which point "the suntan becomes a mark of class distinction just as the aristocratic 'milk and roses' [complexion] had been" (1975:80).

> For many . . . holiday-makers, acquiring a sun tan became the principal reason for taking a holiday. Sun tan is in every sense a cult with its own obsessive ritual, its sacrifices, its specialized costume and implements. Many tourists who come from tem-

perate regions experience great difficulty in acquiring a tan; they have to suffer to become beautiful. It is physically painful for them to change their skin, to become this different desirable creature at play on the beach, worshipping the sun. To attempt this transformation and to fail is social disaster.

Not only does sunburn make its victim un-attractive (the raw rather than the cooked), it makes it painful for them to be touched by others. A minor industry has grown up around this fear. We are offered a whole range of products (many of them perfectly useless) that claim to enhance the tanning process—remove the pink and painful intermediate stage and make the final result a deeper, more coppery gold. (Turner and Ash 1975: 81)

Apparently, however, there is a point beyond which the progression of the coveted suntan is not desirable, "for a sun tan that has gone beyond gold/brown to near black is generally considered less attractive" (1975: 82):

Since it is a phenomenon of white, bourgeois, capitalist states the sun tan craze does not imply any real breaking down of the barriers of colour and race. It merely flirts with the idea of the erotic aspect of colour, and perhaps symbolises a partial absorption into "the System" of blackness, thus rendering it less threatening. . . . (ibid.)

Clearly, the foregoing reconstruction of the evolution of the cult of the suntan is, to a large extent, speculative. Nonetheless, such an exercise serves to give pause for reflection upon an aspect of tourism, the ideological underpinnings of which are hardly ever brought to consciousness.

The Great Escape

"The prime motivation to engage in tourism," as Bukart and Medlik (1975:55) suggest, "is to be elsewhere and to escape, however temporarily, the routine, constraints, and stresses of everyday life." The physical/geographical aspect of this escape is fairly obvious; less so, perhaps, is the element of fantasy which is also an integral part of the touristic impulse to escape: "Disney Land and Disney World are phantasies—phony if you like—but the most successful tourist attractions in history. Are Mickey Mouse and Donald Duck phonies?" (Donald Lundberg 1974; cited in Hiller 1976:106)

The dual nature of the element of escape in the touristic impulse is, of course, well recognized by the marketers of tourism. A short-list of some of the slogans (cited in Hiller 1976:101-2) which have been thus engendered is instructive:

— "We've created a world unaffected by the world." (Pan Am)

— "You are sentenced to fifty weeks hard labour every year. Quantas offers executive clemency."

— "Come to Eleuthera and run away from today."

— "In a world of bad air, poisoned water and litter, there are still a few virginal places. Enjoy. Quickly." (Jamaica, ca. 1972)

The escapist impulse of tourism also tends to be reflected in the overt behavior of the tourist, a tendency which sometimes results in a diminution of the propriety of that behavior:

> Good conduct, if not internalized, is often enforced by awareness of the ways in which important "others" will react. Travel is a way of escaping these censors. . . . By confining the scope of his sensitivity to censors at home, whom he has temporarily escaped, the tourist permits himself the indulgence of misconduct abroad. The man on a spree at a resort, the one who shouts at waiters and clerks, the woman who wears shorts into a cathedral, the traveler who talks disparagingly about the country he is visiting, might never at home so contravene the demands of etiquette. (Pool 1965:120)

Immanent Critique

Tourism, as noted at the outset, is an economic reality of major proportions. It is, as Turner and Ash (1975:11) put it, "no trivial phenomenon." Moreover, tourism is almost universally perceived to be—as was also noted earlier—an enormously efficacious medium of economic development. Herman Kahn declares that:

> In country after country tourism has been the major source of economic development, of foreign exchange, of good jobs for unskilled people. It is labour intensive. And we think of tourism as literally being God's work, because it is helping those who need help the most. It is the most effective method I know of raising incomes in the poorer parts of the world. Well, "most effective" is too strong. Overseas labour is the most effective, but tourism is the second most effective. And by the way, it is about as effective as oil, or better. (Kahn 1980:11)

Wherever it achieves predominance, tourism becomes the quintessential sacred cow of economic development. "All . . . differences yield to a united front," as Gordon Lewis (1972:130) observes in the case of the U.S. Virgin Islands, "when the total image of the [tourism] economy is challenged." Perhaps because of this, there is a tendency in development planning to proceed in apparent oblivion of the body of *critical* thought that has evolved in response to tourism, including in the BVI. Before returning to our more idiographic concern—i.e., tourism economy in the BVI—we shall, therefore, briefly note a few instances of this critical perspective.

The work of Louis Turner and John Ash (1975)—to which ample recourse is taken in this chapter—has been referred to rightly by one scholar (Hiller 1976:101) as a "pioneering critique of tourism". Turner and Ash were not, however, the first to register dismay at the sociocultural impact of the burgeoning tourism industry. Arthur Koestler, for example, anticipated much of the critical argument which began evolving in the early 1970s, in an acerbic commentary on a vacation which he had taken in Fiji in the late 1960s:

> The explosion of the tourist industry and its culture-eroding fall-out are still regarded as a minor nuisance. They are more than that. All over the world the tourist trade is an increasingly important factor in the national economy. In some countries it takes first or second place, and in some the number of tourists per annum outnumbers the total native population. It is a plague of locusts which brings the natives material prosperity and cultural corruption, eroding traditional ways of living, contaminating arts and crafts with the vulgarity of the souvenir industry, and leveling down indigenous cultures to a uniform, mechanized, stereotyped norm. (Koestler 1969:20)

The significance of the Turner-Ash treatise, however, lies in both the wide sweep of its critical vision and the audacious perspicacity of its observations and assertions:

> Tourism is . . . a visible result of the fourth of the great waves of technology which have changed the social geography of the world since 1800. First the railways opened up the continents, carrying the food and materials which made possible the great nineteenth-century industrial cities. Then came steam ships which served as the sinews allowing the Empire builders to stretch across the globe to take what they wanted from their colonies. . . . Finally we have the aeroplanes which when linked with rising affluence, has led to a whole new tribe—the Mass Tourist. The barbarians in our Age of Leisure. The Golden Horde.
>
> It is perfectly legitimate to compare tourist with barbarian tribes. Both involve the mass migration of peoples who collide with cultures far removed from their own. There is, however, one major difference. The old Golden Horde (a Tartar Empire led by Genghis Khan's successors) was a nomadic non-monetary people which threatened the settled urban civilization of Europe. Today

the pattern is reversed. Tourists come from the industrialized centres but, this time, it is they who are fanning out through the world, swamping apparently less dynamic societies, including the few preindustrial ones which still remain. In the past, it was the great commercial centres of the world like Constantinople and Vienna which were threatened. Today, it is the Nomads of Affluence, coming from the new Constantinoples—cities like New York, London, Hamburg or Tokyo—who are creating a newly dependent, social and geographic realm: The Pleasure Periphery. (Turner and Ash 1975:11)

Obviously, such pronouncements would hardly be endearing to those involved in tourism, whether as purveyor, dependent, or consumer.

Others have approached tourism more explicitly as an instrument of metropolitan imperialism, stressing the disparity of power whereby the nature of tourism development is controlled (cf. Nash 1977). At the level of the individual tourist, the derivative manifestations have by now achieved the dubious and unfortunate status of caricature:

The North American vacationer who insists on American fast-food hamburgers, coffee with his meals, hot running water in his bedroom and the use of the English language is a familiar image. Here is a person from a highly industrialized country expecting, even demanding, that his vacation life abroad meet expectations he has come to take for granted at home. Beyond this vacationer there often stands a metropolitan touristic infrastructure that, in effect, sees that his expectations are met. (Nash 1977:35)

It is also argued that tourism sets in motion an irreversible process of cultural commoditization whose "very subtlety prevents the affected people from taking any clear-cut action to stop it" (Greenwood 1977:137).

Perhaps this is the final logic of the capitalistic development, of which tourism is an ideal example. The commoditization process does not stop with land, labour and capital but ultimately includes the history, ethnic identity, and culture of the peoples of the world. Tourism simply packages the cultural realities of a people for sale along with their other resources. . . . The loss of meaning through cultural commoditization is a problem at least as serious as the unequal distribution of wealth that results from tourist development. (ibid.)

Nor is the critical response to tourism limited to what might be perceived as being disgruntled academics, as the following Hawaiian vignette—to cite a non-Caribbean example—illustrates:

Mayor Frank Fasi of Honolulu . . . urged the legislature to enact a hotel room tax hoping to ease the tax burden of local residents. We are fast becoming peasants in paradise he said. The recent Rotary International convention brought 15,000 Rotarians to Honolulu, each spending from $50 to $90 a day (ca. 1969). A group called the "Hawaii Residents Council" mailed mimeographed pleas to Rotarians urging them not to spend money here. We are losing our shirts and souls to the soaring cost of living and the excessive greed that tourism brings, the leaflets said. There is little in Hawaii that you cannot buy for less in your hometown. (cited in MacCannel 1976:165)

With the foregoing digression on the tourist phenomenon as backdrop, we shall now resume our analysis of tourism economy in the British Virgin Islands.

THE GROWTH AND CONSOLIDATION OF TOURISM ECONOMY IN THE BRITISH VIRGIN ISLANDS

It is important to note the political milieu within which the rise of a tourism-based economy in the British Virgin Islands occurred.

Setting the Stage

The hiatus between the abolition of the British Virgin Islands legislature in 1902 and its reconstitution in 1950 constituted a period during which little development of any sort occurred.

The islands, still on the last rung of the constitutional ladder, passed through political doldrums in which nothing of real significance occurred. Commissioners came and went, taxes were levied and collected, the magistrate's court sat each Wednesday mornings to hear petty cases and a puisne judge of the Supreme Court of the Leeward Islands visited once a year to try the occasional criminal offenders and the interminable disputes over land. (Harrigan and Varlack 1975:152)

After 1950, the politico-constitutional apparatus of the BVI underwent relatively rapid transformation, reflecting, in part, the exogenous impetus of post-war metropolitan decolonization concerns. In 1965 a constitutional review Commission was appointed, chaired by Dr. Mary Proudfoot of Oxford (cf. Harrigan and Varlack 1975:167). On the basis of the recommendations of that Commission, members of the BVI Legislative Council conferred in London with officials of the Colonial Office on 4 October 1966 (ibid.:170).

In the meantime, Dr. William Phillips, a United Nations economic advisor, had been appointed to make "Recommendations on Measures for Accelerating Economic and Social Development" of the Colony. The connection between constitutional advancement and development planning within the colonial context was quickly recognized by British Virgin Islanders. In commenting on the Phillips Report's assertion that British grant aid could be eliminated by 1991 (Phillips 1966:17), the local Development Advisory Committee took the opportunity to stress

> the advantage, not only from the point of view of the British Government but from that of local self-respect (*particularly with constitutional development in prospect*), of eliminating grant-aid on recurrent account as rapidly as possible, and . . . [to express the hope] that these will lead the British Government to grant, if necessary, special treatment to the Colony in order to achieve this objective which is now within measurable distance. (Report of the Development Advisory Committee 1966:40 [emphasis added])

In 1967, the process initiated with the establishment of the Proudfoot Constitutional Review Commission culminated in the establishment in the BVI of a system of government based upon the British Westminster model. The Virgin Islands Constitution Order of 1967 as amended in 1976,

> provides for a Ministerial system, with the Governor [formerly, Administrator] retaining responsibility for defence and internal security, external affairs, the civil service and the administration of the courts. The Governor also continues to hold reserved legislative powers necessary in exercise in his special responsibilities but in other matters is normally bound to act in accordance with the advice of the Executive Council. The Executive Council is comprised of the Governor as Chairman, one ex-officio member (the Attorney General), the Chief Minister, appointed by the Governor as the elected member who appears best able to command a majority and three ministers appointed by the Governor on the advice of the Chief Minister.
> Following general elections in 1979 provision was made for a fourth Ministry and there was redistribution of subjects assigned to Ministers. . . .[1]
> . . . The Legislative Council consists of a Speaker, chosen from outside the Council, one ex-officio member (the Attorney General), and nine Elected Members including the Chief Minister, returned from nine one-member electoral districts. (BVI Territorial Report 1981:6,7)

This constitutional development also resulted in the reorganization and expansion of the civil service. Thus, the administrative-bureaucratic apparatus necessary to effect the economic development which was being planned, was concurrently created.

Plans and Politics

It was noted in the Phillips Report ("With Recommendation on Measures for Accelerating Economic and Social Development") that "there has been a consensus for a number of years that the development of the British Virgin Islands must, of necessity, rely primarily on tourism, or the vacation industry . . . to achieve its development goals" (1966:2).

The socioeconomic problems which such development would seek to address were enumerated as follows:

1. A heavy reliance, present and prospectively, on tourism as the principal means for raising levels of income and providing employment opportunities;
2. A static or declining agricultural industry due to relatively low returns to farmers coupled with;
3. A drift of younger members of the work force to the American Virgin Islands for employment;
4. Lack of capital resources by Government sufficient to provide the necessary infrastructure and facilities to speed up the growth of tourism and revitalize the agricultural sector;
5. Insufficient local Government revenue to cover local Government expenditures;
6. Inadequate education and health facilities; and
7. Relatively low level of human resource development, which results in shortages of many of the skills needed to carry out development. (Phillips 1966:2,3)

It might be noted here that there was, apparently, some concern regarding overemphasis on tourism as development strategy—consensus notwithstanding—since the Report suggested that the "heavy reliance . . . on tourism" was one of the problems which should be resolved by properly planned development.

The problem-identification process led to the recommendation of the following development objectives:

1. To provide steady increases in levels of income and consumption per head;
2. To increase the well-being of the British Virgin Islands rural inhabitants and other low-income groups primarily by raising their productivity and thus their income-earning capacity;
3. To generate employment opportunities at a rate sufficient to provide productive work for new entrants to the labour force and lower the number of those seeking employment abroad;

4. To stimulate economic activity in the fields of tourism, agriculture and, to the extent feasible, in light industry and the service industries;

5. To educate and train British Virgin Islands citizens in order to equip them for effective participation in the process of economic and social development;

6. To provide electric power, water, transportation and communication services adequate to meet foreseen demands;

7. To progress with health and social welfare development;

8. To achieve a position of financial self-reliance free from the need for subsidization by the United Kingdom Government. (Phillips 1966:3,5)

In the final analysis, however, the stimulation of "economic activity in ... tourism" was considered the optimal means by which most of the other development objectives could be attained. "If one accepts the proposition that the development of the territory rests principally on its success in building up the tourist and vacationer industry," the Phillips Report reasoned, "then one must accept private initiative and private investment as the vehicle for achieving development." On the other hand,

Government's role in this situation is to provide certain basic facilities such as harbours, airports, roads, communications and utilities. Government also has a very important role to play in attracting or introducing both local and foreign capital investment to be made in hotels, guest houses, private residences, stores, restaurants, and other facilities which will make extensive tourism a reality. (1966:7,8)

The basic postulates of the Phillips Report as enunciated above were accepted by the BVI Government. The Report formed the basis of the British Virgin Islands' Development Plan for the period 1966-1971 (cf. Report of the Development Advisory Committee 1966). During this period, Government undertook a series of infrastructural development projects, including: major road-work, airport runway extension, island-wide electrification, and construction of a deep-water port facility. Concurrently, radio and telecommunication services were vastly expanded. The infrastructural prerequisites which would "make extensive tourism a reality" were, thus, being put into place.

While this infrastructural development was occurring, Government had also been successful in attracting considerable foreign capital investment. Of all of these, the development proposed and begun by the British firm Batehill Ltd was the most significant, both in terms of scale and unforeseen sociopolitical consequences. It might be useful, therefore, to consider the Batehill case in some detail.

On 20 January 1967, after several months of negotiation between Batehill Ltd. and the Government of the British Virgin Islands, agreements were signed for the development of sizeable areas of land on Tortola and Anegada. These agreements are known, respectively, as the Wickham's Cay and Anegada Development Agreements There were, in fact, three separate agreements, two of which related to Tortola and the third to Anegada. The Agreements (as abridged and presented in Bryden 1973:151-2) are noteworthy:

> Agreement No. 1 (Tortola) In return for allowing the Tortola Development and Trust Company Ltd. to reclaim some 60 acres of land, the government [was] to receive not more than 5% for roads, car parking and amenity space (3 acres)—a Crown grant being given to the company for the remainder of the land. In addition the government undertook to: (a) waive customs duties payable on plant, equipment and materials for the purposes of the reclamation works; (b) grant privileges and concessions . . . (re: customs duty and income tax relief) to the company, any subsidiary company, any associated company, all shareholders to the extent of at least 5% of issued share capital of the company or any subsidiary or associated company, and, further, all companies formed by such shareholding persons or companies with the intention of carrying out commercial activities on the reclaimed land including the construction of buildings. . . .

> Agreement No. 2. (Tortola) . . . [concerned] the reclamation and development of Wickham's Cay and Wickham's Cay Reef, giving the right without obligation for a period of 15 years to reclaim a further area of land adjoining that covered by Agreement No.1. Upon reclamation the government [would]: (a) give a Crown grant to the company for the land reclaimed, the mangrove island, and the certain area of foreshore . . . ; (b) give the company the right in perpetuity to 'control, restrict and govern the use of the Marine Area' created by the reclamations, 'and to levy tolls' save in respect of local bona fide fisherman. In return for this the company [would] cede 1 ½ acres of land to government on the reclaimed area. However, the government committed to provide sewage [sic] to each plot. . . .
> Further, the government agreed to provide water and electricity supplies to consumers on the reclaimed land. The same concessions [were] given in respect of concessions under Agreement No. 1.

With respect to the Anegada Agreement, Administrator Martin Stavely, in a radio address on 7 February 1967, gave an interesting *ex post facto* rationale for the signing of the Agreement. "It could never be justified", the Administrator maintained, "for a government—any government—to provide the full range of facilities for a small, isolated community of two hundred people. The only course," therefore, "was to grant sufficient concession to make it worthwhile for someone capable of doing so, to do it" (cited in Bowen 1976:76). The concessions were considerable:

> Agreement No. 3 (relating to Anegada) For the sum of $1.00 the government granted the option to lease the greater part of Anegada island (about 8,000 acres) to the Development Corporation of Anegada. . . . The agreement specified the terms of this lease, which [was] for a period of 199 years. In return for this, the following rents [were] payable:
>
> (a)   Year 1 – a peppercorn
> (b)   Year 2 – $5,000
> (c)   Year 3 – $10,000
> (d)   Year 4 – $20,000
> (e)   Year 5 – 199 – $30,000 per annum . . . .

> There were virtually no restrictions on the type of density of development permitted on the land. The lessee [was] responsible for the provision of electricity, drainage, sewage. The lessee [was] entitled to draw upon underground water supplies and charge for this service. Roads [would be] constructed by the company, but maintained by government.

> Furthermore, the company undertook to meet the initial cost in the first instance of: the public service portion for an air terminal; the fire safety equipment for an air terminal; a police station; customs offices; a small hospital; a post office.

> The government [would] be "liable to repay all such costs to the Lessee with interest" at 1/2% above the company's borrowing rate, such liabilities being met out of the rents payable to government under this agreement. . . .

> The government covenanted . . . that throughout the term of the lease "all persons, firms, companies or corporations . . . resident or conducting activities of whatever description" within the area of land and on the lessee's land [would] be exempt from all taxation on profits, income, capital and death duties arising by reason of such residence or the conduct of such activities. . . .

> The company [would] be exempt from customs duties in respect of plant, equipment and materials imported for the carrying out "by or at the instance of" the lessee of all public services or utilities on Anegada, and for all construction works in relation to the lessee's land for a period of ten years. (Bryden 1973:151-2)

Given the enormity of these concessions, it is hardly surprising that there soon evolved a feeling that the British Virgin Islands had been shortchanged in the negotiations which produced the Agreements. John Bryden's general observations regarding the phenomenon of such "extraordinary agreements" in the Commonwealth Caribbean context are most apposite:

> The large investors were in a seller's market, so to speak. Negotiations were often initiated and concluded at Cabinet level, with little coordination or consultation within the administrations. Serious investors came equipped with a team of highly qualified and experienced negotiators and a well thought out negotiating position, while on the government side there was generally absence of a firm and agreed negotiating position and a lack of experience and qualified negotiators. It would be very surprising indeed if, in these circumstances, governments were able to get anything like a fair share of the potential benefits. (1973:139)

During the period under consideration (mid- to late-1960s), the white population of the BVI had risen from a few dozen to several hundred (see Table 1). Since the Wickham's Cay-Anegada development schemes, as well as much of the other major investment which had been attracted to the BVI, were white-owned, the evolving feeling of "foreign exploitation" almost inevitably took on racial undertones. It should be noted, however, that the burgeoning numbers of immigrants from other Caribbean countries as a consequence of the development spurt of the mid-1960s were also a matter of concern for British Virgin Islanders. "In short," as one observer puts it, "the presence of large numbers of immigrants, both black and white, filled Tortolans [sic] with a brooding sense of unease" (Bowen 1976:80).

By early 1968, a Road Town-based, self-styled "political pressure group" had emerged, charging the Government with having sold out to the expatriate developers and calling for "Positive Action". This became both the group's name and its rallying cry. Increasingly, as Harrigan (1982:24) contends, "the islanders had to deal with a subtle form of [expatriate] arrogance, and responsible people talked about the creation of a society whose essential features would not differ greatly from those of Rhodesia as a distinct possibility."

Within this ambience, the assassination in the U.S.A. of Dr. Martin Luther King in April 1968 constituted the critical incident which heightened and mobilized support for the Positive Action Movement. A demonstration was called, which

> gained a fair measure of public support, but it turned out to be more of an anti-government rally than a march in respect for King, for there were more placards denouncing the Government and demanding Positive Action than any other sort of slogan. The marchers also barricaded white businesses and forced them to close their doors out of respect, they said, for King. (Bowen 1976:82)

Over time, a series of acts associated with the Positive Action Movement—such as, for example, a night-time raid on the Road Town police station—resulted in a diminution of wide-based popular support, much of which had, in any case, been largely covert.[2]

The political agitation had not, however, been lost on the Government. Recognition of the widespread discontent over the Wickham's Cay-Anegada Agreements, as well as the concern over what was being perceived as uncontrolled development, prompted Government to appoint a Commission of Inquiry in 1969 to study the Agreements and to make recommendations pertaining thereto. Ultimately, the Government decided to abrogate the Agreements and to acquire the Batehill Ltd. interests in consideration of the sum of $5.8 million, which amount was obtained as a loan from the British Government.

By 1971, much of the infrastructural work (roads, electricity, etc.) which had been initiated in the mid-1960s had been completed. This also coincided with a down-turn in Caribbean tourism, all of which was reflected in a slow-down of development activity in the Territory. Much of the blame for this economic declension, however, was attributed to the attrition of investors' "confidence and goodwill" (cf. Bryden 1973:139) as a consequence of the BVI government's abrogation of the Wickham's Cay and Anegada Development Agreements. Thus, a British Foreign and Commonwealth Office report observed:

> Development slowed down considerably. Many expatriate entrepreneurs left the Territory and immigration figures fell. The building of hotels and tourism enterprises was stopped. Money was in short supply, the cost of living rose and there was no longer full employment. (United Kingdom Foreign and Commonwealth Office 1973; cited in Howell 1978:84)

Tourism and Development

The relative decline in economic activity experienced in the British Virgin Islands in 1971 notwithstanding, the economic growth which had occurred in the Territory during the preceding decade had been quite remarkable. By 1962 the BVI Government had initially adopted tourism promotion as a "firm policy" of development strategy, and the Gross Domestic Product (GDP) stood at $2,251,000. By 1965, this figure had risen to $3,157,000, an increase of approximately 40%, which was largely attributable to the impact of the construction and commencement of operations of Rockefeller's Little Dix Bay Hotel on Virgin Gorda. This, it was suggested in the Phillips Report, "provided a striking example of the profound impact that a luxury vacation facility of only fifty rooms can have on an economy the size of the British Virgin Islands" (1966:2).

By 1970, the GDP was $15,947,000. Of this figure, the construction sector accounted for $4,813,000 while tourism ("hotels, restaurants, boat charters") accounted for $1,178,000 (see Table 2). The economic growth occurring in the BVI during this period was dubbed a "Sunny Success Story" by the Financial Times (of London):

> So far, all is going remarkably well. The last five years have been a considerable success story, and it may well be that nowhere else in the British Caribbean has there been such fast growth. It has been orderly growth, too, for the most part, and has not yet spawned the social, economic or political troubles that bedevil some of the other islands in the British West Indies. (Graham 1969:19)

During this same period, the value of imports rose from $856,596 in 1960 (Table 30) to $2,960,800 in 1965, to $10,223,574 in 1970. In 1971, the value of imports fell to $8,849,578, reflecting the economic down-turn which, as previously noted, was attributed by some to a decline in investors "confidence and goodwill" (Table 4). Similarly, the GDP declined to $13,769,000. As the 1970s drew to a close, however (1978), the GDP had more than doubled this latter figure, to stand at $28,510,000. The relative contributions of construction and tourism had now become inverted, with "hotels, restaurants and boat charters" accounting for $4,900,000 and construction for $3,340,000. Throughout this period, the value of domestic exports—that is to say, agricultural produce (fruits and vegetables), livestock, and fresh fish—declined fairly steadily from $182,398 in 1960, to $98,845 in 1965, to $42,608 in 1970. Tourism was now clearly the predominant sector of the BVI economy.

After the Batehill/Wickham's Cay-Anegada Development debacle, Government began to reassess its tourism/development strategy. Accordingly, in 1972, the United Kingdom firm of Shankland Cox and Associates was commissioned to produce "A Development Plan for Wickham's Cay" (hereafter referred to as the Shankland Cox Report 1972). The essence of the development strategy recommended to Government in the Report was one of "controlled growth in the interests of both the people and the tourist" (1972:42). The Report further cautioned that it was imperative to "strike a balance between the need to develop . . . tourist attractions for the benefit of the economy, without at the same time destroying what make them attractive in the first place" (1972:48). Thus, restrictions were recommended regarding hotel size and sites, as well as regarding further land subdivision for what is sometimes called "residential tourism"[3] (cf. de Kadt 1979: passim).

But perhaps the main innovation of the Shankland Cox Report was the recommendation that major emphasis be made on developing the Territory's marine resources. In operative terms, this meant promoting the development of the yachting/charter-boat sub-sector of the tourism "industry." Thus, with this basic premise fully accepted by the mid-1970s, a United Nations-prepared development plan for the Territory noted that at locations where land attractions are scarce or can only be developed at great expense, as in the BVI, boat chartering offers a good tourism development alternative. By capitalizing on sea attractions and minimizing on land infrastructure and superstructure facilities, chartering offers bargain basement opportunities for tourism development. (UNDP 1976:26)

The growth of the charter-boat industry in the British Virgin Islands has been truly remarkable.[4] In 1969, two charter-boat companies—The Moorings and Caribbean Sailing Yachts—began operations in the BVI, with 6 boats and 25 boats respectively. At the time of the rendering of the Shankland Cox Report, with its positive recommendations regarding charter-boat tourism as development strategy, the charter-boat fleet stood at 69 boats, with a third company (Fleet Indigo) holding 7 of this total. By the end of the 1980, the number of BVI-based charter-boat companies had risen to 12, with a total fleet of over 300 boats (see Table 5). Indeed, with the largest such fleet in the region (cf. Jackson 1981:13), the British Virgin Islands were advertised as "The Yachting Center of the Caribbean."

Within the overall context of the predominant tourism sector of the BVI economy, the ascendancy of the charter-boat sub-sector has been striking. In 1973, total visitor expenditure amounted to $8,300,000, of which $4,664,000 was contributed by hotel tourists and $2,300,000 by charter-boat tourists (Statistical Abstract . . . 1974). In a relatively short time, however, expenditure by charter-boat tourists exceeded that of hotel tourists. Thus, by 1977, with total visitor expenditure amounting to $18,610,000, charter-boat tourists contributed $9,425,000 of that amount, against $7,760,000 by hotel tourists. In 1981, total visitor expenditure had risen to $74,277,000 of which amount charter-boat tourists accounted for $55,929,000 while hotel tourists accounted for $14,931,000 (see Table 6). As might be inferred from these figures, the majority of the tourists who "vacation" in the BVI are charter-boat tourists. In 1980, for example, of 93,260 total overnight tourists, 25,752 stayed at hotels while 58,650 stayed aboard charter-boats. (Tourism in the BVI . . . 1981)

Some definitional clarification might be in order at this point. The term "charter-boat" is defined in the BVI Cruising Permit Ordinance of 1976 as "any vessel for hire, with or without crew, conveying passengers for payment or reward." Of the total fleet of 320 boats in 1980, a minority of some 45 boats were crewed. The overwhelming majority of the BVI-based charter-boats, then, are chartered without crew, the phenomenon being known as "bareboat" chartering.

Bareboats are mainly of fiberglass construction, designed mainly for pleasure cruising, with emphasis on comfort, easy handling and maintenance, and shallow draught for shallow water. Bareboats are equipped with hot and cold showers, heads (toilet), bunks, stove, and ice storage. Boats are of standard design, with companies operating between three to six different designs in their fleet. . . . Boats currently chartered range in length from 31' to 50' and in beam (maximum width) 10'6" to 14'1". Each boat is chartered with dinghy, average length of 10ft., and usually equipped with an outboard engine. (Jackson 1981:14)

The investment represented by these bareboats is considerable. Each one of Caribbean Sailing Yachts' forty model CSY 44's—a 44-foot, 7-bunk cutter—cost approximately $132,000 at 1980 prices. By way of further example, the Moorings 1980 fleet of 82 boats included thirty-two 8-bunk Morgan-Moorings 46's, at approximate costs of $165,000 each (see Table 7). It should be noted, though, that the investment represented by these vessels is largely effected by means of an ingenious financial device known as a "lease-back":

Most of the bareboats are owned by North Americans, who purchase the boats and lease them to a company, under what is termed a "lease back" arrangement. The life of the lease ranges from three to seven years, (average five years), after which the boat is returned to the owner or sold. During the life of the lease, owners are allowed to use their boats between two and four weeks per year, and can deduct expenses of the trip for tax purposes. Owners also benefit from investment tax credit and tax concessions from the depreciation of the boat which can be written off in about seven years. During the lease, owners receive quarterly or annual payments to assist in mortgage payments and pay no operating expenses. (Jackson 1981:20)

While the lease-back arrangement is obviously advantageous to both the BVI-based charter-boat company and the North American investor-owner—"boat sales [are] reported to be one of the major sources of income for companies, without which charter operations may sometimes not be feasible" (Jackson 1981:37)—the economic benefit derived from this by the British Virgin Islands is open to question:

Bareboat companies act as brokers when individuals purchase new yachts under the lease-back arrangement and at the end of the lease arrangement. The commission on sales [varies] from 10-15%. Most of this money never enters the BVI, since transactions are frequently done through company offices in the United States. (ibid.)

Nonetheless, charter-boat tourism is an important source of revenue for the BVI Government. In 1980, Government revenue derived from this source included:

— 5% import duty on new boats = $450,000.

- cruising tax from local and non-local boats = $383,826.
- Annual License and tonnage dues = $9,500.
- Trade License fees for bareboat companies, marinas, boat yards and direct support businesses = $9,600.
- Departure tax from charterers = $91,000. (Jackson 1981:38)

Tourism Ascendant

The decennia of the 1960s and 1970s witnessed the transformation of the British Virgin Islands from an essentially autarchic, petty-commodity / smallholding economy (see Chapter 3) to a tourism-based economy, within which the charter-boat sub-sector was predominant.[5] The BVI tourism industry was predominantly foreign-owned. Tourism thus constituted the transformational medium by which the BVI economy was linked ". . . to the market and therefore to capitalist exploitation" (Werlhof and Newhoff 1982:89), following a post-emancipation interregnum of metropolitan disinterest.

A Government report provides the following synopsis of the BVI tourism economy as of 1981:

Passenger arrivals in the British Virgin Islands rose in 1981 to 233,084. Arrivals by sea increased 15% to 147,748, by air 6% to 85,336. 42% of passenger arrivals entered through West End and 29% through Beef Island [Airport].

Tourist arrivals in 1981 were 154,484, a 5% increase over the 1980 totals. 85,355 arrived by sea and 69,129 by air. Over-night tourists at 90,615 declined 3% in 1981 from the 1980 figure of 93,260. The increase in cruiseship passengers accounted for the overall increase in tourist arrivals in 1981.

Hotel room capacity increased 4% to 674; one charter boat company went out of business in mid 1981 and the number of boats fell 13% to 244.

Occupancy rates for charter boats fell in 1981 but there were some improvements for the hotel industry. The rates were 54.7% and 48.7% for all hotels and charter boats respectively.

Average length of stay was 8 nights. Visitors' expenditure was estimated at $73.6 million in 1981. (BVI Territorial Report 1981:44)

The dependence of BVI tourism on the U.S. market is underscored in another Government document:

The recession in the U.S.A. plus the increase in the rate of the U.S. dollar against other currencies have resulted in an overall decline in the number of overnight tourists. This in part has been compensated by a slight increase in the average length of stay and by an increase in the number of Cruiseship Tourists. Due to an increase in room/boat capacity the occupancy rates have declined even more sharply and the sector as a whole showed a sluggish performance for the 1981/82 season. Since there will be no likely improvement in the U.S. economy before the end of 1982, it is to be expected that the performance of the tourist sector will not improve for the 1982/83 season. Partly as a result of the disappointing performance of the industry for the last two years at least two major hotel construction plans have been postponed and one charter-boat company went out of business. (BVI Government Project List 1982:4)

This document also notes that "the domestic-value-added generated by tourism [in the BVI] is fairly low due to high leakages and lack of linkages with the domestic production sector." It is suggested that "this situation could be improved by (a) an increased output of the agricultural and fisheries sector, (b) an increase in local hotel/charter-boat management and ownership, and by (c) and increase in skilled and trained manpower availability" (ibid.).

The exogenous vagaries of tourism notwithstanding, however, the growth of the BVI economy continued. Indeed, each year since 1978—at which time the BVI ceased being grant-aided by the United Kingdom—the Government had realized surpluses of revenue over expenditure. In 1978 this amounted to a surplus of $1.3 million—"as a result, the general revenue balance deficit became a surplus of $667,000, while at the end of 1979, a further larger surplus on that year's operations meant that the reserves of the Territory rose to nearly $2.7 million". And it was anticipated that reserves at the end of 1983 "should, for the first time, stand at over $4 million" (BVI Budget. . . 1983: iii-iv).

With some justification, therefore, the official view of the socio-economic state of the Territory was one of confident optimism. The Chief Minister, the Honourable H. Lavity Stoutt, declared, in his 1983 Budget Address to the British Virgin Islands Legislative Council:

Throughout 1982, economic and financial instability have remained central to the problems of many of our neighbours in the Americas. Governments have come and gone; currencies have fluctuated, at times wildly; the international banking system has been under constant and erratic pressure; delayed debt repayments have reflected large scale foreign exchange deficits in countries as far apart as Mexico, Poland and Argentina. World recession, commercial retrenchment and business failures continue; with output stagnating, stocks being run down and only faltering recovery in the economies of developed countries. Unemployment is at record levels since the days of the Great Depression of the 1920s. In the United States and the United Kingdom alone, there is a generation of potential adults, who have never worked in a regular job. It is a frightening social and human reality of our time.

I invite you to compare all this with our own way of life. The British Virgin Islands are blessed in many respects. Ours may be a small country with a small population; yet we use one of the world's stabilizing and trading currencies as our official tender; we have a nominal public debt because we live within our means; we contribute handsomely to our own development; we have no exchange controls; and there is a spirit of free enterprise in commerce and business, with the encouragement of a democratically elected government. We have no grinding poverty or widespread suffering; unemployment does not divide the community into those who work and those who do not; and we remain on terms of friendly co-operation with our immediate neighbours in the "other" Virgin Islands and beyond. (BVI Budget . . . 1983;i-ii)

Clearly, the British Virgin Islands had reached an inflection point, a moment of dramatic socioeconomic change brought about by the consolidation of tourism as development strategy. The ensuing ambivalence manifested in the public discourse is demonstrated in the next chapter.

5

Perceptions of Tourism and Development

Against the background of the sanguine official assessment of the socioeconomic state of the Territory at the start of the 1980s, we now consider some perceptions by British Virgin Islands residents regarding development and its primary motive force, tourism.

This chapter begins with the presentation of material transcribed from the tape-recorded proceedings of a symposium on "Social Change: Implications for the British Virgin Islands," held in Tortola on 21-22 May, 1982, under the auspices of the British Virgin Islands Mental Health Association. The conceptualization and design of the Symposium had been my responsibility, undertaken as part of a doctoral internship in which I served as anthropologist-consultant bilaterally to the Association and to the Government's Mental Health Programme.

From McWelling Todman's extraordinary oral-historical *tour de force*, to Elihu Rhymer's wry observations, the dialogue presented below affords perspicuous insight into British Virgin Islanders' perceptions about their existential circumstances.

INTROSPECTIVE ASSESSMENTS

Aspects of Social Change: Excerpts from a Symposium

The moderator, JOSEPH S. ARCHIBALD, Q.C., a prominent local barrister, introduces the first speaker, fellow-lawyer, McWelling Todman: "Among those gathered here are some of the closest friends I have on earth. And everybody knows that whenever we meet, we not only discuss but we argue vociferously. And we never agree on anything. You need not ask whether I agree with Mac Todman on everything. All the courts wonder how we are such good friends and yet we've fought so much. I'm going to ask Mac Todman to lead off the discussion.

McWELLING TODMAN, Q.C., is a Barrister-at-Law and President of the British Virgin Islands Bar Association. His career has encompassed the roles of teacher, Administrative Assistant to the Commissioner of the BVI (ca. 1949), and Senior Assistant Secretary in the Federal Government of the West Indies. After studying law at the University of London, Mr. Todman returned to the BVI in 1967 and established a private practice.

Mr. Todman is Chairman of the Public Service Commission and of the Economic Development Advisory Committee.

The problem is where to really begin. You know, I began life as a young man firmly convinced that lawyers were parasites, and I didn't go to the Bar for many, many years because that was a deeply held conviction. Lawyers, especially in Western Society, were parasites. And, in fact, I didn't see law as a social service—something to serve the community. But, in my practice of law on the 15th of this month [May 1982] I celebrated my 20th year of public service . . .

J. S. ARCHIBALD (moderator)

He's 20 years "retired."

McWELLING TODMAN

. . . and in the practice of law in this Territory. I came back here with the intention of being a country lawyer, you know. I said, "All right, I'll go to court once in a while", and "I'll do this once in a while", and "I'll live easily and quietly". Of course, the most hectic time I've had in my life is since I've been back in the Virgin Islands. Because I came back here when things were just beginning to change.

I notice that everybody speaks of "the last 15 years". But nobody has said why the last 15 years is the watershed. '67 was the year when you had the Ministerial System introduced. That was the year when locally, the collective representatives became responsible for the executive authority in this country. People didn't have to go and see "the Commissioner" or the "Administrator" anymore. It took a long time, of course, hammering that into heads, especially of the English residents, that going to the Governor was a waste of time. He's no longer, under the constitution, authorized to do anything but sign documents, kiss the babies and hold receptions. It's in the hands of your Chief Minister.

I had gone for this course to Trinidad, for example, where, when the Ministerial System was introduced in Trinidad and Tobago in its fullest form, Dr. Williams made it very simple. He simply moved (if you know Port-of-Spain) the complete paraphernalia of the Ministries from around the Red House and moved it to North Port-of-Spain. If you came from Tunapuna or Arima and you wanted to see a Minister or wanted to do something Ministerial, you no longer went around the Red House, which was associated with the Colonial Secretary and the Colonial Governor, you went to North Port-of-Spain. So that, eventually, without having to propagandize the whole thing, the man in the street came to realize that, in fact, the Colonial Secretary was no longer a body, was no longer important. You only went to the Red House to go to court, not for administrative purposes. And then, when the Federation was set up, he had the *coup de grace*. Where is the Governor General going to live? Dr. Williams said, "All right, I'll answer. We'll send the Governor of Trinidad and Tobago to live in Tobago, and we'll give the Government House to the Governor General." Now, if you remember at the time at which this was done, there was only one flight a day between Trinidad and Tobago. So the Governor was isolated. He was a Crusoe on Crusoe's Island. And this was the difference between the colonial—a crown colony government—and a ministerial government.

And '67 is significant in the minds of everybody because that is the year when things really started to happen. Because the man out at Meyers or the man out at Butu Mountain could come in to an elected representative, put pressure on him, twist his arm and get him to respond. You couldn't get the Governor to respond. You couldn't get Dr. Wailing to respond, but you could get Lavity Stoutt and all his colleagues to respond.

Turning now to the question of land alienation. I came back here in 1967, and one of the things that struck me forcibly was how, in fact, we had a number of Englishmen going around the countryside without cash, without money. They were, as all people who migrate, men on the make. They were like the men who came across from Normandy with William the Conqueror—all men on the make. The settlers who came here in the 17th Century, who went to Virginia and all the other places—all men on the make. Nothing wrong about it. That is how the world is populated and grown. But these men were going around the countryside to peasants who had never seen a thousand dollars at any one time in lump sum, who had land for which they had been having to pay taxes. It was only a shilling a year, but it was a time, of course, when a bag of coal—charcoal—sold for 20 cents, and you had to spend two weeks in St. Thomas running around the town all day with it on your head in a pan to get it sold.

A shilling a year for land tax was a lot of money. But, Mr. Rockefeller traveled here in '61 and he pushed the price of land up to one hundred dollars an acre. And then, of course, before his hotel was finished, they got a thousand dollars an acre in Virgin Gorda.

And these people were going about the hillside to Mr. X up in the mountains and saying, "I would like to buy your land. I'll pay you five hundred dollars an acre if you sign a contract." The man hasn't got five hundred dollars an acre to make the payment, but he would then get on the next plane to London, and he would sell it out to his colleagues over there, come back and make a good profit. And I can show you an article from the Financial Times where, in fact, one such person was boasting how he'd make a killing.

Well, I spoke to people like Henry Creque, who's been my good friend all these years, and other people involved, and said something had to be done. I had just come from England after living there for several years and knew what it was to be a West Indian living in England. I had gone and stayed in France on a holiday with my family and got back on the ferry steamer and the whole boat-train was held up because we were the only Black people on the train and the Immigration had to be convinced that we had a right to come to the United Kingdom. But the Germans and the Italians and the Dutchmen and the Spaniards and everybody just went ahead. So I said to the Ministers at the time, I said, "Why do you draw a distinction between an Englishman and an American? If you tell the American he must get a licence, why not the Englishman? He's as much an alien in the BVI as the German or the American." Now I wasn't the first person to say this. But I had a little bit of influence. And, of course, the result is that in 1969 the law was changed to make every non-belonger—even including the Kittitian and Antiguan, because we wouldn't draw any distinction—subject to licensing procedures.

The last ten years was the point at which this wholesale transfer of beach, chunks of land, from belonger hands to non-belonger hands was curtailed. That's when it started slowing down. Well, one of the results was that if you take a map of the BVI and look at it, you'll find that a considerable bit of the land had been alienated, but not only in recent times. If you start at the Western end of the island, Belmont Estates never got into native hands. So, if you go down to the point at West End and you draw a line right across from coast to coast—from the south coast to the north coast, west to the office building (the customs building) and back—all that land between there was never in native hands. It never passed from the old planters to the natives. You go up to Pasea, and that's a fascinating story. You can read the story in Dr. Harrigan's and Dr. Varlack's book, and if you want some more direct help, you can ask Mr. Ovie Shirley to show you his grandfather's will, where he again re-tells the story there as to how Mr. Cookman robbed him from getting Pasea and Fahie Hill Estate. But that, again, never passed into local hands. Paraquita Bay Estate is another one, again, which never really dropped—except for a small part of it—into local hands.

And then you have other areas, of course, which were in native hands, which are no longer native. Let us take Norman Island. Is Norman Island held by belongers or non-belongers? Well, in the case of the present owners of Norman Island, they are whites who became black and then white again. Most of them live all over the United States. I think some of them don't even know they have a trace of black blood in them. They've become "white" again. But the question is, is this land alienated or not alienated? It poses a nice legal and sociological question. From my point of view it has become alienated and, therefore, if the Creques were to sell it to somebody else tomorrow really, you're not alienating something that was yours—it was alienated two generations ago. It changes a lot of things.

Now, we change to another period. After Mr. Rockefeller moved into the Virgin Islands, you got places like up in the North Sound, the

Biras Creek land, which, because it had become so burdensome to pay the taxes for it, had become abandoned by the people who owned it. They went off to Santo Domingo and those who stayed behind never paid the taxes. And it was cut up to stand for public sale and there was nobody to buy it. It wasn't worth buying. And so it continued until, as I said, there was this expatriate invasion, people wanted to buy land and then offers were being made. So, you got a whole chunk of it alienated there again because it was an easy way of settling what had become very intense land disputes. And Dr. Eric O'Neal of St. Thomas coming back here in the '50s from Washington, and probably appreciating in a way that a person who had never left the BVI could understand, the value of land as land, went down to Santo Domingo, saw his dying uncles, made a deal with them, paid them a few hundred dollars, came up, went and talked to the Commissioner, made a deal with him, bought it out—title transferred. So he got a big chunk. And you can take several pieces like that. If you take the south coast of Tortola and go right around you'll find there again, big areas which have gone. Maya Cove, which we know as Hodge's Creek, that, again, went in the early years. But at the time which it was sold, it was a burden, it was onerous. The owners, who were manifold, got a few hundred dollars each.

In one case, I remember where there were about 23 transactions done by one realtor in a year. There was not a single one that involved alienation in the sense that you were taking a piece of land from a belonger and transferring it to a non-belonger. And this is one reason why you're getting another phenomenon: the appearance of involuntary segregation. If Belmont looks like a segregated community it is not because, in fact, the people there set out to make it so. It is that when the man comes out from Rhode Island and he wants to buy a house or he wants to buy a lot, when you make an offer to buy you have to find somebody willingly to sell. If he goes to Meyers, he's going to have a headache because they're going to come to Mr. Archibald or to a certain doctor, "I can't let you buy the place where my navelstring is buried, and where my father and mother's bones are buried," and that's the attitude.

Land means something more than just an economic resource, it represents an identity. In fact, you know, I just came back from New York, and when you are up there and you're driving long distances and you see land that is land, land that can be productive, you wonder, "Why does the chap who had lived here for 20-odd years come back to the BVI to fight over a bit of land?" And the difference is this: if he bought 50 acres in New Jersey and cultivated it or built on it, who is he? What is he? He is still one ant on the anthill. He has no identity, he's a nonentity. He comes back to the BVI and if he only puts his house on a little promontory, he's still king of the castle. And this is something that all human beings desire—a sense of identity, a sense of being somebody. Well, so much for land alienation. Now, the question of tourism and investment from abroad.

I was saying yesterday that I was depressed when I heard all the complaints and all the tales of woe about how the outsiders are taking over. And, in fact, I spoke to people about it and I was thinking about it all night last night. The question that remains lingering in my mind is this: "Do we want to be made whole?" You know that biblical text? Do you want to be made whole? Are we prepared to take up our beds and walk? The question has been posed in another form by a poet whose name I can't remember, but the line goes something like this:

> "My very chains and I grew friends
> So much a long acquaintance
> Tends to make us what we are."

The government, through various legislative acts, has put a *cordon sanitaire* around the BVI: You can't remain in the Territory without permission. If you remain in the Territory, you can't start working without permission. If you want to open up a business, you can't start doing it without permission. If you want to buy land, you have to get permission. If you want to lease property for more than a year, you have to get permission. All those barriers, all those obstacles have been put in the way of outsiders coming in and taking over. We are living in a "protected" society. And yet, we're being told, "Oh, this is in the hands of outsiders, the other thing is in the hands of outsiders." Well, on the other hand, is anybody asking themselves the question, "Is there anything we can do to take advantage of the situation— the political and economic and social situation—created by this *cordon sanitaire*?

Now, I have advised a number of Virgin Islanders "Don't put your money in a hotel," for a very simple reason. Those of you who know the Eastern Caribbean will know that they've been growing bananas in Dominica, in St. Lucia, in Grenada for hundreds of years. But the most they can do with the banana crop is put it on a schooner and send it to Barbados or Trinidad. It was left for a Dutchman, Van Geest, to come out here after World War II and organize the industry and create what you now know in the Eastern Caribbean as the Windward Islands Banana Industry. Why couldn't the Windward Islands do it? For a very simple reason: the market is not in Trinidad and Barbados. The market for all those bananas is Europe, and you need somebody with the skill and expertise to organize that market. Unless you could organise the market in England, and in Western Europe, you just don't have a banana industry.

A hotel, as somebody whose name I will not call discovered to his cost some years ago, is not a question of four rooms, four walls, a roof and beds. Your market is in North America, basically. And unless you have the expertise, and the know-how to know how to organize the

North Americans, you're wasting your money in a hotel. People go to Little Dix, not because they want a holiday, they want to go back home and talk over their hedge on Sunday morning and tell their neighbours that they'd been down to one of the Rock Resorts in the British Virgin Islands. It's one-upmanship. You boast about it. Your neighbour can probably only go up to the Catskills. What's the Catskills? Anybody can get in their car and drive there. But not everybody can go and stay at Little Dix, go there and come back and boast that they paid $200 a day. But the point is, because of this thing, when everybody else was complaining they couldn't fill their rooms, Little Dix was having an overflow. And the problem was, where do we put our overflow? If a man has come all the way from Poughkeepsie to stay at Little Dix with his family, you can't tell him you're going to put him in the Wayside Inn. You have to give him alternative accommodations which are at least comparable. I got Andy Flax who was working, at the time, for Little Dix. I spoke to him, I spoke to the Manager and, of course, Andy Flax took off. He was prepared. He took off.

Now, let us see what has happened. Are BVIslanders participating in the tourist industry in any other way? Well, you've got the local hotels. Apart from that, you've got things like ground transportation. It's a vital part of the tourist industry, ground transportation. Tourists come here and they complain of the higher rates you have to pay when you pick up the odd taxi driver. They complain of the fact that they are sometimes surly and rude and discourteous. The hotels at the far end of the island complain that when the plane comes in at the last flight, very often the guests have trouble getting there. It got to the point where all the hotels are beginning to think—and the marinas—of providing their own services. But fortunately, of course, one or two people in the East End section realized that there was an opportunity. Somebody suggested to two or three fellows up there, "Why don't you go to the marinas or to the hotels and make a deal?" Offer your services on a contractual basis: "I will bring you all your guests. The rate will be X dollars per head, whether I have a bus load or I have only one. I will come all the way down to Long Bay at $10 per head even if I have to come there at midnight with one guest." So gradually you began to see these safaris marked "CSY," "The Moorings," "Prospect Reef," "Long Bay." And then, our good friends, the taxi drivers on the Road Town waterfront, woke up to find that they had been completely excluded and preempted from that service. And you know what they did? A client of mine, you know what he did? He led the delegation to the Minister to complain that the East End taxi drivers had gone and set up contracts with all the marinas and hotels and now they didn't have any work. Well, the Minister had a very good answer at the time, he said, "Well, of course, you know, they were born here, so I can't do anything." But there is the difference between those who are prepared to take up their bed and walk and those who were prepared to sit on the waterfront, lean on the car, sport a golden wristwatch on one hand, and a can in the other hand.

Now, the outside capital that came in, I probably have to attack from a different perspective.

One of the many little business groups you have in the BVI—in fact, I will call its name, The Trust Company Association—like a lot of other groups thought that they would extend some hospitality to the newly appointed governor, a few months ago when he came here and they did invite him to a reception one afternoon. I arrived a little late. The crowd was thick, so I got to the door and had to stand just inside the door. A lot of people came and talked to me for quite a while, and looking around the room, one thing struck me most—you had bankers and banking executives, you had trust company executives, you had accounting executives, you had lawyers, and one or two other people. And I said, "You know, if all these people here were to close their businesses down tomorrow"—because they *could* close down; Chase has closed down about four banks in the Eastern Caribbean in the last three years: Grenada, Trinidad, St. Lucia, Montserrat—"if they would close their businesses, within a month the whole economy of this island would come to a dead stand-still." And those who talk about going back to plant sweet potato will suddenly discover what salt butter costs per pound.

Let us take the marinas for example. We grew up in these islands believing that every white man was rich. Once you came from overseas with a white face, you had money. Very few Virgin Islanders understand how small business—and all of the businesses here are small, let us make this quite clear—are run. General Motors or Ford can plan an extension on the basis of earnings most of the time. But the ordinary trader doesn't do business like that. Take the marina, for example. You've got to plan for change, you've got to buy boats, you've got to get them in, you've got to pay staff. Every Friday afternoon, you have to have their pay cheques ready. You can't tell your people who are working for you, "Well, we have to wait for tourists to come in to collect it from them to pay you." You have to pay them. Which means, of course, you operate the business with bank overdraft. Every business which is a business, except the fellow who's around the corner just selling a few fruits and vegetables, operates on overdrafts. So, therefore, the banks come in. No banks, no overdrafts, you can't run your marinas, you can't run your hotels. Just take it for granted.

How did the joint stock banks first come here? Well, let me give you one example. On the first working day of this year, my wife went, as usual, to the Post Office, cleared the letter box. And when she started opening, the first thing that dropped out was a cheque for $715,000. It wasn't mine, it was made out to the Accountant General. What was it for? It was for having performed during the last 12 months, foreign exchange contracts in the BVI. This company is a multi-national, it hasn't got a presence in the BVI. It is registered here as a company, doing business here, but it really doesn't do business here. What it does, of course, instead of going to London or Hong Kong or Zurich, and doing the buying and selling of foreign exchange there, when they've made a contract, when they've entered into arrangements there, when this company is making its arrangements to buy Japanese Yen or Spanish Pesetas or Italian Liras, for certain tax reasons they execute the contract—they perform the contract we'd say—in the BVI. And all that they have to do really, when all the paper work is ready, is send it to the bank. The bank then calls whoever the person is having the power of attorney to sign the documents on their behalf, to sign it.

Now that one company had contributed $715,000 to the Treasury of the British Virgin Islands for having just sent paper here, having it stamped here and sent back to them. But one of the things that strikes me here when you speak to senior Civil Servants in the BVI is how ignorant most of them appear to be as to what keeps the economy ticking, what pays their salary. You hear them making all sorts of wild statements. Go to the Bahamas and you're struck with how the average Bahamian Civil Servant understands what is the nature of his economy. He doesn't want his country alienated. But they understand it.

And this is where the Trust Companies come in. Those men are not here, they are not taking anything away from us, they're not manufacturing anything here, they're not exploiting the Territory. This isn't Carroni, Ltd. or Tate and Lyle or—what do they call the people in Guyana who owned Guyana at one time—this isn't Bookers. They are not taking anything out. All they are saying is "For the privilege of occupying one little spot on the shelf of the Registrar's Office in the British Virgin Islands"—a memorandum and articles—"and for the privilege of being able to use your name"—the name of the Territory—"in saying I'm a British Virgin Islands Company, I'm prepared to pay you so much for filing an annual return and, if we make a profit, which is taxable, we'll pay you an income tax too!" And that's where most of your income tax comes from, not from the locally operating companies. Because, believe it or not, very few of the companies which are operating locally, make a profit. Now, that may come as a surprise, but if you remember, one of your leading bareboat companies went under completely late last year. And in St. Thomas, about three or four of them went out of business in the last year. You realize how precarious business is here. So that, in fact, we are more dependent on outside capital and outside capital flows than most of us stop to think or realize.

If you go to Lower Estate and look at the houses on your left-hand side—the hill side of the road—and look at those on the right side, you'll realize that there is a marked physical difference between them. Not only are the houses on the hill side larger, they are better constructed, they have facilities—car ports and garages and gardens and all sorts of things. What is the difference? The difference is simply this: when the first houses were built, there were no banks and, therefore, you could only build to the extent of the cash you had and such credit as you could get from Lumber and Trading or Maduro's in St. Thomas, or H. Lockhart's Lumber Yard in St. Thomas. J.R. O'Neal was just then beginning to come into his own. When the second set of houses were built, you had the Virgin Islands National Bank, precursor to the First Pennsylvania Bank. The result, of course, you can see.

The point is, it's a community in which we are just moving from a subsistence economy to a community which is a cash economy. It is a beginning of a commercial life and it's not easy to find yourself with anything in which to invest. That's why most British Virgin Islanders who have invested, have invested in real estate. Again, let us take one of the earliest sectors of our economy, transportation by sea. Well, if it was not for "Speedy", we would have to say that the British Virgin Islander has, by default, lost out in that area. In the days when we didn't have a tourist industry and all we were doing was carrying twenty-niners—you ask what is a twenty-niner? A twenty-niner is a British Virgin Islander who went to look for work in St. Thomas. He could only get 29 days at a time, so you had to go in every 29 days and out every 29 days. When you had the twenty-niners you had the local people controlling that industry. The ferryboat industry. Now that there's big money in it—real big money—by default, we've stood by and done nothing. And it was left to the people in St. Thomas. True it is that the owners of the *Native Son* are very largely people of British Virgin Islands descent, and I discovered, again to my surprise, that the Captain and owner of the *Bomba Charger*'s mother is from Jost Van Dyke. And his wife is from Carrot Bay. So, they've got B.V. Islanders. But the fact still remains that, by default, we've allowed that sector to go. Nobody stopped us. But there it is. I don't think I should say more at this point.

J. S. ARCHIBALD (moderator)

You will understand why Dr. Harrigan said yesterday in his opening address that he gave the first draft of his book to Mac to look at. You don't get to hear Mac often, that's why I didn't stop him.

DR. NORWELL HARRIGAN, a British Virgin Islander, Director of the Caribbean Research Institute of the College of the Virgin Islands.

I understand and appreciate what Mac has said. But he has consistently used the phrase, "somebody suggested". Now, when we call names of people who were prepared to take up their beds and walk, those of us who know the story of "take up your bed and walk", know that it was Jesus Christ who told the fellow to take up his bed and

walk. Mac admitted playing Jesus Christ to another case. And I believe a lot of other people here have played Jesus Christ to some other
people. I think that is one of the problems that we have here. People
come from Britain or they come from the States where they have been
exposed to this kind of thing; they can see business opportunities,
they can see where they can jump in and do something. Our people
were never corporate minded, they never learned to be corporate
minded. We're talking about distrust. Every single partnership that
you had here with two people, even if they had to put a jumbie on the
boat, the partnership broke up. Something happened about it. We
were not oriented towards it. I've said this time and again, if you were
a foreigner and you came to me in the government and gave me a
scheme, I would send you home, call a native and tell him to do it, because that is what we need. Mac is right, we need to take up our beds
and walk. But we also need Jesus Christ to tell us, show us where.

ELIHU RHYMER, a British Virgin Islander, and formerly a Permanent
Secretary in Government, is currently Managing Director of Air BVI.

Now, the only quarrel I have with government personally, is that the
corruption is not being directed toward my benefit [audience laugh-
ter]. I don't want to preempt what I am going to say but I think this is
the conflict that is taking place in the BVI. I think we have the whole
thing sometimes upside down. The problem in the BVI is not between
any whites and blacks. We've gotten over that thing, longtime. We
know how to use white people now, much better than they know how
to use us. The problem in this country is that the argument is between
ourselves. Who are going to be the new elites in the BVI? Who are
going to be the rich people? And the Rastas understand that too.

EUGENIE TODMAN-SMITH, M.S.W., is Personnel and Establishment
Officer of the British Virgin Islands Government. She has also been a
teacher and Permanent Secretary.

I particularly want to say something about the Rastas, because I feel
at this point that the Rastas form an integral part of this community.
And there is no point in thinking that they are not going to be here.
We're going to wake up tomorrow morning and they will be here.
They're going to be with us, and perhaps we ought to examine ourselves to find what part we play in causing them to develop the sort of
attitudes which we deplore [applause]. . . . I think, although the
strength of the church, the influence, over the years, is waning, I still
think it has some, especially in some of the smaller churches. The
question I wanted to ask was what was the church doing, since they
so loved the Rastas, to get the rest of the community to understand
the Rastas and to love them as much as the Ministers loved them
[laughter]. The question is what sort of policy should be developed to

take the Rastas into account. They're people who have all kinds of characteristics that we don't really like but I feel they are part of the community like any other group.

DR. PEARL VARLACK, Professor of Education of the College of the Virgin Islands, is co-author with Dr. Norwell Harrigan, of *The Virgin Islands Story*.

If we're going to talk about setting up policy, we're going to have to say what we are going to do about making the next generation able to cope with the kind of evolving situation that we now have. And it seems to me as if the answer to that is education. We have not made any attempt whatsoever, so far as I know, to try and train them to live in this kind of society. We are talking about tourism, but there is more to tourism than watching the tourists come, and driving them around. You don't need very much training to be a good taxi driver. But you need a whole lot of training—everybody needs the training—to be able to deal with the whole impact of tourism. And I'm not talking about training people to be waiters and this sort of thing.

I have, in a lot of ways, written off most of this generation. But I like to look forward, because I always think that there is hope. And I always think that people can do what they want to do with a society of this size. In a small island like this, the problem-solving capacity of the government is immense.

I'm not concerned so much with the curriculum content that people like to talk about. I don't think it matters a whole lot what content you teach. It's how you teach it and whether or not you train those people to think. If you teach me to think I can think about anything. And I can think about a lot of things that you probably don't want me to think about.

We talk about the heritage of these islands—how much we are going to retain, what we are going to preserve. The preservation of that depends on a number of things. Not only what we teach and how we teach it, but who teaches it. Yesterday, from a source that should be reliable we learned that only one-third of the teachers in the High School are local people. I was amazed, I shouldn't have been, but I was. When, in due course, we have that kind of proportion in the elementary school, will we, in fact, be training Virgin Islanders, will they be Virgin Islanders when we have finished with them? This is the difficulty. If you want Virgin Islands children and you want to preserve your cultural heritage you're going to have to train Virgin Islands teachers. Non-Virgin Islands teachers cannot produce Virgin Islands children. It's utterly impossible.

ELIHU RHYMER

Let me tell you a little story. Once, when I returned from the University, I was having an argument with Ralph on his porch in McNamara, which is only one house removed from Mac. But if you know the size of Ralph's voice, and if you know the size of mine, you would know that it was no great difficulty for Mac to have been able to listen to what we were saying. And when Mac could not take it anymore, he shouted out, saying "Tell me something. Rocky [Elihu's father] still have the land in Virgin Gorda?" I said, "As far as I know, yes." Mac then forgets about me. He turns to Ralph and says, "Ralph, what are you all arguing for? Just let a little time pass, and so will his socialism". There's one thing you can say about all of us in the British Virgin Islands—all of us are capitalists.

The society is in change and when a society is in change there's stress. And when a society goes through this kind of change, you have a breaking down of the normal structure of the society and, usually, a state of anomie is created in which people are no longer quite sure of the moral and ethical frame of reference; when leadership in a society seems to be projecting one thing as local preachers on Sunday, and somehow give the appearance of participation in villainy, Monday through Friday.

Social change usually makes us rather suspicious, and when grappling for something to hang onto, you pick up anything and you develop paranoia. Definitely, you do get in every society in this situation, xenophobic attitudes, where you begin to want to direct your anger, your frustration, and who best to direct it against than people who don't quite look like you. It's an identifiable group, it's them. So we'd better watch that, because you see, it could make us quite unfriendly people.

I do want to say on the question of "British Virgin Islands for British Virgin Islanders," many of you may not be aware of it, but I can assure you that there are odd things happening in this society in terms of ownership. It takes a long time for a community to develop prior accumulation, gathering the wealth to do things. When Russia wanted to do it, they simply dropped the iron curtain around the country and they made people literally starve. You just had to do without certain kinds of things. Are you now saying—because if you are, let's say it—that we need to redirect our consumption significantly? If you want to have money to invest in big hotels, ships, sailing around the BVI, then you have to stop eating so much steak. You have to stop buying so many televisions, you've got to save the money. Don't criticize the fellow from outside who comes in. You take his money, you buy steak, you buy TVs, you buy the Tortola Briefcase— it's the great big radio—then still criticize other people because you can't have your cake and eat it.

And I'll say something else. British Virgin Islanders are quite intelligent people. A lot of British Virgin Islanders know better than owning these great big hotels. They have a lot more sense. They're building those little cottages. They don't want Mr. Braithwaite [taxes] to know about it, so they are not publicizing it. British Virgin Islanders are doing their thing and they are smart. Do you know why they don't own the Radio Station? Because they don't make money, and that's it. Anything in the British Virgin Islands that makes money, you are going to have British Virgin Islanders there, even if behind the scene. But don't expect that you are going to see British Virgin Islanders suddenly taking their hard earned money and doing stupidness with it. British Virgin Islanders are not like that. They will put their money in things that will work, or else they're going to carry it down the road and give it to Chase Bank or Barclay's Bank, who's going to invest it for them.

I think the ideas that have come out are good. But you've got to create the political framework to achieve it. As long as you have in the British Virgin Islands the "nook" concept of electoral politics—electing them from the nook, that's what I call the constituency system—then you are going to get the product of the nook. And if you get the product of the nook, you're going to get the thinking of the nook. And put the thinking of the nook together, you're going to get nook-nook. You have got to create a new kind of political structure, you have got to create a situation in which the young and the intelligent are not completely and totally frustrated by the greedy and the ignorant. All I am trying to ensure is that some of us can appeal generally to the people of this country to get elected. They're not going to get a certain caliber of people elected from the nook. You've got to go to this country and give the Virgin Gordians, the Anegadians, the people from Road Town, the people from East End, the people from West End, the people from Jost Van Dyke an opportunity to pick some of us from all over. In other words, get some of us there at large and you'll see the difference. We're going to still have the nook. But mix it up so you get a different type of political animal who is capable of generating the political will to achieve the kind of objectives of which we are talking. My first political speech.

EMERGENT THEMES

On further pursuing some of the issues raised at the Symposium in the course of field study, a number of recurrent themes surface. A few of the more salient of these are presented below via (pseudonymous) informants' assertions. These fieldwork-derived documentaries—informants' musings, assessments and considered opinions—are placed within the context of a further elaboration of our earlier discussion of tourism as phenomenon. In this manner, "an anthropological link" is established "between private . . . expression and the . . . marketplace of issues and ideas" (Gwaltney 1980: xxvi).

One of the more insistent of these emergent themes relates to the issue of servility and, conversely, of hostility as regards tourism. It might be noted here that the ubiquitousness of this concern is reflected in a considerable body of material within the tourism literature. "The problem," as Professor Jose Villamil of the University of Puerto Rico observes, "is that the line between friendliness and servility is a thin one when it is a commercial requirement. This tends to generate hostility which breaks out intermittently" (in Sethna 1979:54). It is also suggested that "catering to guests is a repetitive, monotonous business, and although questions posed by each visitor are 'new' to him, hosts can come to feel that they have simply turned on a cassette. Especially late in 'the season', it becomes progressively harder to rekindle the spontaneity and enthusiasm that bids guests truly welcome" (Smith 1977:6). Moreover, in the Caribbean, the colonial legacy is also a factor, as Jean Holder, Executive Director of the Caribbean Tourism Research and Development Centre, points out:

> Purchasers of the tourism product . . . tend to see themselves especially when in post-colonial destinations, as playing a different role from that [which] they normally play when they purchase other types of products or even the same product in their own country. The visitor to the Caribbean therefore often sees himself not only as purchasing a holiday, but as doing the country an economic favour, and bringing it sociologically and culturally in touch with civilized behaviour. He sees himself as being part investor in the country and part guest of the government, hence the type of attitudes he brings to the area and the letters written by him to Caribbean ministers of tourism and even to prime ministers, complaining of matters more fittingly referred to the offending hotelier or restauranteur. He sees himself as the Caribbean people see him—an alien distant from the indigenous population, experiencing a two-week fantasy with socio-economic implications. (1979: 12)

Invariably, however, the problem is perceived as being one merely of host-attitude. The policy solution, therefore, tends to resort to the institution of so-called smile campaigns—"Barbados is a smile wide"—producing a phenomenon which might appropriately be dubbed "the Rictus Syndrome".

> Such campaigns are grotesque. Why should whole nations be brainwashed into living a lie? Coffee-growers are not expected to smile as they work. Sri Lanka tea plantation workers would kill anyone seriously asking them to feel perpetually grateful to the British housewives who keep them from starving (just). No, it is one more victory for The Smile—that forced, tired, strained, purely commercial grimace which has become the meaningless symbol of service industries the world over. However, there is something vitally different between, say, Avis instructing its employees to smile at clients, and a national policy by which governments in countries like Jamaica, the Bahamas, Fiji and Bar-

bados instruct their citizens to "appreciate" the symbols of their poverty. Both are pure commercially inspired actions—but the governments are graphically enmeshed in a neo-colonial situation. Despite their formal political independence, they still cannot actually do without their former masters. In "Be Nice" campaigns, they are convincing themselves to grin and bear it. (Turner and Ash 1975:195)

The Issue

In London—or New York—visitors take the occasional surly waiter or preoccupied desk clerk in stride; in the Caribbean, they are apt to feel threatened. On a stroll through Piccadilly—or Rockefeller Center—tourists don't expect the locals to greet them with smiles, but they read hostility into sober expressions on the faces of passers-by in the islands.

— Robert Stock, "Of Tourism and the Soul: The Caribbean Dilemma," *The New York Times*, 13 June 1975.

ARTHUR WILKINSON is from the United Kingdom. He has been living in the British Virgin Islands for the past two years and works as an accountant with a hotel in Tortola.

The service is so bad in the islands that it leads to frustrations on the part of the tourist. Unfortunately, if you complain about the service, it will only get worse. Regardless of whether or not a person smiles in New York or London the service is usually good.

If they could only teach the locals what "customer service" is all about. It would be a major break-through in the islands.

NAN ARUNDEL, a British Virgin Islander, is a teacher in the secondary school system.

This is really an attitude developed and fostered in the main by the pattern of advertising the Caribbean and its people abroad. We're portrayed as poor, smiling people, lolling in our Calypso culture and given to wild abandon. More realistic portrayal of people and their societies is needed as well as greater contact between Caribbean people and tourists.

SUSAN HINKSON is from Ohio, U.S.A. She has lived in the BVI for eight years and works in the charter-boat industry.

As a consumer in the States, I don't appreciate surliness or remoteness in clerks or waiters any more or less than in Tortola. Friendliness of passers-by on the streets is often a factor of community size.

In towns of comparable size in the States, people recognize or greet each other just as happens in Tortola.

MIRIAM EDNEY, a British Virgin Islander, is currently a student at a North American University.

> We are taught to wear the fake smile for the benefit of the tourist. Perhaps we are expected to assuage their fear of being a minority in a black country. A minority, moreover, with whom historically we have had, to say the least, a relationship of mutual distrust and dislike. When the West Indian goes abroad, furthermore, he would be naïve to expect such treatment from his counterparts. The same tourist he must smile with here wouldn't give him the time of day in his [the tourist's] country.

FRANCIS NUGENT is from the U.S.A. He has lived in the Virgin Islands—both U.S. and British—for the past twelve years. Mr. Nugent is manager of a major charter-boat company in Tortola.

> The concept of coming to "Paradise" where the "natives" always wear a big smile and live in relaxed bliss is promoted to attract those tourists. Realistic or not, the tourist is coaxed by media hype to expect warmth and congeniality and are threatened especially because they do not know how to react when faced with a different culture which does not project this expected hospitality.

JAMES SLANEY, a West Indian, is a development planning consultant with an international agency.

> In the case of the Caribbean the variable of race is critical to such responses by visitors. I do not think that a white visitor would "read hostility into sober expressions on the faces" of white Barbadians when visiting Barbados.

Another recurrent theme evinced in the field study concerns the question of degree of economic benefit which the British Virgin Islands derives from tourism.

Economist-statistician Vaughan Evans, writing in 1976, noted that in the British Virgin Islands,

> the operating losses of tourist/sector companies are, indeed, so large that the British Virgin Islands must be unique in the world in having a corporate sector which seems at an overall operating deficit. The problem common to most developing countries of the expropriation abroad of the large operating profits of foreign owned companies is entirely reversed in the British Virgin Islands. There is in the British Virgin Islands a sizeable inflow of money from abroad in order to

subsidize the operating losses of British Virgin Island companies. (Evans 1976:5)

Presumably, these circumstances have since changed. But in any case, to focus on the putative cash-flow problems of foreign investors in the BVI is to engage in an exercise in obfuscation. For, as Charles Geshekter (1978:68) contends,

> trying to ascertain net balances on travel accounts from data based on gross tourist receipts sometimes seems like trying to nail jelly to a wall. No one seems to know for certain how much foreign exchange is retained in destination countries, and the corporate practice of transfer pricing manipulates figures, moving multi-national profits from one country to another, further complicating the exchange. . . . The 1975 Economic Survey of Kenya estimated that "tourist visitors spent a total of K£26.5 million in 1974" but admitted that "no reduction was made for the cost of imported goods and services used in the tourist trade". One expert [Young 1973:145] contends that, since tourism generally "requires an import of capital goods, expanding the tourist industry can actually be a net loser of foreign exchange even though it may show a surplus on current accounts".

Moreover, "in the context of the Caribbean," as econometrician John Blyden (1973:146-7) maintains,

> taking incentives and infrastructure together, it would not be unduly misleading, on the evidence . . . , to suggest that governments have had to match the contribution of the private investors almost "dollar for dollar' in monetary terms. Although some of this public investment earns revenue over and above tourist receipts, it is suggested that, even taking this factor into account, it would be highly misleading to ignore the cost which is borne by the government in any calculation of the costs and benefits of tourist development.

The Issue

Only half of what a foreign tourist pays a travel agency for a vacation in most [Third World] countries ever gets into the economy of those countries, and much of the remaining half that does, goes to imports to accommodate tourists.

> — Association for International Cooperation and Development, Denmark – *Tourism Study*, 1982.

While most respondents were in essential concurrence with the above proposition, the instances below are illustrative of the spectrum of opinions elicited.

CHRISTOPHER LONGDEN, a British Virgin Islander, is a business manager. The firm by which he is employed is a part of the tourism sector.

The challenge is there for the BVI to create the conditions whereby a greater percentage of the tourist dollar can remain with the local economy.

FRANCIS NUGENT (Expatriate, charter-boat company manager)

I expect this is true—if not an overstatement—especially in the bare-boat industry, where the cost of airfare far exceeds the cost of a yacht for 4-6 people for a week.

ARTHUR WILKINSON (Expatriate, hotel accountant)

That is probably a true statement. When I went to Rio de Janiero on vacation I booked through an agency in London. I stayed for three weeks at a cost of $650.00. The nightly rate in the hotel was only $20.00—a rip off!

PAULINE WYNNE is from Michigan, U.S.A. She has been residing in the British Virgin Islands for about one year and is an assistant manager at a hotel in Virgin Gorda.

Perhaps the airfare portion of the fee is diverted to other places, but the "accommodation" portion certainly aids the whole economy of a given area, with wages, goods, services, etc. being the result of the accommodation dollar.

Clearly, then, British Virgin Islands residents' perceptions regarding tourism and development constitute a wide spectrum. Not surprisingly, individual instances fall at both ends of the spectrum, with tourism being variously perceived as unqualified good or as unqualified abomination.

For most indigenous British Virgin Islanders, however, tourism seems to constitute what one informant (ANNE KORTRIGHT, below [p.122]) refers to as a "two-edged dilemma": the dependency of the Territory on tourism evokes apprehension, while at the same time the material gains that are regarded as being its concomitants are acknowledged. These varying degrees of ambivalence are lucidly displayed in the narratives by both British Virgin Islanders and expatriates which follow.

Shades of Ambivalence

JANE SHANNON is a British Virgin Islander. She is a senior civil servant whose work in one of the government ministries involves considerable dealings with tourism. She is a woman of strongly held convictions and remarkable candor.

As it is a wise child that knows his father, it is a wise BVIslander who knows just what the interest of the tourism industry is, at least as far as that interest concerns Government.

No effort has been made or is being made to chart a course for our tourism development. The Tourist Board, which is charged with the implementation of policy, has yet to state a policy, except the platitude "we want quality tourism," with no guidelines given on how to obtain this "quality". While all nations are striving to professionalize their tourism plant we seem hell bent on "business as usual", thinking that the visitor will come anyway, if even there is no well thought-out promotional plan to entice him to our shores instead of going elsewhere.

Our tourism controls us, when it should be the other way round. Because there is no well thought-out plan of tourism development and promotion, we are forced to be satisfied and deal with tourism as it is conceived by the "outside" private entrepreneurs. Unlike Bermuda where the Government controls the quality and quantity of tourism, here the private tourism investor controls both quality and quantity of what is the Government's largest income producer. The situation is not helped by having a Tourist Board whose membership comprises the very persons who now control tourism privately. This may account for the fact that to date it seems impossible to get simple hotel legislation for the policing of this vital industry.

Very little effort is made to get the visitor to try "things local". Because we do not raise the quality of beef for steaks (we are told), they must be imported from the visitor's country to satisfy his tastes. This could be the reason for the proliferation of Kentucky Fries, McDonalds, Arbies in the Caribbean. The visitor has left home, but he wants the amenities of home where he takes his vacation. The host country must provide these amenities if it wants the visitor's dollar and the likely place to turn is, of course, the visitor's home country.

There seems to be a move afoot to keep the locals out of certain segments of the tourism industry. There has been secondary education here from in the late 1940s and by now there should have been a cadre of trained locals to fill almost any position in this territory. No study has been done to ascertain just what the job market will be in the near future and what skills will be needed with a view to preparing locals to fill these positions. Further, companies are not mandated—when given licences—to train locals if even an outsider is employed in the first instance. The allegations of officials who are willing to close their eyes to some unsavory employment practices for a consideration are rampant as brush fires during a hot California summer.

There is no "grinding poverty" in the BVI depending on where you look or who is doing the looking. Because of our "open door" immigration policy, we have in our midst persons from other islands who are almost unable to earn a subsistence income. This lack of earning power coupled with unbridled fertility has given us substandard enclaves in areas such as Purcell and sections in Long Bush. While it seems as if in some areas there is economic progress, it is limited to specific segments of the community. Our social development seems to have stagnated and the leadership needed to move us forward in areas of social development is sadly lacking.

We, in the Caribbean, the Pacific and other island resort areas have been portrayed as happy, contented natives just awaiting the appearance of the visitor. We are not supposed to have worries or problems. Those are reserved for our benefactors, the tourists. In our mad rush to "develop" our tourist industries, we are forced to picture only gyrating dancers, smiling waiters, or steel-band men having a good time. The visitor came to us to leave his troubles behind, so dare us to show him anything but a smiling face.

In our community, because of a very weak cultural heritage and no efforts being made to shore up that weakness, we are easy prey to the negatives of tourism. We are expected to pray to the altar of the tourist dollar, with our eyes closed to the moral decay it also brings. Each visitor brings his own peculiar behaviour patterns and the native of the host country must be strong in his own cultural beliefs to be able to withstand the onslaught—sifting through the new, the different, and sometimes the downright indecent, and be able to make a moral judgment.

The average British Virgin Islander of average age is a docile being, but if there is resentment—and there is—it is not of the visitor, but of what is perceived as to what he brings. The anything-goes attitude of some of the visiting women, their outright disregard for values in the host country, has created an attitude of blatant disrespect for local females by some sections of the male population in the host country. You hear such phrases as "what these girls [native] here playing, 'tis a white woman I got." When you match the words with the man, you are given cause to wonder if the "white woman" he "got" is in her right mind.

It is impossible to know where you are going until you are sure from whence you came. The Virgin Islander, unlike many of his peers in other Caribbean islands, has very little sense of heritage. Our cultural roots were uprooted and purged of all vestiges of our past. Very little effort has been made or is being made to anchor us to what little is left of our cultural heritage. Old-time things are scorned and have to make way for modern ways. All ties with the past 20-40 years are wiped away and viewed with shame. No one wants it known that there was a time when we did not have sanitary facilities, a stereo and television. If we were sure and proud of our cultural heritage, this certainty of who we are would have served as a bulwark against the erosions of the different cultures against which progress has thrown us.

FRANCIS NUGENT (Expatriate [U.S.A.], charter-boat company manager)

I am concerned that the development of the BVI is too dependent upon the tourist industry and feel it is extremely fragile due to that fact.
I feel that to insure continued stability in the local economy, the government should make every effort to attract and develop light industry and other non-tourist oriented businesses, as well as local agriculture.

I suppose my experience is limited to my individual work experience, but certainly our employees, to a great extent, realize their live-
lihoods are directly related to the level of tourism. However, because
the industry is so time-intensive (i.e. the bulk of business occurs between December and May) it is difficult to keep this realization always in the forefront. I think this is *my own* end-of-season burn-out
speaking.

I believe that most BVIslanders would *prefer* to have an equally,
significant income which was non-tourist related. (wouldn't we all!)—
i.e., the income associated with tourist development is desirable, but
the aggravations and philosophic sacrifices which are associated are
often difficult to justify.

Incidentally, while some tourists may be somewhat insensitive to
local culture, I don't hear BVIslanders complaining about rudeness,
as was inferred in a recent San Juan Star article. Perhaps we deal with
an exceptional group, or perhaps our staff brings out the best in these
otherwise self-indulgent clods!

In our experience, where BVIslanders are in all but top general
management positions, difficulty in "counterpart training" lies in almost total absence of basic educational/communication skills. The
standard coming from the BVI High School is appalling. When a top
manager cannot write a letter, the potential for his assuming general
managership is not very realistic and certainly the employer cannot
be held responsible for that basic shortcoming.

A vocational training center would be a big asset. Personal experience is that very few BVIslanders who are qualified and have skills
and personalities suited to skipper work want it. Most have good full-
time jobs.

Based on my exposure to the U.S. and BVI during the past twelve
years, it seems to me that, unfortunately, there is very little evidence
remaining in any of these islands of the traditional crafts and values.
With the exception of Crucian quadrille dancers, a few local restaurants and foodstuffs, annual carnivals, and the local boat builders and
fishermen in Tortola, tourists and resident alike are hard pressed to
find anything unique to this area produced by its people. As long as
most workers can make more in the tourist industry than in the pursuit of traditional tasks such as fishing, straw-weaving, agriculture,
etc., this will undoubtedly remain so. I fear that these traditional

skills and values will be lost to the present and future generations who may be forced to seek non-tourist related means of support in the future.

I can only compare the BVI to having lived in the USVI, which is *not* desirable. All in all, government restrictions seem to have had a positive effect on the growth and employment situation here.

JAMES SLANEY (Expatriate, development planning consultant)

The social repercussions of development in the BVI perhaps is reason for Government and public concern. In a free enterprise economy, where tourism is the leading sector, one should seek the best possible balance between non-belonger and belonger[1] involvement in key business or economic activities in the interest of fairness and future social stability. A similar balance should be sought for the same reasons in key employment positions. It is in the interest of both Government and private enterprise to seek jointly to erode constraints that prevent the achievement of such balance, such as the shortage of local entrepreneurship ability and job skills and perhaps what might be termed the hesitation of commercial banks to support local investment projects.

Foreign investors are very concerned with political and economic stability but they are also ("genuine" and non-genuine ones) very concerned with tax concessions. In fact, one suspects that most of the major development projects undertaken by expatriates were encouraged because of the tax concessions offered.

Tourism can be damaging to a local culture by eroding and transforming it beyond recognition in certain aspects. Countries that push tourism as a key industry can help to minimize such impacts by (a) striving to amplify national culture in its various forms for the benefit of residents and visitors; (b) seek through public concensus to determine what aspects of traditional living need to be reinforced or preserved. For example, in the BVI, no one should want to suggest to a farmer that he maintain a donkey for transporting agricultural produce if he wants to have a competitive and rewarding business; of course, unless a donkey is all he can afford; (c) seek to screen out development projects that have obvious components that could directly erode local culture.

There are certainly frequently expressions of concern on the part of BVIslanders on the "tenuous base of tourism and the sometimes undesirable social effects" [cf. Lett 1982] but, from my experience, very few examples of outright resentment. Rather, comments point to, for example, the need to diversify the economy, encourage a greater degree of local involvement, promote fairness and equity in employment practices, etc.

It is also probably true that many persons feel that the interests of some groups are perhaps better served than others. So, one often hears complaints registered against the industry although most people believe that tourism is essential for the economic well-being of the BVI.

In the final analysis, there are some good examples to be drawn from the BVI's experience. Certainly, if yacht chartering is viewed as a desirable component of the tourism industry, then the BVI's experience is one that a number of countries in the Caribbean would want to copy if that was possible. The BVI's resources—i.e., anchorages, numerous islands, pleasant sailing routes—are unique for sailing, and so will perhaps remain the most important attraction for bareboat chartering.

However, beyond the attraction, the numbers of charterers, and the money circulation, the "promise" of BVI tourism must be assessed in view of what Caribbean peoples consider desirable in respect of tourism. In the future, I suspect that they will consider desirable—beyond just the creation of jobs—better distribution of management jobs in tourism between belongers and non-belongers, better opportunities for local economic involvement, and perhaps land tenure controls that slow down the rate of land transfers from local to non-local ownership.

MIRIAM EDNEY (British Virgin Islander, university student)

We compare favourably with our neighbours. Our poor are not as poor as those of other islands but the fact is that they do exist—at least relatively speaking—a fact somewhat masked by the tendency of even the poor here to try to live Hollywood style.

We have become very Americanized, adopting not always the better features of the American or, more broadly, Western culture. Disco is in, reggae, calypso, etc. is out. Gerry curls are in, natural hair is out. At least among the young.

I do not think that BVIslanders are generally aware of the undesirable effects of tourism. On the contrary, I think that the opposite case is the reality. Even in tourism, the LDCs get the short end of the stick. The big hotels are foreign-owned, therefore, profits are repatriated to England or wherever. Luckily, we use U.S. dollars so money spent on imports to feed the tourists does not deplete us of precious foreign exchange. Not so with many of our neighbours. Certainly, I think the economic returns on tourism are exaggerated. But in our case, with little else to depend upon, some return is, I guess, better than nothing.

Tourists are largely invisible when they come here. Because the major attraction is boating, we see little of them. I was shocked to be told that our tourist arrivals approached those of Antigua. It is disturbing that local non-whites have so little a share in the growth industry of this country.

Here, as probably everywhere else, the dollar has become omnipotent. The government, for instance, brags that there is plenty of money around, which is supposed to make us believe that all is fine. While there may or may not be plenty of money, money itself should not be the criterion for progress, but rather how it is used.

BENJAMIN DRUMMOND is a British Virgin Islander. Trained in Economics, Mr. Drummond currently works in the private sector, after having worked for several years in the civil service.

There has been indeed a fair amount of progress in socio-economic development of the BVI over the past two decades, and the momentum established seems sustainable through the 1980s. However, economic development has also meant a change in the character and tone of the community because of a too rapid increase in the numbers of immigrants, both Black and White. Local culture and way of life seem swamped by outside influences, since the local capacity to absorb the influx was over-strained. Also, it is perhaps too early to boast about the economic well-being of the community, since the economic base of tourism is sensitive and therefore not very reliable. Seven years of plenty may well be followed by seven years of famine.

By and large, the BVIslander seems content with the status quo. One reason for this may be that he is by nature a quiet person, accepting too blindly the laws of the powers that be. On the other hand, given the past experience of the island as a poverty/stricken agricultural community, say from after Emancipation to the nineteen-sixties, it is understandable that the people of the islands would regard earnings from tourism, and the raised standard of living that they have experienced as a result as a Godsend. And would be prepared as a result to tolerate a fair measure of social ill-effects to ensure that the islands do not revert back to their former poverty-stricken state.

PAULINE WYNNE (Expatriate, assistant hotel manager)

I think that there is undoubtedly some local resentment of tourism, particularly among people who are aged. They remember "the good old days" fondly and resent the changes tourism has brought to their homes. Almost all older people everywhere remember that it used to be better than it is now. Young people are mostly not resentful.

It is an unfortunate trait of the average North American that he or she does not bother to take the time to find out about the area of the world they're visiting. Most tourists do not even know the coordinates of longitude and latitude of their holiday area.

At times, some tourists may seem rude, but they are mild, wonderful—even most welcome at their rudest—compared to British sailors from Navy vessels. They are rude, crude, and much else undesirable.

Tourism is an important factor in world trade. It puts the idea forth that all cultural and ethnic groups must unite even stronger to preserve their own identity. And one's own identity is something worth preserving. We must work toward an equitable balance of world knowledge and knowledge of one's self.

Our tourism industry is young and it is a resource that will fund, clothe, educate and house BVIslanders. It is physically easier to work eight hours a day and receive a weekly pay-cheque than to till the land and hope for rain to grow food. Why would the young BVIslander want to die at 62 like his father, from having worked too hard in the sun all his life? As time goes by, the young man knows he can live 15 years longer—at a more comfortable place than his parents —by being a boat mechanic. Tourism is that young man's ticket to a longer, easier life. But it must not reach the eroding shape of USVI proportions. Easy! Easy! Easy! Slow! Slow! Slow!

ANNE KORTRIGHT, a young British Virgin Islander, is a self-described "government functionary". Like many persons in the higher regions of the public bureaucracy, she began her career as a pedagogue.

The BVI must be careful. This state of apparent socio-economic well-being cannot last in the face of increases in expatriate population, both "Down Islands" and European/American. The percentage of BVIslanders in managerial positions in private enterprise is still re-markably low. We are told that there are no locals to fill the positions, which justifies the importation of expatriate expertise—most times from America or Europe.

One of the problems the BVI labour force is beset with is an al-most constant migration from the islands and the tendency of the school system to train people in docility. Students are not trained to be effective, much less, efficient. They are trained to be secretaries (How can you be an effective secretary if your grasp of English is poor?), but rarely for management positions. Therefore, one shouldn't be surprised that of those locals left after migration, few are prepared to acquire managerial positions. On the other hand, few companies owned by non-belongers bother to train locals to fill man-agerial positions. Still, the flow of permanent migration seems to be slowing down and one sees belongers returning home with skills and managerial experience. Yet it would seem that the tendency is still to pay this ready-made local manager less than a white counter-part brought in from outside.

Tourism presents the BVI with a two-edged dilemma. What the BVI is trying to do is to control it as far as possible, exploit it for the good of the BVIslanders and to still make attempts at diversifying the local economy, the philosophy being that if one has to prostitute one-self in order to live, do so, but avoid the pimp to maintain control over what you sell. And prepare yourself for a time when you can do better!

Most BVIslanders see the tourism industry as a necessary evil, something to be controlled as much as possible by BVIslanders for our benefit not for the benefit of the industry. If it were otherwise, we'd have Sheratons, Hiltons, Holiday Inns sinking the island and crowding the beaches, and we'd permit any and everyone to come in and stay as long as he or she wanted.

Those from the "developed" countries who can afford to travel are generally white, middle or upper class. They have preconceived prejudices of people who live in the "underdeveloped" world, who are generally brown or black. They have also been sold a tourist package where darkies laugh or smile all day and are pleased to wait hand and foot on the tourist, who represents the wealth their economies are dependent on. The "underdeveloped" world also has a notion that all tourists are white, wealthy, and liberal with their money.

Some tourists arrive to the destination and act according to the stereotype of the "ugly American" (even if they are French, German or Dutch) and are, in their behaviour, offensive and perhaps do not consider the social mores of the country they are in—like wearing bikinis on main street or bathing nude on a public beach. Many are not prepared for the resentment this may trigger in the local person.

British Virgin Islanders tend to be reserved people. We pride ourselves on our "good sense". Tourists are generally on vacation from their good behaviour and good sense and become very uninhibited. So, behaviour which may not normally be acceptable in their countries, should somehow become acceptable in the BVI. Tourists do not consider that they are paying us a visit or courtesy call. They are "on" vacation to let it all hang out all over us, and resent any attempt to ask for constraints. They impose this behaviour on us. Generalization, of course. One sometimes meets very nice tourists.

In the BVI, a country which has no foreign exchange problem and in which the standard of living is generally quite high, the people are proud. We are proud even in our "poverty"; we didn't know we were poor and therefore did not develop a so-called culture of poverty. Whites and others from the so-called developed countries are not used to proud Blacks. We make them uncomfortable, because, behaviourwise, we either take them or leave them, and are quite prepared to leave them.

BVIslanders should look at St. Thomas, USVI as an example of unplanned growth. Similar ill-effects could occur in the BVI if we don't try to regard St. Thomas as an example of what could happen. All aspects of West Indian life have been ignored except for those which could be exploited for the American dollar. The native U.S. Virgin Islander—native not meaning "born-there" but "from-there" for generations back—has been almost completely over-run, exploited, used, and now finds himself even disenfranchised in a mock election where candidates are not necessarily from there, and where the only requirements for anyone voting is to have established residence for a very short period of time. At this rate, no amount of "slowing down" is going to change the fact that the USVI no longer "belongs" to Virgin Islanders.

Partly because we developed far behind other nations in the Caribbean and can look at them as examples of what we want or don't want to happen here, we are in a position to be able to pick, choose and refuse. But we don't know how long this can last in the face of overwhelming currents of world change and the strength (military, media, propaganda, etc.) of the U.S., which all the world is increasingly unable to resist. The BVI is trying as much as possible now to stick our fingers in the increasing numbers of holes in the dyke. But I suppose it's just a matter of time before we too are swept away.

PART III

REPRISE

6

The Present as History

Fort Charlotte's guns are silent now,
Fort George's flag is down;
No sentry guards Fort Shirley's brow,
Defenseless is Road Town.

The whites who manned these ancient forts
Have vanished like the dew;
Their barks have left our friendly ports,
Likewise the pipes they blew.

But lo! I see they're coming back;
They're coming back to stay.
A hearty welcome they'll not lack
From Ebo, Kru, or Vey.

— A. Osorio Norman, "Tortola's Ancient Forts," ca. 1920

In commenting on the historical significance of the West Indian colonies to the European predators as they fought each other for the right to exploit the New World, Eric Williams contends that "the West Indian colonies assumed an importance that appears almost incredible today, when one looks at those forgotten, neglected, forlorn dots on the map" (Williams 1970:88). Conversely, another scholar, Gordon Rohlehr (1974:85), counters that "it is not the decline of the West Indies that should engage our sentiment, but rather their endurance as a perennially fertile hunting ground for everyone except the people who live there".

> The exploiters of this [current] age preserve a much greater sense of propriety. . . . The bauxite of Jamaica, Guyana, and Surinam, the oil of Trinidad and Venezuela, and even the sunshine and the beaches of most of the islands still seem to be exploitable commodities and provide the enterprising descendant of the slave trader and planter with his adequate pound of flesh. (ibid.)

Polemic aside, it might be useful to attempt to place the current phenomenon of the Caribbean territories' collective role as "a perennially fertile hunting ground" briefly in historical perspective.

At the risk of some redundancy (see Chapter 1) it must be reiterated that the European imperial incursions in the Caribbean had as a primary objective the establishment of what have been designated "colonies of exploitation" (Beckford 1972), created for the purpose of local commodity production for sale in the metropolitan marketplace. The sugar plantation constituted the prototypical productive format in this type of colony, and the productive process itself rested on the backs of enslaved African laborers.

> The African slave trade and slavery itself were intimately bound up with the spread of European military and colonial power and with commercial developments, especially in overseas capitalistic agriculture. . . .
>
> Moreover, the development of plantations to produce commodities for European markets was a vital first step in the history of overseas capitalism. (Mintz 1974:9-10)

From the outset, the European plantation colonies in the Caribbean were characterized by the externality of their orientation. That is to say, the plantation economy existed for the benefit of the imperial metropole. Thus, as Sidney Mintz argues, "the 'economic development' of the islands was largely responsible for their 'underdevelopment' at a later time" (1974:44). Plantation economy, "as developed by the Europeans, was adapted to the assimilation of the Caribbean territories to their metropolises only in ways that made the territories themselves increasingly backward, relative to the economic growth of the metropolises" (ibid.). The eminent nineteenth century British economist John Stuart Mill was not trying to be facetious when he referred to Britain's Caribbean colonies merely as a locale "where England finds it convenient to carry on the production of sugar, coffee, and a few other tropical commodities" (cited in Beckford 1972:44-5).

To be sure, the emancipation of the slaves did not signal the complete demise of plantation economy in all the colonies. Over the years, the sugar plantation continued to exist, and sometimes to thrive, as a more or less viable socioeconomic formation. By 1970, for instance, the volume of sugar production from the British Caribbean was estimated to be "10 times the level of 1935 and 20 times that of 1900" (Craton 1974:286). The continuing externality of the economic linkages associated with the revivification of Caribbean plantation economy has given rise to a feeling by some observers that the more things change, the more they stay the same. Michael Craton has very accurately summarized the argument:

> The phoenix-like sugar plantation is symbolic both of a neo-colonialist conspiracy to restrict the Third World Caribbean to the role of primary production under external exploitation, and

also of an even more subtle tendency to perpetuate the socio-political patterns of slavery days. (ibid.)

This latter-day plantation economy has, of course, undergone various transformations, but these have only served to exacerbate the mis-development of the host territories.

> The emergence of the vertically integrated corporate plantation enterprise has really served to preserve the character of the slave plantation system. The three characteristics of that earlier insti-tutional environment—appendage in overseas economy, total economic institution, and incalculability[1]—have been preserved and strengthened in the period since Emancipation. . . . The plantation still dominates the economic life of the region. It owns and controls the use of the best land, has access to credit and technology, owns all the factory capacity for the rudimentary processing of plantation crops in the islands, provides services for the marketing of the export staples (shipping, insurance, overseas distribution, and so forth), and influences government policy in fundamental ways. (Beckford 1972:48)

Similarly, the plantation syndrome continued to manifest itself in the social structure of the post-emancipation era. Emancipation of the slaves left the plantocracy in its familiar position at the top of the social pyramid with the base comprised of

> a mass of [formerly] enslaved Africans who were . . . left to their own devices at emancipation while their owners received cash for value lost. In between, there grew up a skilled professional and trading middle class advancing into a local capitalism, sub-servient to the needs of imperialism, counting all their blessings of status, wealth, conspicuous consumption and opportunity as flowing from a foreign domination and culture. (Arnett 1967:xxi)

A caveat must, however, be entered here, for as we have seen in the case of the British Virgin Islands, the nineteenth century decline of the local plantation economy quickly ushered in the complete obliteration of the plantation system.

Upon the demise of the British Virgin Islands plantation economy, there followed a period which lasted for roughly a century (ca. 1860s to 1960s)—the post-emancipation interregnum—during which time the forms of production (subsistence agriculture, fishing, livestock, and char-coal) of the new social formation (see Glossary, Appendix) were not such as to evoke the interest of the imperial center. The agriculturally marginal British Virgin Islands had simply become unattractive—to revert to George Beckford's schema—as a "colony of exploitation."

The post-emancipation interregnum is invariably described in terms of socioeconomic decline caused by metropolitan neglect. Thus, we have earlier noted a Government report of 1907 positing that

> the history of the British Virgin Islands since 1815 has been one almost uninterrupted record of retrogression and decay. . . . The Virgin Islands during these years were almost forgotten and no interest was taken in their inhabitants either in England or elsewhere.

More recently, this theme of metropolitan neglect has been reiterated by two native British Virgin Islands scholars, Drs. Norwell Harrigan and Pearl Varlack (1975:115), who observe that

> by 1900 the helplessness and hopelessness of the islands due to economic degradation had reached serious and scandalous proportions and the British Government belatedly bestirred themselves.

While the historical record provides ample justification for such moral indignation, it is here suggested that the situation was less one of neglect (which imputes moral responsibility to the Colonial power) than of economic disinterest. This is because "infrastructural spending by metropolitan interests," as Codrington argues, "tends to be determined in most cases by actualities and possibilities of surplus extraction" (1977:201). With the demise of the sugar-based plantation economy, these "actualities and possibilities" no longer obtained in the British Virgin Islands.

As might be expected, similar conditions of agricultural marginality produced similar effects elsewhere in the Caribbean (cf. Lowenthal and Clarke 1977:516). Collectively, these agriculturally marginal imperial territories today constitute what Ulf Hannerz has referred to as the "other Caribbean":

> It has intimate links to plantation America and shares much of its traditions, but it has no large plantations and is oriented instead toward the sea. Scattered islands in the eastern Caribbean could be considered representative of it, and in the past the Bahamas and Bermuda further to the north shared several of its characteristics. In the western Caribbean, it may be seen in a historical network of English-speaking societies, constructed between the seventeenth and the nineteenth centuries, with economies which have involved piracy, wrecking, fishing, turtling, seamanship, logcutting, smuggling and small-scale agriculture in mixes which have varied over time and between different territories. (Hannerz 1974:20)

In the British Virgin Islands, the situation of imperial disinterest persisted, by and large, until, with the cessation of North American tourist-travel to post-Castro Cuba (1959 onwards) and the consequent burgeoning of tourism elsewhere in the Caribbean, the tourism potential of the colony became apparent. At that point (early 1960s), with the possibilities—if not the actualities—of surplus extraction fairly evident, "infrastructural spending by metropolitan interests" ensued. A decade later (1970s), the British Virgin Islands had been transformed from a smallholding/petty commodity economy into a tourism-based economy. With the more or less concurrent emergence of the Territory as an important "off-shore" banking center (see Chapter 5), the British Virgin Islands economy was once again appended to the world economy to a degree which had not occurred since the heyday of the plantation era.

It is instructive to examine the demographic correlates of these historical developments. Again, at some risk of redundancy, we note that at the apogee of the plantation economy in 1805, the population of the British Virgin Islands peaked at 10,520 persons, of whom 9,220 were blacks and 1,300 were whites. By 1834, the year in which slavery was abolished, and by which time the BVI plantation economy had gone into irrevocable decline, the total population had fallen to 6,815: 6,338 blacks, 477 whites. Thenceforth, with the BVI no longer viable as a "colony of exploitation," the white presence continued to decline—from 32 in 1891 to 2 in 1901. As recently as 1960—the dawn of the era of tourism—the population stood at 7,771 blacks, 47 whites. The Osorio Norman (1920s) poem with which this chapter began therefore exhibits an almost uncanny prescience: with tourism—the new "King Sugar"—fully consolidated, the 1980 census indicates a total population of 11,152 persons, of whom 9,941 were blacks and 778 were whites (see Table 8).

This resuscitated metropolitan interest might well be viewed with some ambivalence. Clearly, there is a danger that marginal territories such as the Cayman Islands, Anguilla, the British Virgin Islands, and so on, having more or less fortuitously avoided some of the more invidious aspects of the perpetuation of plantation economy, might now be heading almost ineluctably toward the re-institution of a latter-day, transmogrified plantation economy. This new economy is based not upon the cultivation and exportation of sugar cane, but upon the attraction and processing of what might more or less facetiously be called a North Atlantic variety of "homo touristicus". In commenting on this phenomenon—with specific reference to the Cayman Islands, but with fairly obvious implications for the rest of the "other Caribbean," including the British Virgin Islands—Professor Hannerz observes that

> [in] tracing the history of the islands from their days as a frontier society, different from much of the rest of the Caribbean, it may seem as if the tourist economy is finally forcing [them] into a mold which [they share] with many other parts of the region. And the difficult questions [they] may have to face are thus fa-

miliar from elsewhere. There are observers of tourist economies who point out that these are highly sensitive to international recessions, and that a reputation for political instability is so damaging that repression may be allowed to grow instead. There is also the question what happens in the long run in a successful tourist economy: When [native] families have sold all that land which is so attractive to outsiders, and when their men have built the houses which the new owners want on their land, what will they do next? What jobs will be open to [indigenes] in the new economy in the long run? Will they become a proletariat of beach hustlers, bar tenders, and local maids, with a few entrepreneurs in those crevices of the local economy left unattended by foreign business? Will the men start going back to sea, feeling the salt water beating their faces again? (Hannerz 1974:184)

The British Virgin Islands have now reached the point in their socio-historical evolution where the provision of adequate answers to these questions is a matter of considerable urgency. It would be most distressing if an absence of a sense of historical perspective and an overemphasis on historical uniqueness were to blind this until-recently "neglected" territory to the centripetal force of a mode of development which, in the long run, is completely homogenizing.

Afterword

Bill Maurer

IN THE SUMMER of 2008, when Michael O'Neal invited me to write this afterword, the United States Senate Finance Committee was holding hearings on the offshore financial services business in the Caribbean, and its potential or actual threat to United States revenue collection.[*] One of the witnesses brought up the BVI in rather unflattering terms, claiming that it permits anonymous incorporation (it does not) and that it is virtually unregulated (it is not). Reaction in the BVI was swift: commentators on one of the territory's online discussion forums wrote (spelling and punctuation as in the original):

> They STOLE us from our home land, CHAIN us like dogs in the bottom of their ships, THREW over the ship those of us who were to weak and sick, BRANDED us with hot iron when they sold us to the highest bidder, WIP and BEAT us to death for free labour, LEFT us to die after they made their wealth on these islands but GOD was on our side and we SURVIVE now the GREAT USA the one that we help built with force free labour is at it again. Now they trying to take away our daily bread, like they did with caribbean banana, so many travel restriction into their land for us and none for them into our land, the same money we make all goes back to them as we produce notting and have to import all from them, so to all in the SENATE/CONGRESS who want to now kill the caribbean islands for the WEALTH they now have because of OFFSHORE BANKING and IBC [International Business Corporation], REMEMBER

[*] I would like to thank Michael O'Neal for inviting me to contribute this afterword, as well as for his enduring support over the years. I would also like to thank Colleen Ballerino Cohen for her mentorship and guidance, and Tom Boellstorff and Julia Elyachar for comments on this short essay. My research in the BVI has been supported by the U.S. National Science Foundation (SES-0516861). Any opinions, findings, and conclusions or recommendations expressed in this afterword are those of the author and do not necessarily reflect the views of the National Science Foundation.

GOD DON'T LIKE UGLY AND HE IS THE ONE AND ONLY
ONE WHO PROVIDES FOR ALL OF US.

God have his waY to make those that benifited from free labour
to now pay those that work for notting so caribbean islands reap
your sweets.

Michael O'Neal's book, of course, is a story of tourism, not finance. But
it was written right at the beginning of the emergence of this "second
pillar" of the British Virgin Islands' economy—financial services—and the
tantalizing references to that industry in this book, as well as the rich
discussion of the enduring influence of the plantation complex, provide
the starting point for this afterword. Indeed, the quotations above speak
volumes about the continuing legacies of slavery and the plantation era.
Those who gained from slave labor—and inherited the benefits slave-
holding conferred—now pay in the form of lost revenue to the people of
the Caribbean whose ancestors used to "work for nothing." This is a cun-
ning commentary on value, its circulation, and its deep histories, histories
that O'Neal's volume helps us better to discern.

While the financial services sector was already implanted in the BVI
during the 1970s and early 1980s, it began to achieve its position as the
territory's second economic engine only after passage of the International
Business Companies Act of 1984. Today, financial services is second in
historical sequence only. As of 2008, the financial services industry brings
in 56% of BVI revenue; its contributions to the rest of the BVI economy far
exceed that of tourism.

Despite these shifts, how precisely to understand the impact of financial services on the BVI remains an open question. There are passages in
McWelling Todman's commentary in Chapter 5 that resonate with the
comments sparked by the U.S. Senate Finance Committee hearings. After
explaining how tourism perpetuates some of the central features of the
plantation complex, with the very real potential for land alienation and a
displacement of British Virgin Islanders from their country, McWelling
Todman goes on a tangent for a few paragraphs about offshore finance.
What struck him in that conversation in 1982 may surprise the contemporary reader. To McWelling Todman, the trust companies' physical absence
upends the plantation story. Financial services, it seemed to him at the
time, contributed to the territory *without* alienation or expropriation.
"Those men are not here, they are not taking anything away from us,
they're not manufacturing anything here, they're not exploiting the Territory. . . . All they are saying is 'For the privilege of occupying one little spot
on the shelf of the Registrar's Office in the British Virgin Islands . . . and
for the privilege of being able to use your name . . . in saying I'm a British
Virgin Islands Company, I'm prepared to pay you so much for Registration
fees . . . and, if we make a profit, which is taxable, we'll pay you an income

tax, too!" (p.105). Offshore finance has made the once-slave free, and has reversed the direction of the flow of value from North American or British metropole to Caribbean colony.

Yet McWelling Todman cautioned that this inflow of capital from financial services might enhance the Territory's "dependency," and that "we are more dependent on outside capital and outside capital flows than most of us stop to think or realize" (p.105). Today, the BVI is more dependent on those flows of capital than McWelling Todman could ever have imagined. With nearly a million companies and now mutual funds and insurance, the BVI is a major international center for finance. This is still little understood by most BVIslanders, some assuming that the business consists chiefly of money-laundering, and others noting the presence of more law firms, more white expatriates walking their dogs in the early morning hours, and more home building on the hillsides.

At the same time, finance is simply the continuation of a pattern of capital flow that has long characterized the Caribbean. An outsider might assume that Panamanian trust companies in the BVI represent some sort of shady inheritance from the Noriega years. And in one sense, they do: capital flight from Panama reached great heights during and after the Noriega regime. Yet older BVIslanders will also recall the history of migration to and from Panama dating back to when the isthmus was first breached by West Indian laborers. The careful observer will also note that these Panamanian-managed trust companies are primarily holding companies for trading firms, and that the territory's place at the center of finance is not just about new money flows but old circulations of goods and people going back to slavery, if not before.

Things have not quite turned out the way McWelling Todman may have foreseen, either, in light of the massive development of physical infrastructure demanded by the growing financial services industry. Wickam's Cay, that strip of land reclaimed from both the sea and the greed of Batehill (discussed in Chapter 4), is now nearly fully occupied. Road Town bursts with three and four-storey office buildings housing lawyers, accountants, and registered agents who set up and manage the trust companies. Pasea Estate is the new home of the BVI Financial Services Commission ("just behind the paint factory," the visitor will be told), the independent regulatory body in charge of ensuring the Territory's compliance with international treaties and standards of best practice, and empowered to take punitive action against wrongdoers. And there are new expatriates, too, occupying homes on the hillsides, accessed by newly paved and graded roads. When asked to characterize the changes that have taken place in the BVI since the 1990s, one longtime expatriate resident immediately offered, "the infrastructure has improved tremendously."

And what of the plantation complex? Does the financial services industry represent another form of expropriation and alienation, as many critics of the offshore world assert (Palan 2003; Hampton and Christensen

2002)? At least from the BVI perspective, the story is considerably more complex, and the historical legacies of slavery, the plantation era, post-emancipation and post-WWII developments charted in this book help to explain why.

Consider Wickam's Cay. There are buildings that house trust company-registered agents, serving as the official address for hundreds of thousands of companies. Take a closer look, however, and you will see that many of those buildings have names, and most of those names are longstanding BVI family names: Frett, Hodge, O'Neal. BVIslanders got into real estate during the tourist boom, but this did not just lead to land alienation. BVIslander landowners have acquired property on Wickam's Cay and elsewhere, or used family land and built office buildings, leasing them to trust and estate planning companies and the law firms and accountants that are ancillary to the financial services sector. Looking at Wickam's Cay today, you could either see the expropriation of the land by the financial services sector—a second coming of Batehill, perhaps—or, looking a little bit closer, you would see land-use patterns bespeaking the deep legacies and durable histories of family, race, class, and party.

Thus, during the U.S. Senate Finance Committee hearings, when Senator Max Baucus made an example of Ugland House in the Cayman Islands for being a five-storey building with over 18,000 tenants—mainly LLCs and other corporate entities registered in the Caymans—he missed a crucial point; namely, that a five-storey building is an important thing in a small place like the Caymans or the British Virgin Islands. The Ugland name itself is of local Caymanian importance, being that of a prominent expatriate Norwegian who made his livelihood in shipping, and has been a prominent supporter of the Cayman's National Trust for the environment and heritage sites. When one witness at the Senate Finance Committee hearing noted that the BVI is "the place to go for quick, cheap, anonymous incorporation," he missed that the BVI has stricter rules around incorporation than several U.S. states, and that the BVI, unlike many OECD countries, regulates and monitors registered agents. This is not to defend the activities taking place offshore, but rather to redirect inquiry toward those activities and their social and political effects locally as well as internationally, rather than resorting to blanket castigation of countries and dependent territories—a too-common practice that relies on thinly disguised racial stereotyping.

The issue of family names and territorial reputations looms large here. One might trace a line of memory from the controversy over the name of Hodge's Creek/Maya Cove, as documented in this book, to the names of the buildings that "house" the trust companies. They may exist only on paper or computer files, yet their address marks real estate in two senses of the phrase: a physical piece of property, and a true legacy, an inheritance from one's ancestors whose names now prominently mark Road Town.

Of course, this business of name and reputation carries a flip side: there are many excluded from this estate, this inheritance of name and all that goes with it. The excluded include immigrants and their descendents, who probably outnumber BVIslanders (however one defines that complicated identity category); and members of BVIslander families not as blessed with landholdings as their compatriots. Elihu Rhymer had foresight when he stated that "the problem in this country is that the argument is between ourselves. Who are going to be the new elites in the BVI? Who are going to be the new rich people?" (p.107).

The question of how first tourism and then finance restructures social and economic hierarchies in the BVI brings us to the very important discussion in this book of "colonies of exploitation" (p.128). If the BVI remains today a colony of exploitation, how does it do so, in what direction, and who is exploiting whom? Trust and estate planners, corporate lawyers, and transnational firms are using the new "resource" of the BVI—its jurisdictionality and its favorable incorporation, trust, mutual fund and insolvency laws; its stable reputation; its status as a regulatory leader in the offshore financial services sector globally—much as plantation-era elites used slavery and monocrop agriculture, or expatriate businessmen and women used tourism to extract their "pound of flesh" (p.127).

Here, finance could be seen as not much different from the plantation economy, characterized by the "externality of its orientation" (p.128). Hence, the serious attention paid to maintaining a stable and tightly regulated jurisdiction, and the concern with the BVI's reputation with multinational investors and multilateral regulatory agencies. Yet, at the same time, other external forces are arrayed against offshore finance, in the name of reducing tax competition but also due to an international politics of race and rank. Some external forces are trying to propel and enhance the financial services industry, while others are trying to constrain if not outright eviscerate it. The clash of elites globally is manifested in the places where debates over globalization, revenue collection and finance touch down, like the British Virgin Islands. Where O'Neal wrote about the servility demanded of the tourism industry, enterprising BVIslanders now seek to teach their compatriots proper manners and the niceties and refinements of cosmopolitan culture—like proper tablesetting and dinnertime conversation—so that they can mingle effectively and with pride with the lawyers and accountants who arrive in the Territory daily.

While the Territory is made increasingly subject to the regulatory might of the large global powers as well as the vagaries of finance and, potentially, the dastardly intentions of transnational criminals, still nothing so characterizes the BVI as vigilance, and, as documented so vividly in this book, the tense dialectic of continuity and transformation. It is fitting that the BVI Financial Services Commission sponsored a float at the 2008 Festival commemorating the emancipation of the slaves. The idea was proposed by the most junior staff of the organization. Carrying Commission employees and their children, and with a lighthouse—the Commission's symbol—mounted atop it, the float slowly rolled down the waterfront. A man with a microphone shouted, "Keep your eyes on the lighthouse, and you won't run aground," as the children threw candy to the crowd.

BILL MAURER, Ph.D.
Professor of Anthropology and Law
University of California, Irvine

References

Hampton, Mark P. and John Christensen
　　2002　"Offshore Pariahs? Small Island Economies, Tax Havens, and the Re-configuration of Global Finance." In *World Development* 30 (9): 1657-73.
Palan, Ronen
　　2003　*The Offshore World: Sovereign Markets, Virtual Places, and Nomad Millionaires.* Ithaca, NY: Cornell University Press.

NOTES

Introduction

[1]The situation is further complicated by the fact that, as Sidney Mintz observes, "Caribbeanist research is not held in very high regard by European and North American social scientists":

> In anthropology, for instance, the rarely articulated underlying assumption of traditional ethnography, with its emphasis on the isolated, remote, "primitive," and "pure" has meant that the islands would serve best as a training ground, a laboratory, a place "to get your first fieldwork under your belt," before turning to the "real" anthropology of Africa, Asia, or the tropical forests and frozen wastes of the New World. Though the terms of reference are of course different, similar perspectives appear to dominate the thinking of scholars in the other social sciences. (Mintz 1974:51-2)

[2] To wit:

> Tortola and Virgin Gorda (Spanish Town), Jos Van Dykes, Guana Isle, Beef and Thatch Islands, Anegada, Nichar, Prickly Pear, Camanas, Ginger, Cooper's, Salt Island, Peter Island, and several others of little value. (Edwards 1793, vol. I:499-500)

[3]Notably, Raghaven 1963, Lewisohn 1965, Dirks 1971, Harrigan and Varlack 1975, Dookhan 1975, Howell 1978, McGlynn 1980, and Lett 1980. Since the completion of the research upon which this volume is based, scholarship has continued to emerge to fill this void, notably Pickering 1983, Harrigan 1986, Maurer 1997, Turnbull 2002, Smith 2009, and Cohen 2010.

[4]During the course of this fieldwork, the author was elected President of the British Virgin Islands Mental Health Association.

[5]The Delbecq Technique is similar, but not identical in approach to the Delphi Technique:

> In a traditional Delphi, the objective is to achieve a consensus among experts on a given issue or problem through a series of questionnaires. After the initial questionnaire is administered and responses are obtained, the judgements are collated. A second questionnaire is distributed that incorporates feedback from the first survey. Ultimately, the "most desirable solution" emerges from the experts' collective knowledge. (Hawkins et al. 1980:17)

Chapter 1 • The Era of the Plantation

[1]Harrigan and Varlack (1975:58) state that "in 1743 the islands produced 1,000 hogsheads of sugar and 1,000,000 pounds of cotton. . . . In 1752 it was noted in England that 'we have little cotton from the West Indies and that chiefly from the Virgin Islands'."

[2]By way of comparison, it might be noted that the demographic figures of the 1805 Virgin Islands census (total population, 10,520) were not to be approximated until the late 1960s/early 1970s, when the 1970 census revealed a total population of 10,484 persons.

[3]The North American Reporter conceded, however, that his description of apparent Tortolian prosperity might not have been completely accurate, "as the observations were made in the height [sic] of Business, when the Enemy's Shott were flying over us" (Log of the S/S Pilgrim, op. cit.).

[4]Trelawney Wentworth's analysis of the decline of British Virgin Islands plantation economy—based on first-hand observation immediately after the hurricane of 1819—is as follows:

> Tortola has been declining for many years, in no inconsiderable degree from the natural poverty of the soil, which might have classed it among the most unimportant of the British possessions in these seas, had not capaciousness of the anchorage pointed it out as a suitable rendevous for the homeward-bound shipping from the neighbouring settlements during the war, whence it became a place of considerable traffic, and for some time enjoyed peculiar privileges as a free port.
> . . . But the termination of the war proved a sudden and serious check to them, and [the hurricane of 1819] may be said to have given the final blow to its political importance (Wentworth 1834:234-6).

[5]Concerning the etymology of the term "colony," we find that it derived from

> The Latin irregular verb, *colo*, whose past participle is *cultum*. The first meaning of the verb was "to till the ground"; it expanded to include every kind of cultivation—of the arts, of philosophy, or even of a person. (Hughes 1975:14)

It soon, however, acquired imperial connotations "to include 'the settlements of Roman citizens in a hostile or newly conquered country'" (ibid.).

Chapter 2 • Manumission and Rebellion

[1]Regarding the Nottingham deed, a contemporary writer provides the following details:

> Samuel Nottingham's original deed manumission is dated in June 1776. He then lived at Long Island, in the province of New York. Owing, probably, to the war which existed at that time between Great Britain and her Colonies, eight years passed before the deed was transmitted to Tortola. It was enrolled in the Roll Office of the state of Pennsylvania, on the 28th of

April, 1784; and it was not recorded at Tortola until 15th of July 1784. The deed itself is thus superscribed:

"Tortola, July the 15th, 1784. Recorded in the Registrar's office, to and for the Virgin Islands, in lib. B, folio 76, 77, 78, 79 and examined by

George Leonard, Registrar"

It is not clear how soon after the transmission of the above deed to Tortola the slaves of Mr. Nottingham were put in possession of their freedom. A farther deed, however, appears to have been necessary, to give validity to the former. This deed bears date at Wellingborough, in Northampton-shire, on the 3rd of October 1789, and purports to be that of Hannah Abbott, the sister, and residuary legatee of Samuel Nottingham, and the executrix (in conjunction with Henry Gandy, of Bristol) of his last will and testament; in which deed she conveys and confirms "to the late servants" of her deceased brother a plantation called Longlook. This deed is super-scribed as follows: –

"Tortola, 16th June, 1790. Recorded in the Register Office of and for the Virgin Islands, in lib F, folios 109, 110 and 111 and examined by

Mark Dyer, Deputy Registrar."

(Review of the Quarterly Review . . . 1824:91-3).

[2]It might be noted in this regard that

The recovery of runaways always mobilized the entire machinery of social control, though in small islands in placid times this was less from fear of encouraging rebellion than because of the loss of the slaves' services. (Craton 1974:178)

[3]Perspective on the phenomenon of slave resistance and rebellion in Virgin Islands plantation society may be further gained by consideration of the following items:

(1) A petition from the Virgin Islands Legislature to the Governor of the Leeward Islands bemoaned the fact that large numbers of Virgin Island slaves are escaping to Puerto Rico where the Spanish government refuses to return them to the masters on the ground that they converted to Roman Catholicism. (C.O. 152/60: Leeward Islands; enclosed in Burt to Germaine, 26 September 1780. Cited in Tyson and Tyson 1974:31)

An Act of 1787, however, closed this avenue of escape to slaves by making it mandatory that a white man be aboard every boat not hauled ashore and properly secured. (Dookhan 1975:82)

(2) In 1789 and 1790 "attempts at arson for the purpose of pillage were so frequent that in the absence of a regular system of police, the young white men of Road Town were constrained to form an association to watch by night to prevent them" (Dookhan 1975:83; citing C.O. 239/11).

(3) Records show that in 1793 "eight slaves, two of them women, cut off their arms with their bills" (Dookhan 1975:83; citing C.O. 239/11).

[4]Working with various sources, Richard Price (1973) has synthesized the following etymology of the term "maroon":

> The English word "maroon," like the French *marron*, derives from Spanish *Cimarron*. As used in the New World, *Cimarron* originally referred to domestic cattle that had taken to the hills in Hispaniola (Parry and Sherlock 1965:14) and soon after to Indian slaves who had escaped from the Spaniards as well (Franco 1968:92). By the end of the 1530s, it was already beginning to refer primarily to Afro-American runaways (Frances 1968:93; see also Guillot 1961:38), and had strong connotations of "fierceness," of being "wild" and "unbroken".

[5]For example:

> Besides the offences considered capital if committed by whites or free coloured persons, there are others which will subject a slave (exclusively) to capital punishment: such are "absence from his owners' service for three months, in one continued space of time, or for six months in two years." "The ringleader of slaves, above sixteen years of age, running away in gangs of ten or more, and remaining out for ten days," is also liable to be punished capitally, as are slaves for "mutinous or rebellious conduct;" for "procuring arms and meditating their escape to different countries;" for "any acts committed, contrary to the safety of these islands;" and, in some cases, "for striking a white person;" though it is for each of these offences discretionary with the justices, whether the punishment of death shall be indicted or not. (Parliamentary Papers: 1824)

[6]In a similar vein, and by way of comparison, Karen Olwig's research on St. Johnian plantations indicates that the slaves were quite perceptive regarding differential social status within the superordinate group. Moreover, the slaves were very often able to use this comprehension to their own advantage:

> On the 24th of April 1847, a case is reported to the St. John judge and administrator where a manager by the name of John Franklin Glasco got into an argument with unfree Johannes concerning whether cattle from Johannes' owner, Judge Berg's plantation had intruded on the property of the plantation which Glasco manages. Johannes is reported to have said: "Do you know whom I belong to? I belong to Judge Berg (chief judge on St. Thomas), you are a come-and-go, my master is head-judge. You, pskaw! You a shitting ass Blanco!" Later on Johannes says, "you come here to put a pair of breeches on Mr. Hill's back, you come here to make Hill rich? (Hill is the owner of the plantation which Glasco manages). You come here to make negroes work, ho? You come here to lick negroes to make them run away? you make your houseboy run away the other day? you come here to make money? take care the judge get them (i.e. the money) from you." Johannes is tied and Glasco brings him back to the plantation to which he belongs, where the slaves yell at Glasco in Dutch Creole: "Blanco, Blanco, mothei; break se kop!" (Whitey, Whitey, kill him; smash his head!) Shortly afterwards Glasco is requested to leave the island by the plantation owner, Mr. Hill, who feels that his own position on

the island is being threatened by the slaves' hatred for Glasco, who has shown little understanding of local mores and a lack of respect for the leading plantation owners. (Politi-journal 1847-1860; cited in Olwig 1977:405n; English in the original)

[7]St. Christopher (St. Kitts) and/or Antigua, both several hundred miles and two full days' sail from the Virgin Islands.

[8]Deemed agriculturally marginal for a variety of environmental/ecological reasons—such as the rugged nature of the topography, relatively poor soil conditions, and so on.

[9]Mintz and Price (1967:22) offer an intriguing conceptualization of the genesis of fictive-genealogical kinship systems in Afro-American (broadly considered) society:

> Various shreds of evidence suggest that some of the earliest social bonds to develop in the coffles, in the factories and, especially, during the long Middle Passage were of a dyadic (two-person) nature. Partly, perhaps, because of the general policy of keeping men and women separate, they were usually between members of the same sex. The bond between ship-mates, those people who shared passage on the same slaver, is the most striking example. In widely scattered parts of Afro-America, the "ship-mate" relationship became a major principle of social organization and continued for decades or even centuries to shape ongoing social relations.

Moreover,

> in Jamaica, for example, we know that the term "shipmate" was "synonymous in their [the slaves'] view with 'brother or sister'" . . . "the dearest word and bond of affectionate sympathy amongst the Africans" (Kelly 1838:45, cited in Patterson 1967:150); and that "so strong were the bonds between shipmates that sexual intercourse between them, in the view of one observer, was considered incestuous" (Patterson 1967:150). We know also that the bond could extend beyond the original shipmates themselves and inter-penetrate with biological kin ties; shipmates were said to "look upon each other's children mutually as their own" (Kelly 1838:45, cited in Patterson 1967:150), and "it was customary for children to call their parents' shipmates 'uncle' and 'aunt'." (Patterson 1967:150; cf. Patterson 1972:163-4)

Chapter 3 • Between Plantation and Tourism: The Post- Emancipation Interregnum

[1]Writing after his visit to the West Indies in 1839—a trip which included a sojourn in Tortola—Joseph Gurney, a proponent of emancipation and free labor, expressed disapproval regarding the invidious imposition of rents on the recently freed blacks:

> To require of the tenant the regular payment of such rent, and legally to eject in case of non-payment of it, are neither of them proceedings to which any reasonable objection can be urged. But to require not merely

that the tenant should pay rent, but that he should work on a certain estate, at a certain rate of wages, and for a certain number of days in the
week, and to eject him if these latter provisions are not complied with—
appears to me to be unjust in principle—a recurrence, as far as it goes, to
the old system of slavery. It is the compelling of labor by a penal infliction. (Gurney 1840:246)

Not one to shy away from proffering advice to his peers, Gurney tendered the
following recommendation as an alternative approach to labor relations:

Taking it for granted then, that both justice and policy dictate a total sur-
render of every contrivance to compel the labor of the peasantry, what are
the means of which we are left in possession for procuring that labor?
I answer: First of all—fair though not extravagant wages, paid with
undeviating regularity, at a stated hour, once every week, and paid without any reference whatsoever to rent. The more I enquire into the difficulties which have arisen on some properties in Jamaica, the stronger is my
conviction of the importance of the regular and frequent payment of wages. A credit in account has a much weaker influence as a stimulus to action, especially on uneducated minds, than money placed in the hand.
(Gurney 1840:249)

[2]These figures are from Harrigan and Varlack 1975:195.

[3]See, for example, Professor Ben Cousins' recent article, "What is a 'Smallholder'?" (2010).

Chapter 4 • The Era of Tourism

[1]The responsibilities or portfolios of the Ministries at the time were distributed
as follows:

(a) *Chief Minister*
General Co-ordination of the work of Ministers; Tourism and Investment Promotion; Development Planning; Finance taking in all
subjects in purview of the Financial Secretary; Industrial Development; Public Relations and Information; Wickhams Cay Development; Trade and Industry.

(b) *The Minister of the Environment*
Housing; Agriculture; Fisheries; Lands (including Crown Lands) and
Land Registry; Minerals: Conservation; National Parks (Historical
and Archeological sites and Museums); Forestry; Co-operatives; Sur-
veys.

(c) *The Minister of Communications,*
Works & Public Utilities
Aviation (including airport management); Ports and Harbours; Post
Office; Public Works including explosives; Telecommunications; Wa-
ter and Sewerage; Electricity; Broadcasting and Television (other
than Government Broadcasting).

(d) *The Minister of Social Services*
Education; Health; Social Security; Community Development and Social Welfare; Immigration and Labour; Prisons; Juveniles; Libraries; Ecclesiastical; Cinema; Scholarships; Cemeteries. (BVI Territorial Report 1981:6,7)

[2]In the intervening years, two of the principal leaders of the Positive Action Movement, Walter L. deCastro and Noel Lloyd, have passed away. In 2009, in a ceremony to rename the Palm Grove Park as the "Noel Lloyd/Positive Action Movement Park", Premier Ralph T. O'Neal began his remarks by stating:

Ladies and gentlemen, I stand before you on this historic occasion, everlastingly grateful to the men and women of the one time hated Positive Action Movement for the bravery and courage demonstrated in securing for us all the sixty acres on Wickham's Cay and about three quarters of Anegada.

[3]One retired North American gentleman who lives in Virgin Gorda has suggested that "the solution" to the development problems of the BVI "seems to lie in very selective retirement housing":

Emphasis [should be] on retirement and winter homes. People who spend at least half the year on the island will be more careful of its tranquility and self-respect of their local neighbors. Income from residential settlement can be greater than from tourism and it stays in local pockets. And yet, the residents tend to treat the inns as their clubs. They form a year-round clientele in support of the restaurants. Development will be slower, paced so that local labour can do the construction without importing from other islands. Financing can be local, without needing to skim off profits for off-island investors. Jobs for the native population will be more varied than those from hotels. Local service business will grow up. In the long run, mainlanders also will be beneficiaries. (Hunt 1979:2-3)

[4]Until the publication of Ivor Jackson's (1981) excellent "Study of the Pleasure Boat Industry in the British Virgin Islands," there was little information readily available on the BVI charter-boat industry.

[5]By way of further illustration, 1980 Government revenue from charter-boat cruising tax alone was more than double the total 1960 recurrent revenue—$383,826 versus $186,000.

Chapter 5 • *Perceptions of Tourism and Development*

[1]British Virgin Islands Immigration law provides the following categorizations:

Residents

"Residents" cover all those who are born in the BVI (Belongers), those who have attained status and those expatriates who are permitted to live and/or work in the BVI.

Immigrants

An "Immigrant" is a non-belonger who is permitted to take up residence in the BVI. A passenger is only classified as "immigrant" on his initial entry into the Territory.

Emigrants

An "Emigrant" is a non-belonger who has been resident in the BVI and who leaves for a destination outside the BVI with the intention of taking up residence in another territory. Due to the difficulties posed by the proximity of the USVI, the large number of British Virgin Islanders resident in the USVI and the magnitude of the traffic between the BVI and USVI, belongers cannot be classified as immigrants or emigrants—always as residents—and do not have to complete Exit Cards.

Visitor

A "Visitor" is a person who enters the BVI from a place outside the BVI other than with the intention of taking up residence. Normally a visitor will be in the BVI for a short period of time.

Tourist

A "Tourist" is a visitor whose sole or main purpose of visit is for pleasure—for a holiday, to visit family or friends, for sporting or recreational purposes. It includes all the crew of bareboat charters but not the hired crew of private or charter boats.

Business Visitors

A "Business Visitor" is a person whose primary purpose of visit is in connection with his own business interests, the work of Government or a private concern in the Territory.

Chapter 6 • The Present as History

[1]The phenomenon of "incalculability" derives from the fact that "the commodity flow from stage to stage does not involve any considerable money flows. Accounting takes the form of imputing prices. There is thus a large measure of price indeterminacy" (Best 1968:308).

BIBLIOGRAPHY

Abraham, James

    1933   *Lettsome: His Life, Times, Friends and Descendants*. London: William Heinemann Medical Books.

Achison, James

    1981   "Anthropology of Fishing." *Annual Review of Anthropology*, vol. 10.

Adamson, Alan

    1975   "The Reconstruction of Plantation Labor After Emancipation: The Case of British Guiana." In *Race and Slavery in the Western Hemisphere*. Stanley Engerman and Eugene Genovese, eds.

Althusser, Louis

    1977   *For Marx*. London: NLB.

Althusser, Louis and Etienne Balibar

    1970   *Reading Capital*. New York: Pantheon Books.

Amin, Samir

    1974   *Accumulation on a World Scale: A Critique of the Theory of Underdevelopment*. New York: Monthly Review Press.

    1977   *Imperialism and Unequal Development*. New York: Monthly Review Press.

"Amway Negotiating Tax Treaty for BVI"

    1982   *The San Juan Star*, 11 April, p. 12.

Anderson, John

    1975   *Night of the Silent Drums: A Narrative of Slave Rebellion in the Virgin Islands*. New York: Charles Scribner's Sons.

Aptheker, Herbert

    1977   Discussant: "Slave Revolts, Resistance, and Implications for Post Emancipation Society." In *Comparative Perspectives. . . .* Rubin and Tuden, eds.

Arnett, Vernon

    1967   Foreword. In *The Democratic Revolution in the West Indies*. Wendell Bell, ed. Cambridge, MA: Schenkman Publ. Co.

Baker, E. C.

    1965   *A Guide to Records in the Leeward Islands*. Oxford: Basil Blackwell/University of the West Indies.

Barclay, Richard

    1979   "A Commercial Banker's Attitude Towards Tourism." In *Caribbean Tourism: Policies and Impacts*. Jean Holder, ed.

Beckford, George

    1972   *Persistent Poverty: Underdevelopment in Plantation Economics of the Third World*. New York: Oxford University Press.

    1978   "Peasant Movements and Agrarian Problems in the West Indies: Aspects of the Present Conflict Between the Plantation and the Peasantry in the West Indies". *Caribbean Quarterly*, Vol. 18 (1), March.

Beckford, George (ed.)

    1975   *Caribbean Economy: Dependence and Backwardness*. Mona, Jamaica: University of the West Indies, Institute of Social and Economic Research.

Beckford, William

    1790   *A Descriptive Account of the Island of Jamaica*. 2 vols. London: Printed for T. and J. Egerton.

Belisario, A. M.

    1811   *The Trial of Arthur Hodge*. London: J. Harding.

Best, Lloyd

    1968   "Outlines of a Model of Pure Plantation Economy." *Social and Economic Studies*. Jamaica: University of the West Indies (September).

    1975   "Biography of Labour." In *Caribbean Economy: Dependence and Backwardness*. George Beckford, ed. Mona, Jamaica: University of the West Indies, Institute of Social and Economic Research.

Billerbeck, K. and Y. Yasugi

    1979   "Private Direct Foreign Investment in Developing Countries." Washington, D.C.: World Bank, Working Paper No. 348.

Blackburn, Robin

    1973   *Ideology in Social Science: Readings in Critical Social Theory*. New York: Vintage/Random House.

Bluestein, William

    1982   "The Class Relations of the Hacienda and the Village in Prerevolutionary Morelos." *Latin American Perspectives*, vol. 9 (3).

Boissevian, Jeremy

    1978   "Tourism and Development in Malta." In Tourism *and Economic Change: Studies in Third World Societies*, 6: 37-56

Bontemps, Arna (ed.)

    1969   *Great Slaves Narratives*. Boston: Beacon Press.

Bottomley, Anthony, Michael Hartnett, and Vaughan Evans

    1976   "Is Tourist Residential Development Worthwhile? The Anegada Project." *Social and Economic Studies*, 25: 1-33.

Bowen, W. Errol

    1976   "Development, Immigration, and Politics in a Pre-Industrial Society: A Study of Social Change in the British Virgin Islands in the 1960s." *Caribbean Studies*, 16 (1): 67-85.

Brathwaite, Edward Kamau

1977   Discussant, "Research Problems and Implications for Contemporary Society." In *Comparative Perspectives on Slavery in New World Plantation Societies.* Vera Rubin and Arthur Tuden, eds.

Brislin, Richard

1981   *Cross-Cultural Encounters: Fact-to-Face Interaction.* New York: Pergamon Press.

British Virgin Islands Budget Estimates

1983   Tortola: Office of the Financial Secretary

The British Virgin Islands Economic Development Programme, 1979-1982

1979   Tortola: United Nations Development Programme Socio-Economic Development Planning. (Project BVI/77.001).

British Virgin Islands Territorial Report

1981   Tortola: Office of the Deputy Governor.

Bryden, John

1973   *Tourism and Development: A Case Study of the Commonwealth Caribbean.* London: Cambridge University Press.

Burkart, A. and S. Medlik

1974   *Tourism, Past, Present and Future.* London: Heinemann.

Burns, Alan

1954   *History of the British West Indies.* London: George Allen and Unwin.

Caines, Clement

1801   *Letters on the Cultivation of the Otaheite Cane.* London.

Carkhuff, Victoria

1980   "Swinging Down South." *Sail*, March: 23, 24.

Castello, Manuel

1979   "Immigrant Workers and Class Struggles in Advanced Capitalism: The Western European Experience." In *Peasants and Proletarians: The Struggles of Third World Workers.* Robin Cohen et al., eds.

Caulfields, Mina Davis

1974   "Culture and Imperialism: Proposing a New Dialect. In *Reinventing Anthropology.* Dell Hymes, ed.

"Chief Minister Gives Statement on Present Status of Negotiations...

1982   ...with the U.S. Treasury on the Matter of Double Taxation." *The Island Sun*, 20 November, p. 3.

Clarke, Edith

1971   "Land Tenure and the Family in Four Selected Communities in Jamaica." In *Peoples and Cultures of the Caribbean.* Michael Horowitz, ed.

Codrington, Mitchell

1977   Review of *A History of the British Virgin Islands 1672-1970*, by Isaac Dookhan, and of the Virgin Islands Story, by Norwell Harrigan and

Pearl Varlack In *The Review of Black Political Economy*, Vol. 7:2 (Winter).

Cohen, Colleen B.

2010   *Take Me to My Paradise: Tourism and Nationalism in the British Virgin Islands*. New Brunswick: Rutgers University Press.

Cohen, Robin, et al. (eds.)

1979   *Peasants and Proletarians: The Struggles of Third World Workers*. New York: HarperCollins.

Cohen, Robin, et al.

1982   "Researcher Urges BVI to Rid Sex from Image." *The San Juan Star*, 16 June, p. 10.

Comitas, Lambros and David Lowenthal (eds.)

1973   *Slaves, Free Men, Citizens: West Indian Perspectives*. New York: Anchor/Doubleday.

Coombs, Orde

1974   *Is Massa Day Dead? Black Moods in the Caribbean*. New York: Anchor/Doubleday.

Cousins, Ben

2010   "What is a Smallholder? Class-analytic Perspectives on Small-scale Farming and Agrarian Reform in South Africa." Institute for Poverty, Land and Agrarian Studies, University of the Western Cape (Working Paper 16).

Craton, Michael

1974   *Sinews of Empire: A Short History of British Slavery*. New York: Anchor Books.

1978   *Searching for the Invisible Man: Slaves and Plantation Life in Jamaica*. Cambridge, MA: Harvard University Press.

Craton, Michael and James Walvin

1970   *A Jamaican Plantation: The History of Worthy Park 1670-1970*. University of Toronto Press.

Cross, Malcolm and Arnaud Marks

1979   *Peasants, Plantations and Rural Communities in the Caribbean*. Great Britain: University of Surrey and Royal Institute of Linguistics and Anthropology.

Curtin, Philip

1974   "The Black Experience of Colonialism and Imperialism." In *Slavery, Colonialism and Racism*. Mintz, ed.

1977   "Slavery and Empire." In *Comparative Perspectives on Slavery*. Vera Rubin and Arthur Tuden, eds.

Dalton, George

1972   "Peasantries in Anthropology and History." *Current Anthropology*, vol. 13 (3-4): 385-415.

David, Paul, et al.

1976   *Reckoning with Slavery: A Critical Study in the Quantitative History of American Negro Slavery*. New York: Oxford University Press.

Davis, David B.

1971 "The Continuing Contradiction of Slavery: A Comparison of British America and Latin America." In *The Debate over "Slavery"*. J. Lane, ed.

1974 "Slavery and the Post-World War II Historians." In *Slavery, Colonialism and Racism*. Sidney Mintz, ed.

Davis, Horace

1978 *Toward a Marxist Theory of Nationalism*. New York: Monthly Review Press.

Deere, Carmen

1979 "Rural Women's Subsistence Production in the Capitalist Periphery." *Peasants and Proletarians: The Struggles of Third World Workers.* Robin Cohen et al., eds.

de Kadt, Emanuel

1979 *Tourism: Passport to Development?* New York: Oxford University Press.

1979 "Arts, Craft, and Cultural Manifestations." In *Tourism: Passport to Development?* Emanuel de Kadt, ed.

1979 "Effects of Tourism on Life Chances and Welfare." In *Tourism: Passport to Development?* Emanuel de Kadt, ed.

1979 "The Encounter: Changing Values and Attitudes." In *Tourism: Passport to Development?* Emanuel de Kadt, ed.

Delbecq, A. and A. Van de Ven

1971 "A Group Process Model for Problem Identification and Program Planning." *Journal of Applied Behavioral Science*, vol. 4.

Derman, William and Michael Levin

1977 "Peasants, Propoganda, Economics and Exploitation: A Response to Dalton." *American Anthropologist*, vol. 79 (1).

Diamond, Stanley

1974 *In Search of the Primitive: A Critique of Civilization*. Piscataway, NJ: Transaction Books.

1979 *Towards a Marxist Anthropology: Problems and Perspectives*. The Hague: Mouton.

Dirks, Robert

1975 "Ethnicity and Ethnic Group Relations in the British Virgin Islands." In *1973 Proceedings of the American Ethnological Society*. John W. Bennett, ed. St. Paul, MN: West Publishing Co.

Dookhan, Isaac

1974 *A History of the Virgin Islands of the United States*. Essex, England: Caribbean Universities Press/Bowker.

1975 *A History of the British Virgin Islands, 1672 to 1970*. Essex, England: Caribbean Universities Press/Bowker.

Dougherty, Phillip

1972 "Selling the Sunny *Je Ne Sais Quoi*." *New York Times*, 2 January.

Downing, Theodore

1982   "The Internationalization of Capital in Agriculture." *Human Organization*, vol. 41 (3): 269-277.

Drake, St. Clair

1980   "Anthropology and the Black Experience." *The Black Scholar*, 11 (7): 2-31.

Drescher, Seymour

1977   "Capitalism and the Decline of Slavery: The British Case in Comparative Perspective." In *Compariative Perspectives on Slavery*. Vera Rubin and Arthur Tuden, eds.

Dunn, Richard

1973   *Sugar and Slaves: The Rise of the Planter Class in the English West Indies, 1624-1713*. New York: W.W. Norton and Co.

Dunn, Stephen

1976   "On the Exploitation of Peasants: A Response to Dalton." *American Anthropologist*, vol. 78 (3).

Eadie, Hazel

1931   *Lagooned in the Virgin Islands*. London: George Routledge and Sons.

Edwards, Bryan

1793   *The History, Civil and Commercial, of the British Colonies in the West Indies*. 3 vols. London.

Edwards, Richard, et al.

1978   *The Capitalist System*. New Jersey: Prentice-Hall.

Elkins, Stanley

1959   *Slavery: A Problem in American Institutional and Intellectual Life*. Chicago: University of Chicago Press.

Engerman, Stanley and Eugene Genovese

1975   *Race and Slavery in the Western Hemisphere: Quantitative Studies*. New Jersey: Princeton University Press.

Ennew, Judith, Paul Hirst and Keith Tribe

1977   " 'Peasantry' as an Economic Category." *Journal of Peasant Studies*, vol. 4

Evans, Nancy H.

1978   "Tourism and Cross-Cultural Communication." In *Tourism and Behavior: Studies in Third World Societies*, 5: 41-53. Virginia: College of William and Mary.

Evans, Vaughan

1975   *Statistical Abstract of the British Virgin Islands*. Statistical Office, Finance Department, Road Town.

Fanon, Frantz

1967   *Black Skin, White Masks*. New York: Grove Press.

1968   *The Wretched of the Earth*. New York: Grove Press.

Faulkner, D. E.

1962   *Report on Livestock Development in the British Virgin Islands.*
        Federal House, Trinidad: The Interim Commission for the West In-
        dies.

Finley, M. I.

1968   "Slavery." *International Encyclopedia of the Social Sciences*, ed.
        David I. Sills. Vol. 14. New York: Macmillan/Free Press.

Firth, Raymond

1951   *Elements of Social Organization.* London: Watts.

Fishlock, W. C.

1912   *The Virgin Islands, B.W.I.: A Handbook of General Information.*
        London: Waterlow and Sons.

Fitzhugh, George

[1857, orig.] 1960 *Cannibals All! or, Slaves Without Masters.* Cambridge,
        MA: Harvard University Press.

Foner, Laura and Eugene Genovese (eds.)

1969   *Slavery in the New World: A Reader in Comparative History.*
        Englewood Cliffs, NJ: Prentice-Hall.

Foster, George

1965   "Peasant Society and the Image of Limited Good." *American An-
        thropologist*, vol. 67: 293-315.

Fox-Genovese, Elizabeth

1975   "Poor Richard at Work in the Cotton Fields: A Critique of the Psy-
        chological and Ideological Presuppositions of 'Time on the Cross'."
        The Review of Radical Political Economics, vol. 7 (3).

Franginals, Moreno

1977   Personal correspondence with Sidney Mintz. Cited in Mintz, "The So-
        Called World System. . . ."

Frampton, A. and H. C. Briggs

1958   "The British Virgin Islands: Report and Development Programme."
        Road Town, Tortola.

Frederickson, George M.

1976   "The Gutman Report." *The New York Review of Books*, Sept. 30, vol.
        XXIII (15).

Fronde, James

[1880, orig.] 1973 "The English in the West: or, The Bow of Ulysses." In
        Slaves, Free Men, Citizens. Comitas and Lowenthal, eds.

Frucht, Richard

1971   "A Caribbean Social Type: Neither "Peasant' nor 'Proletarian'." In
        Peoples and Cultures of the Caribbean. Michael Horowitz, ed.

Genovese, Eugene

1971   *Roll, Jordan, Roll: The World the Slaves Made.* New York: Panthe-
        on.

1975   "Class, Culture and Historical Process." *Dialectical Anthropology*,
        vol. 1 (1).

Genovese, Eugene (ed.)

1973   *The Slave Economies, vol. 1: Historical and Theoretical Perspectives*. New York. John Wiley & Sons.

Geertz, Clifford

1962   "Studies in Peasant Life: Community and Society." *Biennial Review of Anthropology*. Stanford, CA: Stanford University Press.

Geras, Norman

1978   Althusser's Marxism: An Assessment." In *Western Marxism: A Critical Reader*. London: New Left Review/Verso Editions.

Geshekter, Charles L.

1978   "International Tourism and African Underdevelopment: Some Reflections on Kenya." In *Tourism and Economic Change: Studies in Third World Societies*, 6: 57-88.

Girvan, Norman

1967   "Regional Integration vs. Company Integration in the Utilization of Caribbean Bauxite." In *Caribbean Integration: Papers on Social, Political and Economic Integration*. Sybil Lewis and Thomas Matthews, eds. University of Puerto Rico: Institute of Caribbean Studies.

1975   *Aspects of the Political Economy of Race in the Caribbean and the Americas*. Atlanta: The Institute of the Black World.

Goveia, Elsa

1965   *Slave Society in the British Leeward Islands at the End of the Eighteenth Century*. New Haven: Yale University Press.

Graburn, Nelson

1977   "Tourism: The Sacred Journey." In *Hosts and Guests*. Valene Smith, ed.

Graham, John

1969   "British Virgin Islands: Sunny Success Story." *The Financial Times*, 12 August, p. 19.

Gratus, Jack

1973   *The Great White Lie: Slavery, Emancipation and Changing Racial Attitudes*. New York: Monthly Review Press.

Gray, Lewis

1941   *History of Agriculture in the Southern United States to 1860*. New York: P. Smith.

Green, Reginald

1977   "Toward Planning Tourism in African Countries." In *Tourism: Passport to Development*. Emanuel de Kadt, ed.

Greenwood, Davydd

1977   "Culture by the Pound: An Anthropological Perspective on Tourism as Cultural Commoditization. In *Hosts and Guests*. Valene Smith, ed.

Gurney, Joseph John

1840   *A Winter in the West Indies, Described in Familiar Letters to Henry Clay of Kentucky*. London: John Murray.

Gutman, Herbert

1975   *Slavery and the Numbers Game: A Critique of "Time on the Cross".* Urbana: University of Illinois Press.

Gwaltney, John

1979   "Up from Malinowski: Notes on Native Anthropology." *Notes from ABA* [Association of Black Anthropologists] vol. 6 (3-4).

1980   *Drylongso: A Self-Portrait of Black America.* New York: Random House.

Hall, Douglas

1964   "Absentee-Proprietorship in the British West Indies, to about 1850." *Jamaican Historical Review*, vol. 4 pp. 15-34. (Reprinted in Comitas and Lowenthal 1973).

1971   *Five of the Leeward Islands 1834-1870: The Major Problems of the Post-Emancipation Period in Antigua, Barbuda, Montserrat, Nevis and St. Kitts.* London: Ginn/Caribbean Universities Press.

Hannerz, Ulf

1974   *Caymanian Politics: Structure and Style in a Changing Island Society.* Stockholm: University of Stockholm.

Harewood, Jack

1975   "West Indian People." In *Caribbean Economy.* George Beckford, ed.

Harrigan, Birney

1986   "The Political and Economic Dynamics of the Tourist Industry in the Virgin Islands." Ph.D. dissertation, University of Pittsburgh.

Harrigan, Norwell

1982   "Social Change in the British Virgin Islands: An Overview." Keynote address, delivered at the BVI Mental Health Association Symposium of Social Change, Tortola, BVI 20-22 May, 1982.

Harrigan, Norwell and Pearl Varlack

1970   *The British Virgin Islands: A Chronology.* Tortola, BVI: Research and Consulting Services, Ltd.

1975   *The Virgin Islands Story.* Essex, England: Caribbean Universities Press/ Bowker.

Harrington, Michael

1976   *The Twilight of Capitalism.* New York: Simon and Schuster.

Harris, Marvin

1968   *The Rise of Anthropological Theory: A History of Theories of Culture.* New York: Crowell.

Haskell, Thomas

1974   "Were Slaves More Efficient? Some Doubts About 'Time on the Cross'." *The New York Review of Books*, vol. XXI:14. (Sept. 19).

1975   "The True and Tragic History of 'Time on the Cross'." *The New York Review of Books*, 22:15 (October 2).

Hawkins, Donald, et al. (eds.)

1980   *Tourism Planning and Development Issues.* Washington, D.C.: George Washington University.

Hiller, Herbert

1975   "Escapism, Penetration and Response: Industrial Tourism and the Caribbean." *Caribbean Studies*, 16 (2): 92-116.

Hobsbawn, E. J.

1973   "Peasants and Politics." *Journal of Peasant Studies*, vol. 1 (1).

Holder, Jean

1979   "Transforming Caribbean Tourism—A Question of Attitudes." In *Caribbean Tourism: Policies and Impacts*. Jean Holder, ed.

1983   "Fighting the Tourism War Together." *The Island Sun* (Tortola), 19 February, pp. 13-14.

Holder, Jean (ed.)

1979   *Caribbean Tourism: Policies and Impacts*. Barbados: Caribbean Tourism Research and Development Centre.

Horowitz, Michael (ed.)

1971   *Peoples and Cultures of the Caribbean: An Anthropological Reader*. New York: The Natural History Press/Doubleday.

Horowitz, Michael (ed.)

1971   "A Typology of Rural Community Forms in the Caribbean." In *Peoples and Cultures of the Caribbean*. Michael Horowitz, ed.

Howell, Christopher

1978   "Tourism in Tortola, British Virgin Islands: Perceptions Toward Land Carrying Capacity." Ph.D. dissertation, University of Florida.

Hsu, Francis

1973   "Prejudice and Its Intellectual Effect in American Anthropology: An Ethnographic Report." *American Anthropologist*, vol. 75: 1-19.

Hughes, Everett C.

1975   "Colonies, Colonization and Colonialism." In *The New Ethnicity: Perspective from Ethnology*. 1973 Proceedings of American Ethnological Society. John W. Bennet, ed.

Hunt, Sydney

1979   *How to Retire in the British Virgin Islands: Virgin Gorda*. St. Thomas, USVI: St. Thomas Graphics.

Hurston, Zora Neale

[1935]   1970 *Mules and Men*. New York: Harper and Row.

Hymes, Dell (ed.)

1974   *Reinventing Anthropology*. New York: Vintage Books.

Irish, Georgia Lee

1980   "Life in the '30s as Remembered." *Virgin Islands Daily News* [St. Thomas, USVI] 50th Anniversary Edition, August 1.

Jackson, Ivor

1981   *Study of the Pleasure Boat Industry in the British Virgin Islands with Emphasis on Charter Boats*. World Tourism Organization. (Available from Chief Minister's Office, Tortola).

Jenkins, Charles

    1923   *Tortola: A Quaker Experiment of Long Ago in the Tropics*. London: Friend's Bookshop.

Jenkins, C. L.

    1980   "Tourism Policies in Developing Countries: A Critique." *International Journal of Tourism Management*, 1 (1), March: 22-29.

Johnson, Dale

    1982   "Observations on Rural Class Relations". *Latin Perspectives,* vol. 9 (3).

Johnson, R. Boyd

    1978   "The Role of Tourism in Tongan Culture." In *Tourism and Behavior: Studies in Third World Societies*, 5:35-68. Virginia: College of William and Mary.

Jones, Robert

    1980   "The Low-Key Islands." *Sports Illustrated*, 4 February, pp. 52-59.

Jones, W.

    1968   "Plantations". *International Encyclopedia of the Social Sciences,* vol. 12. New York: Macmillan/Free Press.

Jordan, Winthrop

    1968   *White Over Black: American Attitudes Toward the Negro, 1550-1812*. Chapel Hill: University of North Carolina Press.

    1977   "Planter and Slave Identity Formation: Some Problems in the Comparative Approach." In *Comparative Perspective on Slavery*. Rubin and Tuden, eds.

Kahn, Herman

    1980   "Tourism and the Next Decade." In *Tourism Planning and Development Issues*. Donald Hawkins et al., eds.

Kidder, Daniel (ed.)

    1852   *Tortola and the Native Missionary*. New York: Lane and Scott.

Koestler, Arthur

    1969   "Fiji." *The Atlantic*, 224 (4), October: 18-25.

Krigger, Marilyn

    1980   "The Virgin Islands: A Kaleidoscope of People." *The Virgin Islands Daily News* [St. Thomas, USVI], 50th Anniversary Edition, August 1.

Lane, Ann J. (ed.)

    1971   *The Debate over "Slavery": Stanley Elkins and His Critics*. Urbana, IL: University of Illinois Press.

Lascelles, Roger

    1976   *Report and Recommendations to the Government of the British Virgin Islands on Tourism Policies*. London.

Lett, James W. Jr.

    1980   "Tourism and Culture Change on Virgin Gorda: Perspectives on Patterns and Processes." M.A. Thesis, University of Florida.

1982   "The British Virgin Islands Tourism Industry: Problems and Pro-
        spects in the 1980's." Paper Presented at VII Annual Meeting, Carib-
        bean Studies Association, Jamaica, 27 May.

Letters from the Virgin Islands Illustrating Life and Manners in the West Indies
1843   London: John Van Voorst.

Levitt, Kari and Igbal Gulati
1970   "Income Effect of Tourist Spending: Mystification Multiplied—A
        Critical Comment on the Zinder Report." *Social and Economic
        Studies*, 19 (3).

Levitt, Kari and Lloyd Best
1975   "Character of Caribbean Economy." In *Caribbean Economy:
        Dependence and Backwardness*. George Beckford, ed.

Lewis, Gordon
1968   *The Growth of the Modern West Indies*. London: McGibbon and
        Kee.

1972   *The Virgin Islands: A Caribbean Lilliput*. Evanston, IL: Northwest-
        ern University Press.

Lewis, Mary A.
1971   "Slavery and Personality." In *The Debate over Slavery*. Ann J. Lane,
        ed.

Lewis, W. Arthur
1936   *The Evolution of the Peasantry in the West Indies*. London: Colonial
        Office.

Lewisohn, Florence
1965   *Tales of Tortola and the British Virgin Islands*. Florida: Interna-
        tional Graphics, Inc.

Lincoln, Shirley
1980   "Travellers' Views of the Virgin Islands." *The Virgin Islands Daily
        News* [St. Thomas, USVI], 50th Anniversary Edition, August 1.

Long, Edward
1774   *History of Jamaica*. 2 vols. London.

Loukissas, Philippos
1978   "Tourism and Environment in Conflict: The Case of the Greek Island
        of Myconos." In *Tourism and Economic Change: Studies in the
        Third World Societies*, 5: 105-132.

Lowenthal, David
1972   *West Indian Societies*. New York: Oxford University Press.

Lukas, J. Anthony
1971   "The Pliant of the Virgin Islands." *The New York Times Magazine*,
        18 April.

Lundbery, Donald
1974   *The Tourist Business*. Boston: Cahners Book.

MacCannell, Dean
1976   *The Tourist: A New Theory of the Leisure Class*. New York:
        Schocken Books.

Madden, R. R.

  1835   *A Twelve Month's Residence in the West Indies*. 2 vols. London: James Cochran.

"The Maldives: An Introductory Economic Report"

  1980   Washington, D.C.: The World Bank.

Mandel, Ernest

  1970   *Marxist Economic Theory*. Vol. 1 New York: Monthly Review Press.

Manigat, Leslie

  1977   "The Relationship Between Marronage and Slave Revolts and Revolution in St. Dominigue-Haiti." In *Comparative Perspectives on Slavery*. Ruben and Tuden, eds.

Marshall, Woodville K.

  1968   "Notes on Peasant Development in the West Indies Since 1838." *Social and Economic Studies*, vol. 17 (3): 252-263.

  1978   "Peasant Movements and Agrarian Problems in the West Indies: Aspects of the Development of the Peasantry." *Caribbean Quarterly*, vol. 18 (1), March.

Maruyama, Magorah

  1974   "Endogenous Research vs. Delusions of Relevance and Expertise Among Exogenous Academics." *Human Organization*, 33: 318-22.

Marx, Karl

  [1852, orig.] 1972 *The Eighteenth Brumaire of Louis Bonaparte*. In *The Marx-Engels Reader*. Robert Tucker, ed.

  [1857, orig.] "The Indian Revolt." *The New York Tribune*, September 16. In *Karl Marx on Colonialism and Modernization*. Shlomo Avenei, ed.

  [1859, orig.] 1972 *A Contribution to the Critique of Political Economy*. In *The Marx-Engels Reader*. Robert Tucker, ed.

  [1867, orig.] 1976 *Capital: A Critique of Political Economy*. Vol. 1. New York: International Publishers.

Maurer, Bill

  1997   *Recharting the Caribbean: Land, Law, and Citizenship in the British Virgin Islands*. Ann Arbor, MI: University of Michigan Press.

McGlynn, Frank

  1980   "Marginality and Flux: An Afro-Caribbean Community Through Two Centuries." Ph.D. dissertation, University of Pittsburgh.

McQueen, James

  1824   *The West India Colonies: The Calumnies and Misrepresentations Circulated Against Them by the Edinburgh Review, Mr. Clarkson, Mr. Cooper, (et al.)*. London: Baldwin, Cradock and Joy.

Meillassoux, Claude

  1973   "The Social Organization of the Peasantry: The Economic Basis of Kinship." *Journal of Peasant Studies*, vol. 1 (1).

Memmi, Albert

  1967   *The Colonizer and the Colonized*. Boston: Beacon Press.

Merivale, Herman

    1841   *Lectures on Colonization and Colonies.* London: Longman et al.

Mills, Frank

    1976   "Production Relationships Among Small-Scale Farmers in St. Kitts." *Social and Economic Studies*, vol. 25 (2): 153-176.

Mintz, Sidney

    1968   "Caribbean Society." *International Encyclopedia of the Social Sciences*, ed. David I. Sills. New York: Macmillan/Free Press.

    1973   "A Note on the Definition of Peasantries." *Journal of Peasant Studies*, vol. 1 (1).

    1974   *Caribbean Transformations.* Chicago: Aldine.

    1974   "The Rural Proletariat and the Problems of Rural Proletarian Consciousness." *Journal of Peasant Studies*, vol. 1 (3): 291-325.

    1975a   "The Social World System: Local Initiative and Local Response." *Dialectical Anthropology*, vol. 2 (4).

    1975b   "History and Anthropology: A Brief Reprise." In *Race and Slavery in the Western Hemisphere*. Stanley Engerman and Eugene Genovese, eds.

    1978   "Was the Plantation Slave a Proletarian?" *Review*, vol. 2 (1): 81-98.

Mintz, Sidney (ed.)

    1974   *Slavery, Colonialism and Racism.* New York: Norton.

Mintz, Sidney and Richard Price

    1976   *An Anthropological Approach to the Afro-American Past: A Caribbean Perspective.* Philadelphia: Institute for the Study of Human Issues.

Montoya, Rodrigo

    1982   "Class Relations in the Andean Counrtyside." *Latin American Perspectives*, vol. 9 (3).

Moore, George

    1979   "Incorporating Offshore." *Caribbean Life and Times*, 1 (2): 35-6.

Muller, Viana

    1979   "The Revolutionary Fate of the Peasantry". *Dialectical Anthropology*, vol. 4 (3).

Mullin, Michael

    1977   "Slave Obeahman and Slaveowning Patriarchs in an Era of War and Revolution (1776-1807)." In *Comparative Perspectives. . .* Rubin and Tuden, eds.

Nash, Dennison

    1977   "Tourism as a Form of Imperialism." In *Hosts and Guests: The Anthropology of Tourism*. Valene Smith, ed.

    1978   "An Anthropological Approach to Tourism." In *Tourism and Economic Change: Studies in Third World Societies*, 6: 133-152.

Nash, June

    1981   "Ethnographic Aspects of the World Capitalist System". *Annual Review of Anthropology*, vol. 10.

Nolan, Sidney D. Jr.,

1978 Variations in Travel Behavior and the Cultural Impact of Tourism."
In Tourism and Behavior: Studies in Third World Societies, 5: 1-
17.

Norman, A. Osorio

[1920] Unpublished Poems. Cited in Harrigan and Varlack, *The Virgin
Islands Story.*

Nunez, Theron

1977 "Touristic Studies in Anthropological Perspective." In *Hosts and
Guests*, Valene Smith, ed.

O'laughlin, Bridget

1975 "Marxist Approaches in Anthropology." *Annual Review of Anthropology*, vol. 4.

Oliver, Melvin L

1976 Review of "Time on the Cross", by Fogel and Engerman, and of
"Roll, Jordan, Roll", by Genovese. *Telos*, vol. 9:2 (Summer).

O'Loughlin, Carleen

1962 "A Survey of Economic Potential, Fiscal Structure and Capital
Requirements of the British Virgin Islands." *Social and Economic
Studies*, U.W.I., vol. 11:3.

Olwig, Karen Fog Pedersen

1977 "Households, Exchange and Social Reproduction: The Development of a Caribbean Society." Ph.D. dissertation, University of
Minnesota.

Parliamentary Papers

1824a "Papers Relating to the Slave Trade: Viz. Copies and Extracts of the
Correspondence Between the Lords Commissioners of the Admiral-
ty and Naval Officers, since the 1st January 1823, not already laid
before the House of Commons."

Parliamentary Papers

[1824]b "Third Report of Commissioner on Civil and Criminal Justice in the
West Indies.

Parliamentary Papers

1825 "Papers Relating to Slaves in Tortola: . . . Information. . . [and]
Judicial Proceedings which have taken place in the Island of Tortola
in consequence of some alleged acts of Rebellion or Insubordination
of certain slaves. . . "

Patterson, Orlando

1967 *The Sociology of Slavery.* London: McGibbon and Kee.

Peck, John and Alice Lepie

1977 "Tourism and Development in Three North Carolina Coastal
Towns." In *Hosts and Guests*. Valene Smith, ed.

Phillippo, James

1843 *Jamaica: Its Past and Present State.* London: John Snow.

Phillips, William

1966 *A Report on the British Virgin Islands with Recommendations on Measures of Accelerating Economic and Social Development.* Tortola: BVI Government (UNDP).

Pickering, Vernon W

1983 *Early History of the British Virgin Islands: From Columbus to Emancipation.* New York: Falcon Publications International.

Pitman, F. W.

1926 "Slavery on the British West Indies Plantations in the Eighteenth Century." *Journal of Negro History*, vol. XI, pp. 584-668.

Pool, Ithiela de Sola

1965 "Effects of Cross-National Contact on National and International Images." In *International Behavior: Socio-Psychological Analysis.* New York: Holt, Rinehart and Winston. Herbert Kelman, ed.

Post, K. W. J.

1979 "The Alliance of Peasants and Workers: Some Problems Concerning the Articulation of Class (Algeria and China)." In *Peasants and Proletarians.* Robin Cohen et al., eds.

Poulantzas, Nicos

1978 *Political Power and Social Class.* London: Verso Editions.

Price, Richard (ed.)

1973 *Maroon Societies: Rebel Slave Communities in the Americas.* New York: Anchor/Doubleday.

Raghavan, Sushila

1963 "Social Stratification in Tortola, British Virgin Islands." M.A. thesis, Brandeis University.

Regatz, L.J.

1928 *The Fall of the Planter Class in the British Caribbean 1763-1833.* New York: American Historical Association/The Century Co.

Redfield, Robert

1956 *Peasant Society and Culture.* Chicago: University of Chicago Press.

"Remarks by the Premier at the Ceremony to Rename the Palm Grove Park to the Noel Lloyd/Positive Action Movement Park"

2009 Government of The British Virgin Islands, London Office, 1 March. http://www.bvi.org.uk/government/pressreleases/premiersremark atpalmgroveparkrename

Report of the Development Advisory Committee

1966 Tortola, BVI Government.

Review of the Quarterly Review: or, An Exposure of the Erroneous Opinions...

1824 *...Promulgated in That Work on the Subject of Colonial Slavery. . .* London: J. Hatchard and Son.

Rice, C. Duncan

1975 *The Rise and Fall of Black Slavery.* New York: Harper and Row.

1977   "Enlightenment, Evangelism and Economics: An Interpretation of the Drive Towards Emancipation in British West India." In *Comparative Perspectives on Slavery*. Rubin and Tuden, eds.

Richardson, Evelyn

1980   "The Fish Market." *The Virgin Islands Daily News* (St. Thomas, USVI), 50th Anniversary Edition, August 1.

Rohlehr, Gordon

1974   "History as Absurdity." In Orde Coombs, *Is Massa Day Dead?*

Rodney, Walter

1981   "Guyana: The Making of the Labour Force." *Race and Class,* vol. XXII (4).

Rose, Willie Lee (ed.)

1976   *A Documentary History of Slavery in North America.* New York: Oxford University Press.

Roseberry, William

1978   "Peasants in Primitive Accumulation: Western Europe and Venezuela Compared." *Dialectical Anthropology*, vol. 3 (3): 243-260.

Rubin, Vera and Arthur Tuden

1977   *Comparative Perspectives on Slavery in New World Plantation Societies.* New York: Annals of the New York Academy of Sciences, vol. 292.

Ruiz de la Mata, Beatriz

1981   "P. R. (Puerto Rico) Firms Exploit Tortola Tax Haven." *Caribbean Business*, 27 May, pp. 1-2.

San Juan Star, The

1982   New York Times News Service Article on BVI-U.S.A. Tax Treaty. 16 January.

Schaw, Janet

1939   *Journal of a Lady of Quality.* Edited by E. W. Andrews and C.M. Andrews, New Haven, CT. (The Journal is based on the author's visit to the West Indies shortly before the American War of Independence).

Schuler, Monica

1977   Discussant: "Slave Images and Identities." In *Comparative Perspectives on Slavery*. Rubin and Tuden, eds.

Selowsky, Marcelo

1979   "Balancing Trickle Down and Basic Needs Strategies." Staff Working Paper No. 335. Washington, D.C.: The World Bank.

Sen, Amartya

1980   "Levels of Poverty: Policy and Change." Working Paper No. 410. Washington, D.C.: The World Bank.

Sethna, Rustum

1979   "The Caribbean Tourism Product —An Appraisal." In *Caribbean Tourism: Policies and Impacts*. Jean Holder, ed.

"The Seychelles: Economic Memorandum"
  1980   Washington, D.C.: The World Bank.
Sewell, William
  [1861, orig.]   1973   "The Ordeal of Free Labour in the West Indies." In
                Slaves, Free Men, Citizens. Comitas and Lowenthal, eds.
Shanin, Teodor
  1971   "Peasantry as a Political Factor." In *Peasants and Peasant Socie-
                ties.* Teodor Shanin, ed.
  1972   "The Nature and Logic of the Peasant Economy." *Journal of Peas-
                ant Studies*, vol. 1:1 (pp. 186-205).
Shankland Cox and Associates
  1972   "Tortola, British Virgin Islands: A Development Plan for Wickhams
                Cay." U.K.: Shankland Cox.
Singleman, Peter, et al.
  1982   "Land Without Liberty: Continuities of Peripheral Capitalist Devel-
                opment and Peasant Exploitation Among the Cane Growers of Mo-
                relos, Mexico." *Latin America Perspectives*, vol. 9 (3).
Skelton, Douglas
  1969   "British Virgin Islands: A More Professional Approach Comes to
                Tourism." *The Financial Times*, 12 August, p. 21.
"The Slave Colonies of Great Britain or a Picture of Negro Slavery drawn by...
  1825   ...the Colonists themselves; being an Abstract of the Various Papers
                Recently Laid Before Parliament on that subject." n.n.
Smith, Adam
  [1776, orig.]   1970   *The Wealth of Nations.* New York: Penguin Books.
Smith, Katherine A.
  2009   "Forging an Identity: British Virgin Islands' Slave Society 1672–
                1838." Ph.D. dissertation, Howard University.
Smith, Valene (ed.)
  1977   *Hosts and Guests: The Anthropology of Tourism.* Philadelphia,
                PA: University of Pennsylvania Press.
Statistical Abstract of the BVI
  1974   Tortola: BVI Government.
Stewart, John
  1823   *A View of the Past and Present State of the Island of Jamaica.*
                Edinburgh: Oliver and Boyd.
Stock, Robert
  1976   "Of Tourism and the Soul: The Caribbean Dilemma." *The New
                York Times*, 13 June.
Stoutt, H. Lavity
  1982   *Annual Development of the Territory Address. Part I: Tourism
                Development.* Tortola: BVI Government Information Office.

Stuckey, Sterling

1971   "Though the Prism of Folklore: The Black Ethos in Slavery." In *The Debate over "Slavery"*. Ann J. Lane, ed.

Suckling, George

1780   *An Historical Account of the Virgin Islands in the West Indies.* London: Benjamin White.

Thompson, Edgar T.

1960   "The Plantation Cycle and Problems of Typology." In *Caribbean Studies: A Symposium.* Vera Rubin, ed.

Todman, McW.

1969   "A Historical Review of Constitutional and Economic Development in the BVI." *West Indies Chronicle*, vol. LXXXIV (1462).

"Tourism in the British Virgin Islands: A Statistical Abstract."

1981   Chief Minister's Office, Planning Unit/Statistics Division (no. 8).

"The Tourist Industry in the BVI"

1973   A Memorandum from the Acting Administrative Officer (E.G. Maduro), Chief Minister's Office, to the Ministries and Administrative Secretaries. Tortola: BVI Government/CMO.

Truman, George, et al.

1844   *Narrative of a Visit to the West Indies in 1840 and 1841.* Philadelphia, PA: Merrihew and Thompson.

Tucker, Robert (ed.)

1972   *The Marx-Engels Reader.* New York: Norton.

Turnbull, Patricia

2002   "Hustling to Host: Everyday Practice, Pedagogy and Participation in British Virgin Islands Tourism." Ph.D. dissertation, University of Toronto.

Turner, Louis and John Ash

1975   *The Golden Hordes: International Tourism and the Pleasure Periphery.* London: Constable.

Tyson, George

1977   *Powder, Profits and Privateers: A Documentary History of the Virgin Islands during the Era of the American Revolution.* USVI: V.I. Bureau of Libraries, Museums and Archaeological Services.

Tyson, George and Carolyn Tyson

1974   *Preliminary Report on Manuscript Materials in British Archives Relating to the American Revolution in the West Indian Islands.* St. Thomas, USVI: Island Resources Foundation.

United Nations Development Programme

1976   British Virgin Islands Physical development Plan. Castries, St. Lucia: Physical Planning Project Office.

United States State Department

1969   *Tourism: Resource for Development—A Study of Benefits to Developing Countries from Investments in Hotels and Motels.* Washington, D.C.

Vandermolden, Harry

    1981   "Tourism and the Territory." *The Island Sun.* 7 March, p. 5.

Van Maanen, J.

    1979   "Reclaiming Qualitative Methods for Organizational Research: A Preface." *Administrative Science Quarterly*, vol. 24.

Vaughan, Mary

    1974   "Tourism in Puerto Rico." In *Puerto Rico and the Puerto Ricans.* A. Lopez and J. Petras, eds.

Verlinden, Charles

    1970   *The Beginnings of Modern Colonization.* New York: Cornell.

Wakefield, E.G.

    1849   *A View of the Art of Colonization.* Oxford: Clarendon.

Walker, Sheila

    1980   "Toward a Native Anthropology." *Notes from the ABA* (Association of Black Anthropologists), vol. 6 (1-2).

Warman, Arturo

    1979   "The Revolutionary Potential of the Mexican Peasant." In *Toward a Marxist Anthropology.* Stanley Diamond, ed.

Waters, Somerset

    1983   "Some Highlights. . . " (Promotional Brochure). *Travel Industry World Yearbook: The Big Picture.* New York: Child and Waters, Inc.

Weisskopf, Thomas

    1978a   "Sources of Cyclical Downturns and Inflation." In *The Capitalist System.* Richard Edwards, Reich, and Weisskopf,, eds.

    1978b   "Imperialism and Economic Development of the Third World." In *The Capitalist System.* Edwards, Reich, and Weisskopf, eds.

Wentworth, Trelawney

    1834   *The West India Sketch Book.* Vol. I. London: Whittaker and Co.

Werlhof, Claudia and H.P. Newhoff

    1982   "The Combination of Different Production Relations on the Basis of Non-Proletarianization: Agrarian Production in Yaracuy, Venezuela." *Latin American Perspectives*, vol. 9 (3).

Wilbur, Charles (ed.)

    1973   *The Political Economy of Development and Underdevelopment.* New York: Random House.

Wilson, David

    1979   "The Early Effects of Tourism in the Seychelles." In *Tourism: Passport to Development?* Emanuel de Kadt, ed.

Wilson, Peter J.

    1973   *Crab Antics: The Social Anthropology of English-speaking Negro Societies of the Caribbean.* New Haven, CT: Yale University Press.

Williams, Eric

    1970   *From Columbus to Castro: The History of the Caribbean 1492-1969*. London: Andre Deutsch.

Wolf, Eric

    1966   *Peasants*. New Jersey: Prentice-Hall.

    1969   *Peasant Wars of Twentieth Century*. New York: Harper and Row.

Woodward, C. Van

    1974   "Seeing Slavery Whole." *The New York Review of Books*, 21:15 (October 3).

Young, George

    1973   *Tourism: Blessing or Blight?* U.K.: Penguin Books.

Zinn, Howard

    1970   *The Politics of History*. Boston: Beacon Press.

APPENDICES

APPENDIX A

Glossary

Emic, Etic:

Emics refer to a variety of theoretical field approaches in anthropology concerned with the inside or native (folk) view of a culture. The concept is based on the formulation of Kennieth Pike. . . who proposed that a model for studying nonlinguistic behavior be devised analogous to the phonetic and phonemic approaches in linguistic theory—hence "emic" and "etic". The formulation is sufficiently ambiguous to allow for a variety of interpretations. However, the main idea is that the subjects one is studying have their own (folk) categories (cognitive categories), assumptions about these categories, taxonomies and part-whole systems in terms of which they logically relate these categories to each other, as well as values concerning items classified according to these categories. To understand the behavior of subjects, then, it is crucial that the field researcher identify the cognitive properties of these emic categories; otherwise interpretations of behavior cannot claim to reflect units of behavior which are meaningful to the people studied.

— Richard L. Stone, 1976. In *Encyclopedia of Anthropology.*
David Hunter and Phillip Whitten, eds.

APPENDIX B

A SYMPOSIUM 00166

Implications for the B.V.I.

ON SOCIAL CHANGE

SPONSORED BY THE B.V.I.
MENTAL HEALTH ASSOCIATION

*Under the Distinguished Patronage of
the Hon. Minister for Social Services,
Mr. R.T. O'Neal, O.B.E. & Mrs. O'Neal*

REEF HOUSE, PROSPECT REEF HOTEL
MAY 20-22, 1982

MENTAL HEALTH WEEK 1982

PROGRAMME
REEF HOUSE – PROSPECT REEF HOTEL

Thursday, 20th May
6:30 pm – 8:00 pm
COCKTAIL PARTY & REGISTRATION

Friday, 22nd May
8:30 am – 8:50 am
OPENING & WELCOMING REMARKS

Michael E. O'Neal, President, BVI Mental Health Association
Hon. Ralph T. O'Neal, Minister for Social Services

9:00 am – 9:30 am
KEYNOTE ADDRESS

Dr. Norwell Harrigan – Director, Caribbean Research
Institute, College of the Virgin Islands
– "SOCIAL CHANGE IN THE BVI: AN OVERVIEW"

9:30 am – 10:30 am
PANEL I. THE LAW AND ITS RELATION TO
SOCIAL CHANGE

McWelling Todman, Q.C. .... Moderator
Anne Henry, Attorney .... Rapporteur

Panelists/Discussants:
Dancia Penn, Attorney
Gerard Farara, Attorney
Freddie Creque, Administrative Officer, Ministry of Social
Services
Robert Bretherton, Chief of Police

10:45 am – 12:00 Noon
PANEL II. THE ROLE OF THE HELPING PROFESSIONS
IN A SOCIETY OF TRANSITION

Ermine Penn, Director, Community Development
Programme .... Moderator
Freddie Creque .... Rapporteur

Panelists/Discussants:
Pat Todman, Psychologist – Director,
Mental Health Division, U.S.V.I.
Laura Lyons, Social Worker
Rodica T. O'Neal, Psychologist
Gayle Shertzer, Social Worker
Barbara deCastro, Social Worker
Dr. Michael Woodbury, Psychiatrist
12:00 – 1:15 pm
BUFFET LUNCH

1:30 pm – 2:30 pm
PANEL III. THE RELIGIOUS DIMENSION

Leslie Reovan, Sociologist,
College of the Virgin Islands .... Moderator
Rev. Joseph Hepburn .... Rapporteur

Panelists/D
Panelists/Discussants:

Fr. Julian Clarke — St. Andrews Anglican Church, St. Thomas
Pastor Silton Browne — Seventh Day Adventist Church
Fr. Robert Granfeldt — St. George's Anglican Church
Pastor Oliver Hodge — Road Town Baptist Church
Fr. John Valentine — St. Williams Catholic Church

2:45 pm – 3:45 pm
PANEL IV. THE POLITICO-ECONOMIC DIMENSION

Elton Georges, Permanent Secretary
to the Chief Minister .... Moderator
Ethlyn Smith, Permanent Secretary, Ministry of
Communications, Works and Public Utilities...Rapporteur

Panelists/Discussants:

Simon Jones-Hendrickson, Professor of Economics,
College of the Virgin Islands
Erik Blommestein, Economist
Robert Mathavious, Economist-statistician
Everett O'Neal, Economist
Hugo Vanterpool, Manager, Devlopment Bank
Brahm Kapur, Economist

4:00 pm – 5:00 pm
PANEL V. EDUCATION, THE FAMILY & SOCIAL CHANGE

Pearl Varlack, Professor of Education,
College of the Virgin Islands .... Moderator
Louis Walters, Acting Permanent Secretary, Ministry
of Natural Resources & Environment .... Rapporteur

Panelists/Discussants:

Charles Wheatley, Chief Education Officer
Quincy Lettsome, Deputy Principal, B.V.I. High School
Rita Frett-Georges, Psychologist – Director,
B.V.I. Mental Health Programme
Ted Mercier, Psychologist

Saturday, 22nd May.
8:30 am – 9:30 am
    PANEL VI   THE MEDICAL PSYCHIATRIC DIMENSION

    Dr. Orlando Smith, Chief Medical Officer .... Moderator
    Millie Ahearne, Matron, Peebles Hospital .... Rapporteur

        Panelists/Discussants:

    Dr. S. Ginandes, Psychiatrist
    Dr. K. Gopal, Medical Officer
    Mr. Vincent Scatliffe, Psychiatric Nurse
    Dr. John Louis – Director, Community Health
      Services, U.S.V.I.
    Dr. Cora Christian, Assistant Commissioner of
      Health, U.S.V.I.

10:00 am – 11:15 am
    PANEL VII.   RESPONSES TO SOCIAL CHANGE

    Carl Dawson, Permanent Secretary,
      Ministry of Social Services .... Moderator
    Janice George, Attorney .... Rapporteur

        Panelists/Discussants:

    Eugenie Todman-Smith, Personnel/Establishment Officer
    Jo De Weese, Psychologist – Assistant Director,
      Mental Health Division, U.S.V.I.
    Lorna Smith, Public Relations Officer, Office of
      the Chief Minister
    Ermine Penn, Director, Community Development
      Programme
    Leslie Reovan, Sociologist, College of the Virgin Islands

11:30 am – 11:45 am
    INTRODUCTION TO THE PLENARY SESSION

    Rita Frett-Georges, Psychologist – Director,
      B.V.I. Mental Health Programme

12:00 – 1:15 pm
    BUFFET LUNCH

1:30 pm – 3:30 pm
    PANEL VIII.   PLENARY SESSION: POLICY
                 IMPLICATIONS

    J.S. Archibald, Q.C. .... Moderator
    Elihu Rhymer, Manager, AIR BVI .... Rapporteur

        Panelists/Discussants:

    Norwell Harrigan, Director, Caribbean Research Institute
    Pearl Varlack, Professor of Education, College of the
      Virgin Islands
    Cyril Romney, Businessman
    McWelling Todman, Q.C. Attorney
    Michelle Abbot-Smith, Information Officer, Office of
      the Chief Minister

    Summary Address: Elihu Rhymer

APPENDIX C

Tables

1. Demographic History by Race, Census Years
    1717 – 1970 175

2. Gross Domestic Product, 1969 – 1978 176

3. History of Trade, 1750 – 1970 177

4. Balance of Trade, 1965 – 1980 178

5. Bareboat Fleet Size 179

6. Visitor Expenditure 180

7. Charterboat Characteristics 181

8. Resident Population by Race 182

Table 1

DEMOGRAPHIC HISTORY BY RACE, CENSUS YEARS 1717 - 1970

Year	Black	White	Mixed[a]	Other or Not Specified	Total
1717	547	795	..	-	1342
1720	1509	1122	..	-	2631
1756	6121	1236	..	-	7357
1774[b]	9000	1200	..	-	10200
1c. 5[b]	9220	1300	(220)	-	10520
1834	6338	477	(1296)	-	6815
1844	6485	200	..	-	6689
1871	..	..	..	..	6651
1881	5235	52	(1546)	-	5287
1891	4607	32	(1189)	-	4639
1901	4906	2	..	-	4908
1911	5526	36	(1473)	-	5562
1921	5046	36	(1158)	-	5082
1946	6469	35	(799)	1	6505
1960	7771	47	(373)	103	7921
1970	8859	676	(153)	137	9672

a 'Mixed' totals are aggregated under 'Black' due to definitional changes over these years.

b Estimates.

(i) N. Harrigan and P. Varlack, "The British Virgin Islands, A Chronology
(ii) 1946, 1960 and 1970 Censuses.

Source: Statistics Office, B.V.I. Government.

Table 2

Gross Domestic Product by Kind of Activity: Current Prices 1969 - 1976 (US$000)

Activity	1969	1970	1971	1972	1973	1974	1975	1975	1972	1976
Agriculture and Fishing	1,149	1,139	1,052	1,085	1,497	1,827	1,959	2,137	2,364	2,577
Manufacturing and Mining	660	945	738	687	805	919	1,258	1,206	1,271	1,700
Construction	4,138	4,813	3,146	2,458	2,285	2,872	3,434	3,071	2,388	3,340
Electricity and Water	228	208	245	265	258	364	359	412	469	495
Retail and Wholesale	1,121	1,263	1,241	1,394	1,699	2,161	2,223	2,564	2,376	2,674
Real Estate/Rent	1,235	1,366	1,420	1,498	1,713	2,213	2,461	2,709	2,933	3,030
Banking and Insurance	407	582	708	659	726	873	913	704	964	1,140
Transport and Communications	1,081	1,306	1,192	1,585	1,483	1,530	1,729	2,002	2,253	2,737
Government	1,081	1,383	1,617	1,864	1,860	2,314	2,272	2,746	2,808	2,938
Professional Services	313	465	447	421	509	550	608	621	497	630
Hotels, Restaurants, Boat Charter	1,119	1,178	1,316	1,502	1,999	2,483	2,699	3,421	3,919	4,900
Other Services	174	179	189	211	237	257	201	269	303	358
Total	12,726	14,827	13,331	13,429	15,071	18,363	20,164	21,864	22,547	26,520
Transfers and Indirect Taxes	804	1,120	438	946	1,201	1,092	1,209	1,433	1,541	1,990
Gross Domestic Product	13,530	15,947	13,769	14,375	16,272	19,455	21,373	23,299	24,088	28,510

Source: Statistics Office, BVI Government

Table 3

HISTORY OF TRADE, 1750-1970

Year	Unit of Currency	Imports into BVI	Exports from BVI
1750	£ Sterling	577[a,b]	26,038
1760	"	577[b]	30,352
1770	"	22,825[c]	43,230
1780	"	37,884[d]	49,023[e]
1790	"	106,162[f]	..
1800	"	216,756[g]	45,987
1810	"	..	52,520
1820	"	13,745[h]	27,785
1830	"	4,139[i]	25,212
1840	"	11,603[j]	15,928[j]
1850	"	5,703	5,133
1860	"	8,247	15,106
1870	"	6,644	6,201
1880	"	4,646	5,384
1890	"	3,994	4,975
1900	"	3,387	2,312
1910	"	8,496	6,610
1920	"	43,413	24,102
1930	"	14,360	11,139
1940	"	18,095	12,297
1950	"	68,526	30,218
1960	U.S. $	356,596	191,155
1970	"	18,223,574	65,328

a 1750 to 1830 figures deal exclusively with exports to and imports from Britain. In these years considerable unrecorded trade took place with the Danish Virgin Islands.
b 1748 - 1764 average.
c 1764 - 1773 average.
d 1774 - 1783 average.
e Peak export years follow in 1782, £161,338; 1783, £137,707 and 1784, £123,308.
f 1772   no records available for 1790.
g Freak year-average between 1799 and 1805, £122,322.
h 1822.
i 1831 (including imports from countries other than Britain).
j 1840 - 1860 figures are 5 year averages.

(i) 1750-1800 figures from Isaac Dookhan's 'History of the Virgin Islands'.
(ii) 1890-1950 figures from Colonial Annual Reports.
(iii) 1960 and 1970 from Annual Trade Summaries

Source: Statistics Office, B.V.I. Government

Table 4

BALANCE OF TRADE 1965 - 1980

YEAR	IMPORTS	DOMESTIC EXPORTS	RE-EXPORTS	TOTAL EXPORTS	BALANCE OF TRADE DEFICIT
1965	2,980,800	98,845	3,752	102,597	2,858,203
1966	4,178,297	70,464	86,511	156,975	4,021,322
1967	3,890,025	87,835	12,072	99,907	3,790,118
1968	6,207,412	144,854	8,732	153,586	6,053,826
1969	8,099,208	49,754	12,774	62,528	8,036,680
1970	10,223,574	42,608	22,720	65,328	10,158,246
1971	8,849,578	103,765	266,772	370,537	8,479,041
1972	7,652,128	71,750	97,847	169,597	7,482,531
1973	9,467,386	98,402	343,014	441,416	9,025,970
1974	11,606,141	52,870	371,756	424,626	11,181,515
1975	13,722,451	39,807	457,388	497,195	13,225,256
1976	14,295,240				
1977					
1978	21,656,162	440,222	372,772	812,994	20,843,168
1979	32,782,746	407,304	997,769	1,405,073	31,377,673
1980	40,494,282	507,934	653,454	1,161,388	39,332,894

Source: Statistics Office, B.V.I. Government

Table 5

Bareboat Fleet Size by Company 1969-1980 (Based on Highest Number of Boats Operated Any Year)

Company	1969	1970	1971	1972	1973	1974	1975	1976	1977	1978	1979	1980[1]	Planned Fleet Size
Caribbean Sailing Yachts(CSY)	25	25	27	32	35	41	41	41	41	56	56	68	66
The Moorings	6	11	18	30	33	33	33	62	62	72	78	82	100
West Indies Yacht Charters Ltd										32	52	46	50
Fleet Indigo				7	10	12	12	15	15	22	24	24	25
Island Sailing								9		9	18	21	44
North South Yacht Charters								2	2	4	8	18	30
Tortola Yacht Charter							5	8	15	16	24	30	50
Latitude 18° 25' Charters Ltd							3	3	3	3	12	12	
Bagatelle													1
British Virgin Islands Bareboats					2	4	5	4	4	4	5	6	6
							3	3	3		3	4	5
Mediterranean Charter Services											9[2]	—	—
Cruising Centre Charters													
Tropic Island Charters											11	11	25
											11	5	25
CMC/ Prospect Reef										6	6	—	—
Total	31	36	45	69	80	90	99	135	142	224	306	331	433

[1] The actual BVI Bareboat Fleet Size in December of 1980 was 320 boats.

[2] These 9 boats are not included in the 1979 total, since they were taken over by Island Sailing and counted in its 18 boats for that year.

Based on questionnaire data

Source: Ivor Jackson (1981), "Study of the Pleasure Boat Industry...."

Table 6

VISITOR EXPENDITURE IN THE B.V.I. 1977 - 1981

U.S. $ 000

	1981	1980	1979	1978	1977
1. Hotel Tourists, Total	14,931	13,178	11,931	9,333	7,760
(a) within hotel	11,869	10,514	9,438	7,410	6,126
(b) outside hotel	3,062	2,664	2,492	1,923	1,634
2. Charter Boat Tourists, Total	55,929	42,773	35,846	12,499	9,425
(a) within boat co.	51,712	38,294	31,614	9,683	7,296
(b) outside boat co.	4,217	4,479	4,233	2,816	2,129
3. Tourists in Rented Accommodation	1,035	999	660	408	313
4. Tourists in Own Acc./with Friends	595	405	568	506	404
5. Cruiseship Passengers	657	501	73	48	-
6. Entered in Own/Foreign Charter Boat	305	170	153	106	15
7. Day Tourists	157	220	232	166	146
All	668	630	698	627	567
VISITOR EXPENDITURE IN THE B.V.IS.	74,277	58,875	50,281	23,714	18,610

Source: Statistics Office, B.V.I. Government

Table 7

Characteristics of Currently Chartered Bareboats (December, 1980)

Design (Make)	No Operated	Length Overall	Width of Beam	Draught	Maximum No.Bunks	No. Heads	Freshwater Capacity (Gals)	Fuel Capacity (Gals)	Maximum Auxiliary Speed (knots)	$ Approx. Cost Today's Prices	Avg Length of Lease (yrs)
(1)	(2)	(3)	(4)	(5)	(6)	(7)	(8)	(9)	(10)	(11)	(12)
CARIBBEAN SAILING YACHTS											
CSY 44 (Ketch)	1	44'	13'4"	6'6"	7	2	400	125	6	153,000	7
CSY 44 (Cutter)	40	44'	13'4"	6'6"	7	2	400	125	6	132,000	7
CSY 37	13	37'3"	12'	6'6"	6	2	175	50	5.5	101,000	7
CSY 33	14	33'4"	10'6"	5'9"	4	1	150	50	5.5	91,000	7
THE MOORINGS											
Gulfstar 50	16	50'	13'8"	5'10"	8	3	400	75	7	175,000	6
Morgan-Moorings 46	32	46'6"	13'6"	6'0"	8	2	330	100	7	165,000	5
Mariner-Moorings 39	8	38'9"	11'8"	6'0"	6	2	200	80	6.5	120,000	5
Gulfstar-Moorings 37	24	37'	11'10"	5'6"	6	2	176	80	6.5	110,000	5
Morgan Out Islander 41 (experimental)	1	41'	13'10"	4'11"			N/I				
CS 36 (experimental)	1	36'	12'	6'0"			N/I				
WEST INDIES YACHT CHARTERS LTD											
CAL 39	19	39'	12'	5'9"	7	2	200	40	7	125,000	3.5
ODAY 37	18	37'	11'	5'0"	6	2	180	40	6	75,000	3.5
Mariner 35	1	38'	12'	5'0"	7	2	220	40	7	124,000	3.5

Source: Ivor Jackson (1981), "Study of the Pleasure Boat Industry...."

Table 8

RESIDENT POPULATION BY RACE (1980 CENSUS)

	Tortola	Virgin Gorda	Jost Van Dyke	Anegada	Other Islands	Totals
Negro/Black	9,352	1,288	122	156	23	9,941
East Indian	33	5	-	-	1	39
White	612	115	10	5	36	778
Mixed	135	16	4	5	5	1??
Other	70	17	-	2	1	?
Not Stated	30	-	-	1	13	?4
	5,322	1,443	136	166	82	11,152

Source: Statistics Office, B.V.I. Government

Index

Abbott, Hannah, 31, 141
Adamson, Alan, 55
Africa, 11, 17, 31, 47, 139
Agricultural Bank, 63
American War of Independence
    (1776-83), 13
Anegada, 2, 90-91, 139
Archibald, Joseph S., 97-98, 106
Arnett, Vernon, 129
Ash, John, 4, 112
average length of stay, tourist, 94
Bahamas, the, 44, 105, 111, 130
bareboat chartering, 92
bareboats, 92
Batehill Ltd, 86, 90
Bates, Kenneth. *See* Batehill Ltd.
Bathurst, Earl, 39, 41-42
Beckford, George, 4, 15, 128-129
Beckford, William, 11, 25-26
Belmont Estate, 100
Belonger, 100, 146
Bermuda, 116, 130
Best, Lloyd, 146
Biras Creek, 101
Bluestein, William, 71
Bomba Charger, 106
Bowen, Errol, 88-89
Brathwaite, Edward, 3
British Emancipation Act of 1833, 14
British Virgin Islander, 97, 112
British Virgin Islands Legislative
    Council, 95
Bryden, John, 4, 87-88, 90
BVI Budget, 95-96
BVI Economic Development
    Programme, 4

BVI Government Report, 56, 60
BVI Legislative Council, 95
Caines, Clement, 19
capitalism and capitalist economy,
    relation to slavery, 13
charcoal, 60, 63-64, 71, 99, 129
charter-boat tourism, 92-93
civic retrenchment, 58
Clarke, Edith, 130
Codrington, Mitchell, 57, 72, 130
Cohen, Colleen Ballerino, i-iv, 133
Coke, Edward, 40
colony of exploitation, 15
constitutional retrogression, 56
construction sector, 90
Cother, Charles, 34
cotton, 11-12, 45, 56-57, 140
Crabb, William George, 41
Craton, Michael, 3, 13, 17-19, 21, 22,
    43-44, 128, 141
Creque, Henry, 99
CSY, 93, 103
culture, 67, 78, 112, 121, 129, 137, 171
Dalton, George, 3, 67, 69
Danish West Indies, BVI's
    dependent relations with, 60
de Kadt, Emanuel, 91
deCastro, Walter L., 145
Deere, Carmen, 71, 72
Delbecq Technique, 5, 139
dependent relations of BVI with the
    Danish West Indies, 60
development strategy, 4, 90-92
Diamond, Stanley, 3
Dirks, Robert, 139

Dookhan, Isaac, 11, 14, 39, 43, 45, 54, 55, 57-65, 139, 141-142

Drake, St. Clair, 2

Dunn, Stephen, 68

economic and constitutional retrogression, 56

economic development, 128

economic disinterest, 130

Edinburgh Review, The, 30

Edwards, Bryan, 20, 22, 71, 139

Edwards, Richard, 46

Emancipation Act of 1833, British, 14

emics, 1-2, 171

Ennew, Judith, 4, 68-70

etic, defined, 1-2, 171

Evans, Vaughan, 113-114

Fahie, John, 12

Faulkner, D. E., 63

Financial Times, 91, 99

Firth, Raymond, 66

fishing, 63, 65, 71, 76, 129-130

Flax, Andy, 103

Foster, George, 3

Frampton and Briggs, 75-76

Fraser, Daniel, 38

French, M. D., 36, 41

Frett, Elizabeth, 29

Geertz, Clifford, 67

Geshekter, Charles, 76, 114

Gordon, William, 41

Goveia, Elsa, 3, 13, 18-21, 23-25, 44

Graburn, Nelson, 77-78

Graham, John, 91

Gratus, Jack, 25

Gray, Lewis, 16

Gross Domestic Product, BVI, 90

Guana Island, 65

Gurney, Joseph John, 3, 52, 65, 143-144

Guyana, 43, 105, 127

Gwaltney, John, 2, 4, 110

Hall, Douglas, 4, 59

Hannerz, Ulf, 6, 130-132

Harrigan, Norwell, 11-14, 27, 29, 44, 54-61, 63, 64-66, 83, 89, 100, 106, 108, 130, 139, 140-144

Hawkins, Donald, 139

heliophilia, 78

heritage, 108, 117

Hetherington, Richard, 32

Hiller, Herbert, 75, 79, 81

Hodge, Arthur, 32, 44

Hodge's Creek, 101

hostility, 110

Hotel Aid Ordinance, 65, 75

hotel room capacity, 94

Howell, Christopher, 90, 139

Hsu, Francis, 2

Huges, Everett C., 140

Hunt, Sydney, 145

Hurston, Zora Neale, 2

immigrants, 121, 137, 146

Irish, Georgia Lee, 64

Isaacs, Wiliam R., 34

Jackson, Ivor, 92-94, 145

Jamaica, 44, 80, 111, 127, 143-144

Jasper Rapsot, 28

Jenkins, Charles F., 62-63

Johnson gut, 55

Jones, W., 15

Josiah's Bay Estate, 33-34, 36, 38-39, 40-41, 43

Kahn, Herman, 77, 80

King, Jr., Martin Luther, 89

King, Richard, 31

Koestler, Arthur, 81

Krigger, Marilyn, 61-62

Lawson, Wilson, 34

lease-back, 93

Lett, James W. Jr., 119, 139

Lettsom, Ruth, 32

Lewis, Gordon, 69, 80

Lewis, Robert, 40-41, 43

Lewisohn, Florence, 139

Little Dix Bay Hotel, 65, 90

livestock, 57, 60, 63-65, 71, 91, 129

Lloyd, Noel, 145

Lockhart's Lumber Yard, 106
Long Bay, 103
Long Bush, 117
Long Island, 27
Long Look, 27, 58
Long, Edward, 23, 46
Longlook, 27-28, 141
Lowenthal, David, 57, 130
Lower Estate, 105
Lumber and Trading, 106
MacCannell, Dean, 4
Manigat, Leslie, 47-48
Marshall, Woodville K., 4
Maruyama, Magorah, 2
Marx, Karl, 49, 67-68
Maurer, Bill, 133-138, 139
Maxwell, Charles W., 39
McGlynn, Frank, 66, 139
McQueen, James, 27-30
Meillassoux, Claude, 3
Merivale, Herman, 12
metropolitan neglect, 130
Mill, John Stuart, 128
Mills, Frank, 4, 69-70
Mintz, Sidney, 2-3, 15-16, 26, 46-47,
     49, 52, 66, 68-69, 71, 128, 139, 143
Moir, A. W., 51
Moorings, The, 92, 103
Nash, Dennison, 82
Native Son, 106
non-belongers, 100, 122
Norman Island, 100
Norman, Osorio A., 127, 131
Nottingham Free People, 27, 30-31,
     39
Nottingham, Eve, 28
Nottingham, Mary, 27, 41
Nottingham, Samuel, 27, 57, 140-141
O'Loughlin, Carleen, 4, 65
occupancy rates, hotel, 94
Olwig, Karen, 46, 142, 143
O'Neal, Eric, 101
O'Neal, Eugenia, iii
O'Neal, Joseph Reynold, 106

Other Caribbean, The, 6, 65, 89, 131
Parliamentary Papers, 3, 33, 35-36,
     39, 41, 142, 161
passenger arrivals, 94
Patterson, Orlando, 3, 16, 18-19, 21,
     24-25, 143
Pearson, Isaac, 41-42
peasantry, 4, 33, 52, 65-69, 144
Peebles, H. W., 62
petty commodity mode of
     production, 2-3, 71
Phillips Report, 90
Phillips, William, 4, 84-86
Pickering, Isaac, 33-36, 43
plantation economy in the British
     Virgin Islands
  boilerman, 21
  British Emancipation Act of
       1833, 14
  colony of exploitation, 15
  conquest colonies, 15
  cotton, 11-12, 45, 56-57, 140
  demographic statistics, 12
  great house, 16
  hothouse, 18
  industrial capitalist economy,
       13
  mercantilist capitalism, 13
  Nottingham Free People, 27,
       30-31, 39
  overseers and attorneys, 22
  physical punishment, 24
  plantation, defined, 15
  protectionism, 13
  provision grounds, 13, 26, 48,
       54
  settlement colonies, 15
  Seven Years War (1756-63), 13
  slave gangs, 22-23, 142
  slavery and subsistence
       cultivation, 25
  slaves' diet, 18
  slaves' housing, 17
  slaves' workday, 18

sugar, 11-13, 15-17, 19-22, 48, 49, 51, 53, 56-57, 63, 72, 128, 130-131, 140
Virgin Islands Slave Act of 1783, 23
plantation system, 2-3, 15-16, 21, 26, 42, 45-49, 69, 71, 129
Porter, George R., 34, 39
Porter, Richardson, 36
Positive Action Movement, 89, 145
Price, Richard, 46-47, 142-143
Privy Council, 31, 36, 38, 41
Prospect Reef Hotel, 76
Quarterly Review, The, 27, 31, 141
Raghaven, Sushila, 139
Redfield, Robert, 69
Report of the Development Advisory Committee, 84, 86
Rhymer, Elihu, iii, 97, 107, 108
rictus syndrome, 111
Rockefeller, Laurance, 65, 76, 100
Rohlehr, Gordon, 127
Santo Domingo, 62, 101
Schaw, Janet, 25
servility, 110, 137
Sethna, Rustum, 111
Shanin, Teodor, 3, 66-68
Shankland Cox and Associates, 91
Shankland Cox Report, 91-92
slavery. *See* Plantation economy in the British Virgin Islands; Plantation system
smallholding, defined, 70
Smith, Valene, 4, 111
smuggling, 57, 64, 130
social change, 4, 97
squatter cultivation, 71
Stewart, John, 26
Stobo, John, 34
Stock, Robert, 112
Stoutt, H. Lavity, 95, 99
subsistence agriculture, 129
sugar, 11-13, 15-17, 19-22, 48, 49, 51, 53, 56-57, 63, 72, 128, 130-131, 140

Surinam, 127
surplus extraction, 72, 130, 131
Thompson, Edgar T., 15
Todman Smith, Eugenie, 107
Todman, McWelling, iii, 66, 97-98, 134-135
tourism, defined, 77
tourist, average length of stay, and hotel occupancy rates, 94
Trinidad, 33, 39, 43-44, 98-99, 102, 104, 127
trust companies, 105
Trust Company Association, The, 104
Turner and Ash, 78-82
Turner, Louis, 4, 78, 112
Tyson, Carolyn, 141
Tyson, George, 14, 141
underdevelopment, 128
value of domestic exports, BVI, 91
value of imports, BVI, 91
Van de Ven, A., 5
Van Maanen, J., 5
Varlack, Pearl, 11-14, 27, 29, 44, 54-56, 58, 60, 61, 63-65, 83, 100, 108, 130, 139-140, 144
Vaughan, Mary, 76
Venezuela, 72, 127
Virgin Gorda, 65, 76, 90, 99, 139, 145
Virgin Islander, 57, 106, 122
Virgin Islands National Bank, 106
visitor expenditure, BVI, 92
Walker, Sheila, 2
Waters, Sommerset, 77
Wentworth, Trelawney, 14, 17, 20, 45-46, 47, 140
Werlhof, Claudia, 72
Wickham's Cay, 90-91
Wickham's Cay and Anegada Development Agreements, 90
Wilbur, Charles, 1
Williams, Eric, 13-14, 53, 54, 98, 127
Wolf, Eric, 3, 66
Young, George, 4, 114

About the Author

MICHAEL E. O'NEAL, Ph.D., is Senior Research Fellow at Island Resources Foundation, an organization with offices in Washington, D.C. and the Caribbean, whose central mission is to assist small islands to meet the challenges of social, economic and institutional growth while protecting and enhancing their environments.

Former President of the H. Lavity Stoutt Community College, British Virgin Islands (BVI), O'Neal had previously served as the first Resident Tutor/Head of the University of the West Indies, BVI Centre. In addition, from 1997–2004, he held appointment as Core Professor at the Graduate College of the Union Institute in Ohio, where he supervised doctoral students in interdisciplinary studies.

Prior to his academic career, O'Neal was a managing director of the business enterprises of J. R. O'Neal Ltd (BVI). He has served on numerous boards and commissions, including the Public Service Commission, the Development Bank of the Virgin Islands, and as Chairman of the BVI National Parks Trust, 2003–2009. He is currently a director of JOMA Ltd, a closely-held, family-owned real estate management and development company.

O'Neal is a member of several professional associations and learned societies, and is a Fellow of the Royal Anthropological Institute (U.K.) and of the American Anthropological Association.

Visit us at *www.quidprobooks.com.*

Made in the USA
Columbia, SC
24 November 2020

25296424R00113